Singing and

Singing and Science:
Body, Brain, and Voice

Jean Callaghan

This edition first published 2014 © 2014 by Compton Publishing Ltd.

Registered office: Compton Publishing Ltd, 30 St. Giles', Oxford, OX1 3LE, UK Registered company number: 07831037

Editorial offices: 3 Wrafton Road, Braunton, EX33 2BT, UK
Web: www.comptonpublishing.co.uk

ISBN 978-1-909082-02-1

A catalogue record for this book is available from the British Library.

Cover design by David Siddall Multimedia (www.davidsiddall.com)
Cover cartoons by Bruce Petty
Illustrations by Richard Collins

Set in Adobe Caslon Pro 10pt by Stuart Brown

Table of Contents

Acknowledgments

My thanks go to the singing teachers—in Sydney, Perth, and London—who have taught me at different stages of my career. Over the years I have met a wide range of performers, researchers, teachers, and students who have continued to stimulate my interest in the singing voice. In our time Richard Miller was an international inspiration to those writing about the singing voice, so when he suggested that my doctoral research might form the basis of a book I was spurred into action. I am grateful to speech pathologist Alison Winkworth for her enthusiasm about the book when it was little more than an idea, and to Noel McPherson for publishing the first edition and, then, 12 years later, approaching me to embark on a second edition. I'm grateful to colleagues Sarah Penicka-Smith and Edward McDonald for their critical reading of the manuscript.

I am delighted with Richard Collins' entertaining illustrations and grateful to Bruce Petty for his permission to reproduce drawings originally displayed at the Powerhouse Museum, Sydney.

Thank you to all the musical friends and colleagues who have provided support for my work with music, laughter, ideas and discussion.

To Ruth and Kate
with love and admiration

Preface

When I began teaching singing 35 years ago I asked myself such questions as 'What is the accepted body of knowledge about singing?' and 'How is *teaching* singing different from singing?' As a student I had encountered the rival claims made by different teachers about how to manage the breath, how to achieve ideal resonance, and so on – knowledge that they had gradually acquired through their own singing and through years of teaching, listening, and observing. Although I knew from experience what worked best for me as a singer, I had no way of knowing whether what worked for me would also work for students of different voice types, with different physiques and different personalities. I was also conscious of the gap between being able to do something and being able to teach someone else to do it. I felt that while an experiential knowledge of the act of singing was important for teaching, so, too, was an understanding of how the voice works physically, of how it operates as a musical instrument, and of how these kinds of knowledge are best conveyed to students.

This motivated a critical assessment of the literature on singing and the teaching of singing, a body of knowledge going back to the 17th century. Much of that literature reflects the fact that player and instrument are one: the singer or singing-teacher author makes no distinction between the knowledge of voice and the practice of teaching. In the 35 years since I began teaching, scientific knowledge of vocal function and vocal health has increased greatly: new technology can show images of brain activity, display the larynx in operation, measure muscular effort, and acoustically analyse vocal sound. It is now possible to take a more objective approach to the singing voice and how it works.

The centuries-old master-apprentice tradition of pedagogy continues, despite a breakdown in many of the assumptions underpinning it, and despite modern educational pressures. However, this continuous tradition is increasingly becoming fragmented, since teachers now confront a proliferation of genres and styles encompassing a wide time span and geographic spread. Teachers must be time efficient and work with students of all voice types and across a wide repertoire.

To meet these demands requires an understanding of the physical factors that safely and efficiently produce the aesthetically appropriate vocal sound, as well as of a teaching approach best suited to a range of students. While there are basic musical and vocal principles that may well be taught in small groups, the need remains for individual work geared to the specific needs and abilities of the student.

In 1998 I published the results of an investigation into Australian singing teachers' knowledge of this area (Callaghan, 1998), based on my own doctoral research involving in-depth interviews of 50 singing teachers at tertiary institutions across Australia. I found that while practitioners demonstrated an admirable commitment to experiential learning and to individual students' development, their knowledge of vocal physiology, acoustics, and health was often at best incomplete, and at worst misinformed. This, too, has been gradually changing, with more research in the area, and publications, courses, and workshops on singing and the teaching of singing making information on vocal function in singing much more readily available.

Since the first edition of *Singing and Voice Science* in 2000 what has changed is the amount of research on the role of brain and mind in music and language, and in psychomotor learning and performance. Since singing involves all of these things, any knowledge of how best to harness the mind for the teaching, learning, and performance of singing is of vital importance for teachers. Another area that has continued to develop is the use of technology, not only in research, but in application to teaching and learning, with commercially-available computer applications to show articulatory manoeuvres and give real-time feedback on the acoustic features of the voice.

This work addresses the need for those working with the singing voice to add to their armoury the relevant knowledge that is accumulating in voice science, teaching and learning, and performance. I identify issues of physiology, acoustics, and health that are pertinent to singing pedagogy and examine scientific understandings of voice relevant to those issues. I then explore thinking on how complex psychomotor tasks such as singing are best learnt and performed.

The main focus of the first edition of *Singing and Voice Science* was an examination of the voice science literature on breath management, phonation, resonance and articulation, registration and vocal health, and the clarification of its application to singing and the teaching of singing. There was also some consideration of the singer as a 'vocal instrument' and of the kinds of knowledge and skills required to teach singing. In this second edition I update the material on the physical aspects of singing, but the emphasis is more on our greatly expanded knowledge of the factors involved in teaching and learning. These are manifold and emerge from research in physiology, medicine, speech pathology, acoustics, linguistics, education, psychology, and neurology.

The book draws on material published in English over the last 40 years, a period marked by technological innovation and the beginnings of inter-disciplinary collaboration and cross-disciplinary communication. It focuses on the vocal technique of the adult voice in singing, with an emphasis on 'classical' genres and styles. Research into voice use in other genres and styles is still in its infancy, but some reference is made to it here.

Singers are distinguished from other performing musicians in two obvious ways: firstly, for singers, their instrument is the whole person; secondly, singers perform language as well as music. In writings on singing and the teaching of singing one strangely neglected area is the relationship between music and language, the relationship between musical text and linguistic text and how these are learnt, embodied by the singer and conveyed to an audience. In this second edition I include these essential aspects of singing in my examination.

In the last 40 years or so much has been published on vocal physiology and acoustics, on cognition, neurobiology, and teaching and learning, as well as singing and voice science, but until recently much of this had not reached the majority of voice teachers. Recently more books have come out attempting to examine the range of factors involved in singing. This second edition builds on the work of Thurman and Welch (2000), McCoy (2006), Nair (2007), Bunch Dayme (2009), Chapman (2012), and Titze and Verdolini Abbott (2012).

The first chapter outlines the long oral tradition of voice teaching that began in Italy early in the 17th century, describes changes that took place in the 19th century, and summarises the new information on voice available in our own time. Chapter 2 gives an overview of the vocal instrument that is the body, drawing a distinction between two essentially different ways of observing and understanding the body: one is the first-person perspective of the singer, the other the third-person perspective of the scientist. Both types of knowledge are necessary for the teacher of singing. This overview provides the background to Chapters 3 to 7, which comprise an exploration of aspects of singing investigated in research studies. This research is assessed and related to practitioner understandings to provide the knowledge necessary for teachers. Chapter 3 deals with breath management, Chapter 4 with phonation, Chapter 5 with resonance, Chapter 6 with registration, and Chapter 7 with vocal health. Chapter 8 deals with the aspects of brain and body, body and mind, involved in singing. The final chapter examines how all the issues discussed in earlier chapters are related to teaching and learning, and makes recommendations for the professional education of singing teachers.

This is an account of how research in voice science and learning in music, language and psychomotor performance can inform our understanding of singing and the teaching of singing. I hope it will prove useful to singing teachers who wish, as I do, to find out all they can about the workings of that superb musical instrument, the human voice.

Jean Callaghan
Sydney, 2014

References

Bunch Dayme, M. (2009). *Dynamics of the Singing Voice* (5th edn.). Vienna: Springer-Verlag.

Callaghan, J. (1998). Singing teachers and voice science: an evaluation of voice teaching in Australian tertiary institutions. *Research Studies in Music Education*, *10*(1), 25–41. doi:10.1177/1321103X9801000103.

Chapman, J.L. (2012). *Singing and Teaching Singing: A Holistic Approach to Classical Voice* (2nd edn.). San Diego, CA: Plural Publishing.

McCoy, S. (2006). *Your Voice: An Inside View* (rev. edn.). Princeton, NJ: Inside View Press.

Nair, G. (2007). *The Craft of Singing*. San Diego, CA: Plural Publishing.

Thurman, L. & Welch, G. (eds.) (2000). *Bodymind and Voice: Foundations of Voice Education* (rev. edn.). Collegeville, MN: The VoiceCare Network.

Titze, I.R. & Verdolini Abbott, K. (2012). *Vocology: The Science and Practice of Voice Habilitation*. Salt Lake City, UT: The National Center for Voice and Speech.

Chapter 1: Science and Singing

> A knowledge of the voice is necessary for everyone,
> but above all this is necessary for a teacher of singing.
> (Bérard, 1755/1969, pp. 61-62)

The oral tradition

Current knowledge about the singing voice exists against the background of a long oral tradition, originating in Italy early in the 17th century and flourishing in the 18th and early 19th centuries. It implied intensive individual study with a master, encompassing musical, vocal, and performance matters relevant to the elegant vocal writing of the time. This approach to singing was later labelled 'bel canto' (beautiful, or fine, singing) and began to take on mythical significance. This master–apprentice approach in one-to-one tuition and imitation of the master singer represents the foundation of singing pedagogy in the Western European art tradition.

Through three centuries of cultural and musical change, the initial precepts and specific practices of bel canto have been so modified that it can no longer be said to exist. A multiplicity of tonal ideals and corresponding pedagogical practices have evolved in different national schools (Miller, 1977), and it may be that multicultural societies – such as Australia, New Zealand, Canada, and the United States – have always embraced a range of ideals and practices. Now, with international travel, international cooperation in performance, omnipresent availability of audio and audiovisual recordings of an extraordinary variety of singing voices and styles, and online information internationally accessible, expectations of what singing is and how it should be taught are changing.

Nevertheless, bel canto ideals and the bel canto approach to teaching live on in writings on singing technique – even in writings directed to different national schools, to vocal technique for repertoire far removed from that of bel canto, and in writings that are scientifically based. While there are now many resources available to singers and their teachers – in print, in audiovisual form, and on the Internet – practitioners continue in the master–apprentice tradition of teaching, and often continue using exercises and technical directives passed on from teacher to pupil over centuries. Because of the profound, pervasive, and continuing influence of the bel canto teaching tradition on singing pedagogy and vocal knowledge, I will begin with an examination of that tradition and of the forces that have made it no longer the complete and self-sufficient model for singing pedagogy that it once was.

1

The history of the development of bel canto has been well documented, both by general music historians (Bukofzer, 1947; Palisca, 1968; Weaver, 1980) and by writers with a more particular interest in singing (Heriot, 1956; Galliver, 1974; Manén, 1987; Celetti, 1991). Bibliographical surveys of bel canto sources have also been undertaken (e.g. Duey, 1951).

The teaching of singing as a solo virtuoso art goes back to Italy in the early 17th century, where it developed in response to the demand for solo vocal virtuosos to sing the new monody and opera. While the poet–lutenist–singer had been a familiar entertainer at courts throughout the Renaissance, he was not primarily a vocal virtuoso. Palisca (1968) quoted a contemporary witness as observing that the solo professional singer began to emerge as an important figure in musical life around 1570. At around the same time, society was giving increasing attention to emotional expression and the cultivation of virtuosity. With the development of opera came the training to meet these demands.

The 17th- and 18th-century tradition of bel canto was based on the continuity of objectives, of technique, and of criteria for musical judgement. It was also dependent on the close relationship between composer and performer, teacher and student, performer and audience. The teacher (who was often also a composer) was an accomplished performer in the musical style who acted as an example to the student. The student practised assiduously and, by trial and error, eventually produced the approved sound, learned what sensations accompanied production of that sound, and thus learned how to reproduce it.

The teaching of the bel canto masters

The bel canto tradition was largely an oral one, which presents obvious – perhaps insuperable – problems to historians aiming to document the practice of the 17th and 18th centuries. There are no recordings of 17th-century vocal sound, and the technical teaching of the singing studio can be deduced only from the writings of singers and teachers, published technical exercises, and the repertoire for which singers were training.

The primary aim of voice teaching was to produce 'beautiful' tone and agility, allied to a sensitive ear. Singers cultivated good breath control for the singing of extended phrases. Voice teachers taught techniques (musical as much as vocal) for emotionally expressive singing and for vocal ornamentation. The tradition emphasized the natural abilities of the pupil and the obligation of the teacher to develop these abilities. The experience of the teacher, as a singer but often also as a composer, was the most important component of the process, and teaching proceeded by example on the part of the master and repeated trial and error on the part of the pupil:

2

In giving the precise rules to a student let the teacher not only tell him
and explain to him, but let him illustrate his meaning by making himself
an example. . . . Let the experienced teacher follow this method and he
will soon be convinced how much more preferable are practical demon-
strations to general rules. (Mancini, 1774/1777/1967, p. 103)

In keeping with the new status of the singer as virtuoso, an understanding of the vocal instrument was expected. In Italy, Tosi (1743/1987, p. x)

advocated 'a little less Fiddling with the Voice, and a little more Singing with the Instrument.' In France, Bérard asserted that:

> A singer who does profound research on the mechanism of the voice will have a great facility in forming high and low sounds. He will command his organs in any way, he will hasten or retard their movement according to his convenience. He will draw from them strong, vigorous, and mellow sounds, as well as tender, light, and mannered sounds. (1755/1969, p. 61)

Many writers emphasized the obligations of the teacher. Tosi, for example, wrote:

> let him hear with a disinterested ear whether the person desirous to learn has a voice and a disposition, that he may not be obliged to give a strict account to God of the parent's money ill spent, and the injury done to the child by the irreparable loss of time, which might have been more profitably employed in some other profession. (1743/1987, p. 2)

There was an emphasis on the innate gifts expected of the singing student: a pleasing appearance, adequate breathing capacity, no malformation of face, mouth, or body, and a good ear. Posture and facial expression were to be 'graceful' or 'natural.' A positive mental attitude, both in study and performance, was advocated. Most of the old masters were interested primarily in breath management and the ability to sing extended phrases. Many of the Italian sources contain rules on where the performer may breathe in long passages and give hints about cutting some notes short in order to obtain needed breath (Duey, 1951).

Theories of phonation were based on incomplete or incorrect information. The anatomy of the throat was well understood for all practical purposes, but the physiology of the vocal organs was not. While some writers presented simplified – and often incorrect – descriptions or diagrams of the vocal organs, these seem to have little to do with their descriptions of vocal technique. Singers made no attempt at conscious control of particular muscle groups. Instead, teachers urged the singer to keep a natural and free muscular balance of all physical faculties in order for the body to respond naturally and quickly to the sense and idea of both text and music. Blanchet was unusual in advocating conscious muscular control of the larynx and, significantly, he was not a musician (Duey, 1951). Perhaps current neurological research and body-use techniques (discussed in Chapter 8) will give us better insight into how best to combine these two approaches.

Teachers gave directions on resonance that were linked to the coordination of respiration and sound production. Singers were concerned with keeping the voice free and producing it orally rather than nasally. The great masters spoke of 'opening the throat,' 'loosening the neck,' and 'singing the tone forward, at the lips.' Many wrote of the different qualities and emotional effects of particular vowels.

All the early writers had something to say about the registers of the voice and how they should be blended. Unfortunately, because these writers formed a great deal of their opinions by observing castrati, the information is now difficult to interpret. Registers were named according to the singer's sensations of sympathetic vibration, for example, the chest or head registers. There is some confusion for modern readers in the use of the term 'falsetto' which may refer to either what other writers call 'head' or to the lighter, breathier tone of the male voice above its full-toned 'head' range. (Register terminology is examined in detail in Chapter 6.)

The earliest Italian writers, such as Caccini (1602/1970), did not advocate use of the head voice. This may be because they wrote for a male public and also because of the narrow range demanded by the early declamatory style. Later writers, such as Tosi and Mancini, considered the head voice to be an essential quality and the blending of chest and head voice to be vital before attempting to acquire agility.

Writers stressed the importance of a good ear and the necessity for precise intonation. It was assumed that the teacher had a good enough ear and sufficient singing experience to be able to identify and correct faults of intonation or tone. The masters generally agreed that moderation in eating, drinking, and living was important to vocal health. Vocal strain was to be avoided in order to preserve the voice. Bel canto developed and flourished within the context of a particular musical style that dominated art music in Italy and many other parts of Europe for over two centuries. Notwithstanding changes and developments within that style, there was little serious disagreement among practitioners from the early 17th century until the early 19th century about the musical function of the singing voice or about what constituted good singing. This musical style formed the accepted context for the teaching of singing.

Over the last 200 years or so, the musical and social assumptions underlying this model for the teaching of singing have ceased to be self-evident. Some of the factors underlying this change are discussed in the rest of this chapter.

New uses of the singing voice

Many musical developments from the late 18th century and during the 19th century contributed to different, heavier demands on singers. Public concerts meant larger venues and larger orchestras, gave increasing importance to the conductor, and contributed to the separation of the roles of composer, performer, and teacher.

During the 18th century, the functions of voice and orchestra in opera had been clearly defined: the orchestra accompanied the singers and played by itself only on specified occasions. The 19th-century desire to blur boundaries led to use of the orchestra not only to create mood but also to enter into the drama as a continuous web of instrumental sound. In the late works of Verdi, for example, the voices compete with a large orchestra employed as part of the drama. With larger concert halls and increasingly chromatic music, the orchestra grew in size and importance, culminating in Wagner's music dramas, in which the orchestra develops the entire action while the voice declaims in melody strictly moulded to the text. These lengthy works, and later the operas of Puccini and the works for voice and orchestra of Mahler and Strauss, all called for hitherto unimagined vocal and physical stamina.

In our time, singing encompasses a wide range of 'classical' styles as well as many other genres and the styles used in them. There are a wide variety of world musics, jazz, rock, pop, and music theatre. The aesthetic expectations in these musics can be very different, and the physical coordinations needed to produce the appropriate vocal sounds quite different. Unfortunately, research into these differences is in its infancy.

Science and singing

The Spanish singer Manuel Garcia (1805–1906) is a legendary figure in vocal pedagogy and voice research. His studies in Naples with Ansani provided him with links to the bel canto traditions of Porpora. His studies in France with his father exposed him to the new style of singing introduced into France by the tenor Duprez in 1837 (Paschke, 1975). His own vocal problems motivated him to invent the laryngoscope, a mirror apparatus used to view the larynx with the intention of showing how it produced sounds and registers (Garcia, 1894/1982). (While we now have videoendoscopy, doctors still sometimes use the laryngoscope to view the larynx.)

Garcia had the idea that bel canto was produced by vibrations of the vocal cords only, caused by a full breath propelled by a bellows-like action of the muscles of the chest, forcing air from the lungs through the vocal cords (*coup de glotte*). On the foundation of his vocal cord theory, Garcia built up a method for the training of singers, published in 1840 under the title of *L'art du chant*. In 1856, he published a revised version of this manual, called *Nouveau traité de l'art du chant*, which became a standard text.

Garcia's development of a method of teaching based on his experimental investigations reflects the growth and increasing importance of the natural sciences in the 19th century. However, his emphasis on the vocal folds and on the separate elements of the vocal mechanism failed to explain their interdependent working. Although his work represented an important advance in scientific knowledge about the voice, it also represented the beginning of fragmentation of knowledge about vocal technique.

The serious attempts at scientific study of the voice continued into the 20th century. Garcia's work was continued by his pupil Mathilde Marchesi (*c.* 1901; n.d., 19–). A scientific stance is also apparent in Emma Seiler's *The Voice in Singing* (1890). Seiler, a pupil of the German acoustician and physiologist Helmholtz, taught singing in America. She advocated study not only of the aesthetic side of the art of singing, but of the 'physiological and physical side also, without an exact knowledge, appreciation, observance, and study of which, what is hurtful cannot be discerned and avoided' (p. 34).

Nonetheless, voice science and vocal pedagogy remained independent of each other, despite such attempts to bring them together. Works describing the mechanism, usually by doctors or physiologists, often emphasized how to avoid vocal problems. Works by singer–teachers more often described the singer's sensations when producing particular sounds, and espoused 'correct' methods for producing 'good' sound. Rarely did the two approaches meet. This division persisted well into the 20th century.

There is still a problem with incorporating the findings of voice science into a theory of singing and singing pedagogy. Scientific studies are often of necessity confined to one or two small elements of the overall mechanism, they often use a small number of participants, and can only test aspects of voice for which there is appropriate technology that is neither harmful nor so invasive or restrictive that it produces unrealistic results. Often the terminology used in voice science and medicine is different from that traditionally used in singing, making interpretation of results difficult.

Singers need the integrated, holistic working of mind and body promoted by the bel canto masters. To help them achieve this economically, singing teachers need the detailed knowledge of the physical aspects of the vocal mechanism that can come from scientific studies, but they also need to know how these aspects are coordinated to produce the aesthetically appropriate vocal tone, and how to convey that information in a way that helps the singer achieve integrated mind–body control of voice in the service of music and language.

Since the 1960s works attempting to integrate the scientific and the experiential, written by singers with scientific interests or doctors and physiologists interested in singing, have become more common. Some of these works are discussed later in this book.

Contemporary voice science

Modern voice science and vocal pedagogy are products of the last 50 years or so. During that period, voice science has been transformed by new technologies that can scan brain activity, view the larynx in operation, measure muscular effort, and provide real-time feedback on vocal acoustics. The period has also seen the emergence of interdisciplinary collaboration between voice specialists in research, clinical, and performance disciplines. Interdisciplinary collaboration and the use of new technologies have raised new questions for voice research, and the answers are leading to a better understanding of how the vocal instrument works and how its health can be maintained. Voice science is both increasing our understanding of the ways in which the performer's voice may most efficiently be employed and, in some areas, confirming the wisdom of traditional pedagogies.

Science for singing teachers

The tradition of vocal pedagogy has been largely an oral one. This tradition continues in our time, despite a breakdown of many of the social and musical assumptions that previously underpinned it and despite the pressures of modern mass education. Today, many of the larger concerns of a rapidly changing society impact on the field of singing pedagogy: science versus art, elitism versus populism, the national versus the international, the rational versus the instinctive.

While many of the precepts of the bel canto masters, based on observation and experience, have largely been proven sound by scientific investigation, such a 'natural,' slow, and generalized approach to the teaching of vocal technique in singing is no longer adequate. The range of vocal styles current in the 21st century means that teachers may need to teach students who wish to train as professional performers in a vocal tradition other than the teacher's own, or to sing for self-expression and amateur music-making. Moreover, the human voice remains the most convenient, portable musical instrument for use in music education and group music-making at all levels (Atterbury & Richardson, 1995; Durrant & Welch, 1995; Welch et al., 2010). To achieve maximum results in minimum time and without vocal strain, a knowledge of vocal technique is useful to the music educator and choral director (Phillips, 1992; Miller, 1995). Most teachers need to work with students of voice types other than their own. Perhaps even more than in Tosi's day, teachers – particularly in post-compulsory education – are required to give strict account of the time and money spent in training singers. To meet these demands requires an understanding of the combination of physical factors that safely and efficiently produce the aesthetically appropriate vocal sound. That understanding also serves as the basis for diagnosing vocal faults.

All these factors – the disruption of a continuous single tradition of vocal pedagogy, the proliferation of vocal styles, the heavy physical demands of singing with electronic instruments or large orchestras in large spaces, fragmentation of sources of knowledge about voice, and new information about vocal function and vocal health – had, by the 20th century, produced a state of some confusion in vocal pedagogy.

This confusion was recognized as early as 1947, when Victor Alexander Fields, in *Training the Singing Voice*, wrote of 'confusion in the vocal teaching profession' (p. 3), and the need to give a pedagogical interpretation to scientific discoveries about the singing voice. Fields isolated a difficulty in singing pedagogy that has since continued to grow and become even more significant:

> The laboratory research worker is often far removed in his thinking from the teaching practices of the classroom or studio. Conversely, the singing teacher often must handle unpredictable personality problems with intuitive insight and improvized instructional techniques that are not readily amenable to experimental analysis. (p. 15)

Fields' book essayed a reconciliation of these points of view through analysis of the working concepts of singing pedagogy embodied in works published in the period from 1928 to 1941. He commented that while there is no lack of printed material on the subjects of singing and voice culture, this material is inaccessible to teachers because it is extremely diversified and fragmentary, and diffusely distributed throughout a variety of books, periodicals, scientific papers, reports of experiments, and published interviews that have never been correlated from the standpoint of a definite vocal pedagogy. His statement, that 'what is written about the singing voice is so often overlaid and interwoven with conflicting theories and extravagant conjectures that misinterpretations are inevitable' (1947, p. 1), pointed to the gap between scientific reports and writings by practitioners. He went on to summarize a mass of critical comment, outlining 21 different categories of complaint voiced by authors, to support his claim that the field of vocal pedagogy stood badly in need of clarification. Fields' aims were to survey and correlate available sources of bibliographic information on methods of training the singing voice in order to provide both a core of organized information for the use of singing teachers and an orientation for research in the field. His bibliographic survey covered pedagogy, breathing, phonation, resonance, range, dynamics, ear training, diction, and interpretation.

Another landmark in 20th-century writings on singing technique, William Vennard's *Singing: The Mechanism and the Technic*, was published in 1949 – two years after Fields' book – and revised and greatly enlarged in 1967. Like Fields, Vennard was concerned with relating aspects of singing pedagogy to the acoustic, anatomical, and physiological facts of voice, but his work is a textbook for teachers and singers rather than a bibliographic survey.

In the nearly 20 years between Vennard's first and second editions, scientific investigation of singing voice grew rapidly. In both editions, Vennard stated his aim as 'to compile under one cover objective findings from various reliable sources and to relate them to the art of singing' (1967, p. iii) and went on to hint at the same difficulties that Fields had articulated:

> As the title indicates, this book is frankly mechanistic. . . . There are those teachers who feel that applying science to an art is quackery, but I believe that our only safeguard against the charlatan is general knowledge of the most accurate information available.
>
> If you are one who has always preferred the empirical approach, perhaps you should read my last chapter first. You may then agree that the knowledge of literal fact is the only justifiable basis for the use of imagery and other indirect methods. Whether you are a singer or a teacher of singing, I hope you will find here truths which you may profitably add to your philosophy, or at least a rationale for harmonizing some of the apparent conflicts in our profession. (Vennard, 1967, p. iii)

These 'apparent conflicts' have not disappeared. In 1973, John Carroll Burgin published a study (*Teaching Singing*) of similar approach and structure to that of Fields, in effect bringing Fields' work up to date by analysing bibliographic data of the period between 1943 and 1971.

In 1978, Brent Jeffrey Monahan identified the need for yet another such study. He acknowledged the work of Fields and Burgin and of Philip A. Duey's systematic analysis of bel canto sources (*Bel Canto in its Golden Age*, 1951). Monahan's research (*The Art of Singing*, 1978) filled in the period from where Duey's work ended to where Fields' began – the period from 1777 to 1927. Like Burgin's book, it followed a similar format to Fields' study. Monahan drew together the earlier research by posing the questions:

> Are traditional concepts retained throughout the years, are they abandoned, or are they interpreted and expanded in the light of modern scientific investigation? When do concepts not mentioned in bel canto writings emerge? Do certain concepts enjoy only fleeting popularity, and is it possible to trace the history of a concept? (p. 4)

Monahan's work is significant in covering the 19th century, a period of change from an emphasis on the empirical methods of the 'old Italian school' to a more scientific approach. During this period, Manuel Garcia's scientific investigations of the singing voice formed part of the general climate of scientific investigations in the fields of anatomy, physiology, acoustics, and orthoepy (theories about the pronunciation of words).

Another work that has clarified some of the sources of disagreement and confusion in the teaching of singing is Richard Miller's *English, French, German and Italian Techniques of Singing: A Study in National Tonal Preferences and How They Relate to Functional Efficiency* (1977). Miller identified basic areas of vocal technique where national approaches frequently stand in opposition to each other: breath management, registration, resonance, vowel formation and modification, vocal coloration, 'cover,' 'placement,' laryngeal positioning, buccal and pharyngeal postures, the attack, vibrato rate, voice classification, and the uses of falsetto. His investigation attributed many national tendencies in singing to language and 'national temperament' factors:

> there are compelling reasons for associating varying national attitudes toward vocalism with overall cultural attitudes . . . vocal techniques are but the means for achieving certain sounds which most please a particular cultural unit. Specific kinds of vocal literature and specific kinds of vocal sounds have evolved which directly correspond to national temperaments. (p. 194)

Miller's comparison of the distinctly national techniques led him to conclude that 'extremes of nationalism in vocal pedagogy often are based upon the distortion of physical function' (1977, p. 203) and that 'a wise singer will look for that internationalization of technique which closely corresponds to the best elements of the historical tradition of the Italian School' (p. 206). It is on this basis that his 1986 book, *The Structure of Singing: System and Art in Vocal Technique*, was predicated. In that book, Miller presented categories of technical problems, exercises to assist in establishing technical skills dependent on optimum physical function, and information on the voice as a physical–acoustic instrument. The introduction articulates – yet again – the problem already outlined by Fields, Burgin, and Monahan:

> any vocal technique involves making assumptions, of varying degrees of specificity as well as of accuracy, concerning the physical production of sound. Differing viewpoints exist with respect not only to aesthetic preference but to the most appropriate physical means for producing the desired sound. (p. xix)

But here a new criterion of judgement was introduced, surely an outcome of late 20th-century scientific certainties about voice:

> The success of any technical approach to singing must be measured by how nearly it arrives at the planned aesthetic result with the least cost.
> Freedom of function in singing ought to count heavily in determining which vocal sounds are most pleasing. The highest possible degree

of physical freedom may well be the best indicator of the reliability of aesthetic judgment on the singing voice. (pp. xix–xx)

As discussed above, conflicts and confusions between the findings of voice science and the traditional assumptions of vocal pedagogy have been noted by Fields (1947), Vennard (1967), Burgin (1973), Monahan (1978), and Miller (1977, 1986). All these works are concerned with clarifying what physical means are used to achieve aesthetically desirable vocal sound. In addition, Miller's work makes explicit a concern that is implicit in many other writings, that is, that judgement of what is aesthetically desirable needs to be informed by judgement about 'freedom of physical function.' For teachers of singing to make a judgement of what is involved in freedom of physical function, they need to be knowledgeable about voice production.

There is still much scientific information relevant to singing appearing in journals in many different disciplines – neuroscience, psychology, physiology, medicine, speech pathology, acoustics, and linguistics, as well as singing and voice science – contributing to the fragmentation of knowledge on voice. In the last 50 years a great deal of scientific material has been published on various aspects of vocal physiology and acoustics. In the last 20 years some of this knowledge has been incorporated into books on singing and the teaching of singing.

Thurman and Welch's comprehensive *Bodymind and Voice* (2000) examines all aspects of singing against a background of the anatomy, physiology, and acoustics of voice. The *Oxford Handbook of Singing* (Welch et al., in press) updates that knowledge. Nair's *The Craft of Singing* (2007) brings together the physical with the aesthetic and applies it to song learning and performance. Chapman's *Singing and Teaching Singing* (2012) applies a range of interdisciplinary insights to singing and teaching singing, with particular emphasis on the Accent Method of breathing, while emphasizing the holistic nature of singing.

This book is concerned with the physical and mental bases of voice production: what we know about how the vocal instrument works. While some reference is made to the publications above, the main focus is on interpreting research findings in the overall context of singing and the teaching of singing. The next chapter gives a brief overview of the vocal instrument, while the following chapters assess the scientific literature on breath management, phonation, resonance, registration, vocal health relevant to the teaching of singing, and how these are brought together by the body, brain, and mind in singing. In the last chapter I return again to issues of teaching and learning, relating the specific physical and mental aspects of voice to broader pedagogical concerns.

References

Atterbury, B.W. & Richardson, C.P. (1995). *The Experience of Teaching General Music*. New York, NY: McGraw-Hill.

Bérard, J.-B. (1969). *L'art du chant* (S. Murray, trans.). Milwaukee, MN: Pro Musica Press. (Original work published 1755.)

Bukofzer, M.F. (1947). *Music in the Baroque Era*. New York, NY: Norton.

Burgin, J. (1973). *Teaching Singing*. Metuchen, NJ: Scarecrow Press.

Caccini, G. (1970). *Le nuove musiche* (H. Wiley Hitchcock, ed.). Madison: A-R Editions. (Original work published 1602.)

Celetti, R. (1991). *A History of Bel Canto* (F. Fuller, trans.). Oxford: Clarendon Press.

Chapman, J.L. (2012). *Singing and Teaching Singing: A Holistic Approach to Classical Voice* (2nd edn.). San Diego, CA: Plural Publishing.

Duey, P.A. (1951). *Bel Canto in its Golden Age: A Study of its Teaching Concepts*. New York, NY: King's Crown Press.

Durrant, C. & Welch, G. (1995). *Making Sense of Music: Foundations for Music Education*. London: Cassell.

Fields, V.A. (1947). *Training the Singing Voice: An Analysis of the Working Concepts Contained in Recent Contributions to Vocal Pedagogy*. New York, NY: King's Crown Press.

Galliver, D. (1974). Cantare con affetto: keynote of the Bel Canto. *Studies in Music*, *8*, 1–7.

Garcia, M. (1982). *Hints on Singing* (B. Garcia, trans.) (rev. edn.). New York, NY: Joseph Patelson Music House. (Original work published 1894.)

Heriot, A. (1956). *The Castrati in Opera*. London: Secker and Warburg.

Marchesi, M. (1901). *Ten Singing Lessons*. New York, NY: Harper and Brothers.

Marchesi, M. (n.d., 19–). *Bel Canto: A Theoretical and Practical Vocal Method*. London: Enoch.

Mancini, G. (1967). *Practical Reflections on Figured Singing: The Editions of 1774 and 1777 Compared* (E. Foreman, ed. and trans.). Champaign, IL: Pro Musica Press.

Manén, L. (1987). *Bel Canto: The Teaching of the Classical Italian Song-schools, Its Decline and Restoration*. Oxford: Oxford University Press.

Miller, R. (1977). *English, French, German and Italian Techniques of Singing: A Study in National Tonal Preferences and How they Relate to Functional Efficiency*. Metuchen, NJ: Scarecrow Press.

Miller, R. (1986). *The Structure of Singing: System and Art in Vocal Technique*. New York, NY: Schirmer Books.

Miller, R. (1995). The choral conductor as teacher of vocal technique. In *On the Art of Singing* (pp. 57–63). New York, NY: Oxford University Press.

Monahan, B.J. (1978). *The Art of Singing: A Compendium of Thoughts on Singing Published Between 1777 and 1927*. Metuchen, NJ: Scarecrow Press.

Nair, G. (2007). *The Craft of Singing*. San Diego, CA: Plural Publishing.

Palisca, C.V. (1968). *Baroque Music*. Englewood Cliffs, NJ: Prentice-Hall.

Paschke, D.V. (1975). Translator's Preface to M. Garcia, *A Complete Treatise on the Art of Singing: Part Two* (pp. ii–xii). New York, NY: Da Capo Press.

Phillips, K.H. (1992). *Teaching Kids to Sing*. New York, NY: Schirmer Books.

Seiler, E. (1890). *The Voice in Singing*. Philadelphia, PA: J.B. Lippincott.

Thurman, L. & Welch, G. (eds.) (2000). *Bodymind and Voice: Foundations of Voice Education* (rev. edn.) Collegeville, MN: The VoiceCare Network.

Tosi, P.F. (1987). *Observations on the Florid Song* (Galliard, trans., M. Pilkington, ed.). London: Stainer and Bell. (Original work published 1743.)

Vennard, W. (1967). *Singing: The Mechanism and the Technic* (rev. edn.). New York, NY: Carl Fischer.

Weaver, W. (1980). *The Golden Century of Italian Opera from Rossini to Puccini*. London: Thames and Hudson.

Welch, G., Himonides, E., Saunders, J., Papageorgi, I., Preti, C., Rinta, T., Vraka, M., Stephens Himonides, C., Stewart, C., Lanipekun, J. & Hill, J. (2010). Researching the impact of the national singing programme 'Sing Up' in England: Main findings from the first three years (2007–10). *Children's singing development, self-concept and sense of social inclusion*. London: Institute of Education, University of London.

Welch, G., Howard, D. & Nix, J. (eds.) (in press). *The Oxford Handbook of Singing*. New York, NY: Oxford University Press.

Chapter 2: The Voice as a Musical Instrument

> What is now proved was once only imagin'd.
> (William Blake, *The Marriage of Heaven and Hell*)

The joint enterprise of the student and teacher is to enable use of the human voice as a musical instrument and aesthetic communicator. That instrument is, of course, the whole person. This is why singing is such a human and moving activity, both for those who do it and for those who listen. In order to help student singers play the vocal instrument to communicate aesthetic meanings, teachers need to know how that instrument works – not just in overview, but in the specifics and their involvement with the larger coordinations. In coming to that understanding, practitioners resort to talking about body and brain, about emotion and vocal apparatus, about music and language, and about perception and cognition. Chapters 3 through 7 discuss voice science findings about the specifics of the vocal apparatus. The description below of the larger coordinations supplies the context for the understanding of the specifics and their applicability in the teaching of singing, while Chapter 8 examines in more detail how brain and body work together, and Chapter 9 the implications of this for teaching and learning.

The soma and the body

The vocal instrument is the body. As Leppert said, 'Whatever else music is "about," it is *inevitably* about the body; music's aural and visual presence constitutes both a relation to and a representation of the body' (1993, p. xx).

But there are two different – and sometimes diametrically opposed – ways of observing and understanding the body. One way is from a first-person perspective, from the inside. This body is the soma. For singers, developing a highly-tuned proprioceptive sense – a knowledge of the soma – is essential in using the vocal instrument effectively, both from a physical and an aesthetic point of view. The other way is from a third-person perspective, from the outside. This is the physical body, characterized by universal laws of physics and chemistry. For scientists, collecting data from observation and measurement of human bodies is essential to an understanding of vocal physiology and acoustics.

Failure to distinguish between these different points of view leads to fundamental misunderstandings and hinders both teacher–student communication and interdisciplinary communication. A complete understanding of the vocal instrument requires both an inside and an outside view: it is this which the teacher of singing requires.

Hearing, feeling, and thinking

The senses are what form the link between the inside and the outside body. It is the human body that sees, hears, feels, perceives, and makes sense of its surroundings. That same body may be thinking language and music while apprehending internal sensations of vibration, movement, and sound, and while attending and responding to external sensations, such as the sound of its own voice and the sight and sound of instrumental accompaniment, other singers, and an audience.

The organ essential to this process is the ear, not only in providing auditory input, but in its control of symmetry and balance. The two functions are intimately related, with the auditory system supplying the brain with data on the nature and location of vibrations in the air (perceived as sounds) and the vestibular system of the inner ear providing data on the position of the body. In any type of music-making these two functions come together. Anthony Storr even claimed that because music can order our muscular system, 'it is also able to order our mental contents. A perceptual system originally designed to inform us of spatial relationships by means of imposing symmetry can be incorporated and transformed into a means of structuring our inner world' (1992, p. 41). Certainly, in singing auditory, vestibular, and oral functions are coordinated as one in responding to thought, emotion, and sensory feedback. This may account for the association over centuries, in a wide range of cultures, of voicing with meditation and spiritual experience.

The ear forms the link between the vocal apparatus and the brain. Both audition (hearing) and audiation (mental hearing) are essential to singing. Audiation also provides the link between music and language and between singing and movement. Audiation is the name given by Edwin Gordon to the ability to perceive and comprehend musical sound that is no longer present, or that may never have been present: 'Audiation is to music what thought is to speech' (1993, p. 13). This ability is essential for all musical thought. Serafine (1988) proposed that a theory of music is at the same time a theory of music cognition and musical thinking. She defined cognition in music, in listening as well as in composing and performing, as 'an active, constructive process' (p. 7), dependent on perception, but not the same as perception. Music listening is a unique thinking process where the 'art form is not considered a clearly specified external object, but rather an internal, subjective entity springing from mental operations' (p. 233).

Alfred Tomatis' work built on this knowledge that 'one sings with one's ear' (1991, p. 44), working on 'good auditory receptivity' and 'good self-listening' (p. 49). He emphasized that the right ear is dominant in singing, because 'in the feedback loop of self-listening, which connects the hearing apparatus to the larynx, the right ear will be closer to the organs of speech than the left' (p. 50).

16

Speaking and singing/language and music

The process of hearing, perceiving, and remembering sound forms a loop with the production of sound. In speaking and singing, the sounds being produced by the vocal mechanism are constantly being fed through this loop, dictating what is produced by the vocal apparatus. Even when the physical sound is not there, we are able to audiate the music we see notated or are about to improvise, just as we are able to hear mentally what we read silently or what we are about to say. Audiation, then, is a process involving physical hearing, perception, cognition, and cultural conditioning.

In recent years, the likelihood of physical and mental links between music and language has been reinforced by investigation into foetal and neonatal development. The foetal sound environment is dominated by the sounds of the mother's body, the sounds of her respiratory and digestive systems, and her movements and phonations (Abrams & Gerhardt, 1997). Infants in the womb react to both unstructured noise and to music with movements that their mothers can feel (Storr, 1992, p. 9). It seems that the origins of both music and language lie in the connection between the neural development of the foetus and this early sound environment. After birth, the affective expressions of crooning, cooing, and babbling develop into speech and song (Storr), with the distinction between speech and song often unclear (Welch, 1994).

Alone among musicians, singers have the joy – and the difficulty – of dealing with words as well as music. Introducing language into the music raises issues related to meaning, phrasing, style, memory, and the need to know several languages. Even more basic, however, is the fact that articulation of words affects the whole instrument: breath management, laryngeal function, and resonance. There is little point in teachers having a good abstract knowledge of vocal anatomy, physiology, and acoustics if they do not have sufficient knowledge of articulatory phonetics to appreciate how the working of the instrument is affected by the demands of different languages.

Then there are the similarities between language and music as semiotic systems using the medium of sound. Specific relationships may exist between music and the meaning of the words, or in the structural relationships between music and text. Under structural relationships between music and linguistic features, two groups may be identified: (1) the relationship between music and linguistic features such as lines, rhyme, and stanza which are present only in poetry; and (2) the relationship between music and linguistic features found in language at large, such as stress, length, tone, and intonation (Nettl, 1964, p. 282). Full understanding of a song thus rests not only on music or words, but on more general linguistic understandings, as well as understanding of the music–language relationship in bodies of vocal music, and in particular compositions.

17

The vocal instrument

Regarded as a musical instrument, the voice consists of an actuator (the energy produced by the respiratory apparatus), a vibrator (the vocal folds), and a resonator (the vocal tract). These body parts must be aligned posturally to maximize their coordinated working, be directed by the brain to produce the requisite pitch, loudness, duration, and timbre, and must respond to higher-level demands such as musical phrasing and text articulation.

Control over pitch and loudness requires control of the airstream and of the vocal folds. Pitch is the perceptual correlate of phonation frequency – the repetition rate of the glottal pulses – which is mainly determined by the tension and mass of the vocal folds. Loudness is the perceptual correlate of intensity, which is determined by the amount of excitation that the glottal waves deliver to the air in the vocal tract (Baken, 2005). This depends largely on the interaction between subglottal pressure and the resistance of the vocal folds to the airflow. Resonance factors may also influence the perception of loudness. Control over pitch and loudness together is a feat of fine coordination, because the singer must judge by feel the amount of subglottal pressure and glottal resistance and the appropriate vocal fold adjustment required to sing high soft notes, to sing low loud notes, and to manage crescendo and diminuendo (Callaghan, 1995).

The vocal folds consist of multiple layers, each having different mechanical properties and each subject to different adjustments from the laryngeal muscles. Hirano (1988) contrasted this structure with the structure of the strings of many musical instruments and with the vocal folds of other animals, pointing out that the human structure is particularly well adapted to singing. The complex adjustments possible within each layer and between layers mean that the voice is capable of finer tuning than is possible on string instruments.

The ability to sing the required relative durations (rhythm) requires coordination of the whole singing instrument in response to a clear mental concept of the musical demands. This coordination depends largely on breath management – the ability to inhale in the time available and to manage the flow of breath to meet the demands of music in relation to length of phrase, leaps, and dynamics (Callaghan, 1995).

The timbre of the voice is determined by the functioning of the vocal folds in the production of the voice source and the acoustic filtering of this sound through the configuration of the vocal tract. The shape of the glottal pulses determines the potential quality of the note sung. The glottal wave may be smoothly varying (rounded) and contain little energy at the higher overtones; or it may have a sharp 'corner,' (changing in slope) and contain relatively more energy at the higher overtones (Rothenberg, 1984).

Turbulence and perturbation are also part of the voice source. Some turbulence is perceived as a softness, or velvety quality, in the sound. More turbulence might be heard as breathiness, or perhaps huskiness, and too much turbulence contributes to the perception of hoarseness (Baken, 2005). Female voices have a longer open phase and a posterior opening, creating aspiration noise in the region of the third formant, which is perceived as a breathier quality than that of male voices (Mendoza et al., 1996).

The voice source produced by the vibrating vocal folds is a spectrum of tones, comprising the fundamental (the lowest frequency or pitch of the note) and the overtones or harmonics at integer multiples of the fundamental. The air in the vocal tract acts as a resonator, selecting out frequencies from the sound source according to the configuration of the tract. Frequencies that fit the resonator optimally are formant frequencies, and it is the partials closest to these formant frequencies that are transmitted with increased amplitude (Sundberg, 1987).

The timbre of a note, both in regard to vowel quality and voice colour, depends on the formant frequencies. A movement in any of the articulators generally affects the frequencies of all formants. The two lowest formants determine vowel quality, while the third, fourth, and fifth are responsible for personal voice characteristics such as voice type and timbre (Sundberg, 2005). Timbre is linked to perception of pitch through the distribution of formant frequencies characteristic of particular vowels: for example, a pitch sung on /i/, with its high second formant, may be perceived as higher than the same pitch sung on /u/, with its relatively low second formant.

As mentioned above, the length and shape of the tract are changed by the position of the larynx, the shape of the pharynx, the position of the tongue, soft palate, and mandible, and the shape of the lips. The articulators are inter-related, allowing subtle adjustments to vocal timbre. Minor alterations in the configuration of these structures may produce substantial changes in voice quality. These structures are also used for the articulation of words. Therefore, in singing, vocal timbre and production of text are intimately linked. The articulation of continuous text set to music affects the whole instrument: breath management, laryngeal function, and resonance.

Because the singer is the musical instrument, the teaching of vocal tech-nique usually concerns the use of body and mind in achieving particular musical ends. Body alignment, breath management, the attack or onset, reso-nance, aesthetically pleasing tone, word articulation, unifying vocal registers, and extending range (e.g. Husler & Rodd-Marling, 1976; Miller, 1986, 1993, 1996, 2000, 2004; Doscher, 1994; David, 1995; Bunch Dayme, 2009) and issues of health and overall body use (e.g. Proctor, 1980; McKinney, 1982; Miller, 1986; Titze, 1994; Sataloff, 2005; Bunch Dayme, 2009; Chapman, 2012) all affect the instrument.

To facilitate the best use of the body as a singing instrument, the teacher needs an understanding of vocal anatomy, physiology, and acoustics. Vennard pointed out that

> A teacher should know what he is talking about, but that does not mean that he gives a voice lesson as if he were teaching anatomy. All muscles are controlled indirectly, in terms of their effects beyond themselves. (1967, p. 19)

Nevertheless, such an understanding facilitates efficient teaching of the physical skills of singing, provides the basis of diagnosis of vocal faults, and ensures that technical work is informed by principles of vocal health. Information on vocal anatomy and physiology is now easily accessible to singing teachers, not only in scientific texts with some application to sing-ing (e.g. Hixon, 2006; Sataloff, 2005; Titze & Verdolini Abbott, 2012) but in many pedagogical texts (e.g. Husler & Rodd-Marling, 1976; Miller, 1986; Manén, 1987; Doscher, 1994; David, 1995; Nair, 1999; McCoy, 2004; Bunch Dayme, 2009; Chapman, 2012). This book is therefore concerned more with recent studies in vocal physiology and acoustics as they relate to singing.

Control of the vocal instrument

Information is extracted from a vocal utterance by recognition of patterns in the sequence of sounds, the patterns being identified by their boundaries, and by discontinuity in relation to continuity. In an article on the perceptual aspects of singing, Sundberg stated that 'the singer must gain control over all perceptually relevant voice parameters, so that they do not change by accident and signal an unintended boundary' (1994, p. 120). Technical control of all vocal parameters is therefore a prerequisite for artistic expression.

This overall control of the instrument is of overriding concern in the teaching of vocal technique. While it is this concern that motivates most writing on singing technique, only a small proportion of the literature explicitly addresses matters of overall coordination (e.g. Miller, 1986; Doscher, 1994; McCarthy, 2006; Bunch Dayme, 2009). Doscher, whose book is titled *The Functional Unity of the Singing Voice*, wrote of the 'sensuous building blocks' of the art that work as a functional unit (p. 167). McCarthy states that teachers who adopt a holistic approach 'not only bring specialist information and expertise to the relationship, but also importantly, take responsibility for facilitating another's change and growth – mind, body, and soul' (2006, p. 162).

> The essence of vocal technique has been realized when all of the physiological, mental, and emotional factors work harmoniously to produce the desired tone in a spontaneous and dynamic manner. This co-ordination and skill are achieved with proper direction, hard work, and patient, disciplined practice. (Bunch Dayme, 2009, p. 32)

While practitioners most often consider body alignment in relation to respiration, the posturing of the body contributes not only to controlled respiration, but to all aspects of sound production, through the relationships established between the respiratory system, the phonatory mechanism, and the resonators, and through feedback from the muscles to the nervous system. Singers may also call on postural muscles to play an active role in stabilizing the body under considerable stress when producing loud, sustained vocalization over a wide pitch range. Doscher's reference to posture as 'a kinesthetic barometer for the entire body, continually giving us conceptual data on body position, muscle tone, energy potential, and balance' (1994, p. 69) is apt.

While singing teachers devote much time to skills related to resonance, many teachers see conscious control of the larynx as either impossible or undesirable; they assert that in 'good' singing, the performer is unaware of any laryngeal sensation. However, the height of the larynx and its tilt have a quite radical effect on the vocal sound and are well within conscious control. And exercises concerned with the onset of phonation and register-blending primarily involve laryngeal control. Singers also experience the varying laryngeal loading of different vowels and the effect of palatal elevation on laryngeal functioning. There seems to be no reason why the fine laryngeal control used intuitively in many physiological functions such as laughing, crying, and sighing should not be brought under conscious control for singing. With these affective expressions, it is possible to achieve an instinctive balance between breath management, adjustment of the articulators, and laryngeal action.

Theories of tone placement attempt to correlate breath management, resonance balance, and the singer's physical sensations. Differences in timbre have corresponding locations of resonance sensation. Titze (1981) suggested that the singer's sensation of where tone is localized may be related to the localization of pressure maxima in the vocal tract and thus 'singing in the mask' or 'resonating the cheek bones' or 'aiming the tone toward the hard palate just behind the upper incisors' may all be related to achieving an acoustic pressure maximum at a specified location in the vocal tract.

The singer's sensations of resonance may, however, be unreliable as an indicator of timbre, or may differ from the teacher's. In adhering rigidly to one theory of placement for all voice types, there is also the danger of creating uneven timbre across the range and accentuating register problems, since the success of increasing acoustic output with formant tuning varies with fundamental frequency. Again, the danger is that such an approach may become fixed, and freedom of adjustment in response to aural cues may be diminished.

All vocal functions are controlled neurologically: the laryngeal muscles position the larynx and achieve adduction of the vocal folds; the diaphragm and intercostal muscles raise subglottal pressure; the muscles of articulation adjust the length and shape of the vocal tract; and the middle ear muscles reduce the sensitivity of the ear just before the initiation of phonation – all in response to a neurological signal (Sataloff, 1992). Recent investigations into the role played in voicing by the periaqueductal grey matter of the midbrain suggest that the re-creation of emotional experience in performance may allow access to subtleties of respiratory and laryngeal muscle patterning and particular vocal qualities integrated in that area of the brain (Larson, 1988; Davis et al., 1996).

Essential to vocal control is feedback. For singers, feedback may come from external sources or from internal sensory sources (Titze, 1982). External sources include the human response of audience, teachers, or colleagues. Internal feedback – visual, tactile, auditory, kinesthetic, and proprioceptive – is usually immediate and directly related to what goes on in the body. The mirror, the simplest form of visual feedback, has been in use in the singing studio for centuries. Recently computer-assisted visual feedback has become available.

Tactile, kinesthetic, and proprioceptive feedback is supplied through sensory receptors located throughout the entire body. Tongue position, jaw position, and tongue contact with the lips, teeth, or palate are monitored continuously during singing (Titze, 1982) and, as previously mentioned, the posture of the body provides proprioceptive feedback that is important in phonation.

Auditory feedback, transmitted from the ear through the brain stem to the cerebral cortex, is also used as a control by the singer. It allows the singer to match the sound produced with the sound intended (Sataloff, 1992; Titze, 1994). Tactile feedback from the throat and muscles also may help with the fine-tuning of vocal output (Sataloff, 1992).

For singers, sensations of vibration constitute a major source of control. Books on voice production for singers and teachers commonly have referred to location of vibration sensations (e.g. Husler & Rodd-Marling, 1976; Proctor, 1980; Miller, 1986), particularly in relation to airflow and resonance. Schutte and Miller (1984) pointed out that these sensations differ from or exceed the vibratory sensations of speech.

Several studies have clarified the source and location of sensations experienced by singers. Sundberg (1990), for example, found that the voice source, particularly the amplitude of its fundamental, was reflected in chest wall vibrations, particularly at the centre of the sternum. Even when the overall sound pressure level remained essentially constant, changing the mode of phonation from pressed to flow increased chest vibrations. This change led to changes in the amplitude of sternum vibrations, providing tactile feedback for phonation at low fundamental frequencies (up to 300 Hz). This would serve as a useful non-auditory (room-independent) signal for voluntary control.

Titze (1994) relates the singer's sensation of where the vowel is localized (focused) to the localization of pressure maxima of the standing waves of the vocal tract. Different vowels have high pressures in different regions, the /i/ vowel having pressures high in the palatal region, the /u/ vowel having pressures high in the velar region, and the /ɑ/ vowel having pressures high in the pharynx. The singer may use these sensations in modifying vowels as needed.

A study by Estill et al. (1984) found support for the common assumption that the palate is active in the production of high frequencies and differentially active depending on the voice quality. The researchers recorded the activity of the levator palatini, palatopharyngeus, the middle constrictor, and the geniohyoid muscles while a singer produced six vocal qualities over a two-octave range. Electromyographic recordings showed, in all six qualities, an increase in muscle activity with increase in fundamental frequency. Since these muscles are located in the centre of the head, their contraction may contribute to the feelings experienced by many singers that the palate is active in the upper part of the range, or in high intensity tones at any frequency.

Vocal control depends, then, on a complex of fine motor coordinations directed by neurological signals and monitored by a range of external and internal feedback.

The physiologically gifted voice

From time to time someone advances the theory that premier singers must be physiologically gifted. In societies where singing has become quite divorced from speaking, where the general populace does not sing (except perhaps at the football stadium), and where the singing of 'high art' music and 'popular' music have become very different, it is commonly believed that elite singers must be physiologically gifted. Researchers, however, have yet to prove this point.

Ingo Titze (1998) relied on theoretical models of voice and physical laws to suggest five attributes of a physiologically gifted voice: a wide cricothyroid space, strong cricothyroid and thyroarytenoid muscles, a thick mucosa with an optimal fibre–liquid concentration, symmetry between the left and right vocal folds, and the ability to activate adjacent muscles selectively. This cluster of physical attributes is analogous to those which may be identified as physical predispositions for playing other instruments (e.g. lip and jaw attributes in brass playing) and can contribute to a fine voice. A wide cricothyroid space makes a wide pitch range more likely. Strong cricothyroid and thyroarytenoid muscles allow efficient length and tension changes in the vocal folds. The quality of the mucosa affects the ability to create the optimal mucosal wave. Symmetry between the left and right vocal folds (and across the entire larynx) contributes to normal vocal fold vibration and good control of pitch, loudness, and onset. The ability to activate adjacent muscles selectively is one required for all skilled physical activity.

In a 1991 article, however, Thomas Cleveland recounted his investigation into the laryngeal characteristics of some premier singers. He used nasal endoscopy to examine the larynges of a number of premier singers and videotaped the examinations. He was disappointed to discover that these premier singers did not have the 'class' larynges he expected; they exhibited the range of difference and asymmetries common across the population. He concluded that each larynx 'is an original, and its potential lies far beyond its appearance' (p. 51).

While certain physical characteristics may amount to a predisposition for singing, learned skills are more important. In reviewing the differences between breathing, phonation, and articulation patterns in speech and singing, Johan Sundberg (1990) identified reasons why singers are 'special'; these relate largely to the ability to meet the heightened demands of pitch, duration, dynamics, and timbre made by many musical genres. The nature and applications of these physical skills will be considered in greater detail in the following chapters.

To see what one thinks, hears, and feels

Since the 1960s, there have been major developments in voice science. In singing, technical matters pose unique problems in that the singer's instrument is the body. The component parts of the singer's instrument consist of many different body parts that are used for other activities and require fine coordination to achieve expressive singing. Any part, or the overall coordination of all parts, of the instrument is susceptible to the singer's general physical, intellectual, and emotional state. Until recently, many of the working parts of this instrument could not be viewed in operation.

Sophisticated instrumentation now makes possible real-time visual and aural feedback on the acoustic effects of particular vocal manoeuvres. Through the use of videoendoscopy, for example, it is possible for a singer to see on a video screen the operation of the larynx as the sound is being produced, other computer analysers give a visual display of the acoustic properties of the sound as it is made, and there is software that demonstrates the buccal movements involved in articulating consonants. Such equipment makes it possible to diagnose vocal problems, to teach more efficiently, and to match specific prescriptions for vocal effort with the acoustic effects they produce.

Since about 1970, many scientific studies of voice have been carried out using technology to view the larynx in operation, measure muscular effort, determine subglottal pressure, and record the acoustic nature of vocal sound. Over the last 30 years it has become more common for writings on singing pedagogy to refer to scientific findings, and for scientific writings to comment on the implications for pedagogy. For these reasons, the following chapters refer mainly to the literature of the last 50 years.

References

Abrams, R.M. & Gerhardt, K.K. (1997). Some aspects of the foetal sound environment. In I. Deliege & J. Sloboda (eds.), *Perception and Cognition of Music* (pp. 77–95). Hove, UK: Psychology Press.

Baken, R.J. (2005). Vocal tract resonance. In R.T. Sataloff (ed.), *Professional Voice: The Science and Art of Clinical Care* (3rd edn.), Vol. 1 (pp. 237–55). San Diego, CA: Plural Publishing.

Bunch Dayme, M. (2009). *Dynamics of the Singing Voice* (5th edn.). Vienna: Springer-Verlag.

Callaghan, J. (1995). Fundamental teaching units of vocal pedagogy: Paper 1. *Australian Voice*, *1*, 1–5.

Chapman, J.L. (2012). *Singing and Teaching Singing: A Holistic Approach to Classical Voice* (2nd edn.). San Diego, CA: Plural Publishing.

Cleveland, T.F. (1991). Vocal pedagogy in the twenty-first century: does the 'premier' singer's larynx show visible differences from the normal singer's larynx? *The NATS Journal*, *47*(4), 50–51.

David, M. (1995). *The New Voice Pedagogy*. Lanham, MD: Scarecrow Press.

Davis, P.J., Zhang, S.P., Winkworth, A. & Bandler, R. (1996). Neural control of vocalization: respiratory and emotional influences. *Journal of Voice*, *10*(1), 23–38. doi: 10.1016/S0892-1997(96)80016-6

Doscher, B. (1994). *The Functional Unity of the Singing Voice* (2nd edn.). Metuchen, NJ: Scarecrow Press.

Estill, J., Baer, T., Honda, K. & Harris, K.S. (1984). The control of pitch and quality, Part I: an EMG study of supralaryngeal activity in six voice qualities. In V.L. Lawrence (ed.), *Transcripts of the Twelfth Symposium, Care of the Professional Voice*, 1983, Pt. I (pp. 86–91). New York, NY: The Voice Foundation.

Gordon, E.E. (1993). *Learning Sequences in Music: Skill, Content, and Patterns: A Music Learning Theory*. Chicago, IL: GIA Publications.

Hirano, M. (1988). Vocal mechanisms in singing: laryngological and phoniatric aspects. *Journal of Voice*, *2*(1), 51–69. doi:10.1016/S0892-1997(88)80058-4.

Hixon, T.J. (2006). *Respiratory Function in Singing: A Primer for Singers and Singing Teachers*. Tucson, AZ: Redington Brown.

Husler, F. & Rodd-Marling, Y. (1976). *Singing: The Physical Nature of the Vocal Organ*. London: Hutchinson.

Larson, C.R. (1988). Brain mechanisms involved in the control of vocalization. *Journal of Voice*, 2(4), 301–11. doi:10.1016/S0892-1997(88)80022-5

Leppert, R. (1993). *The Sight of Sound: Music, Representation, and the History of the Body*. Berkeley, CA: University of California Press.

McCarthy, M. (2006). The teaching and learning partnership Part 2. In J.L. Chapman (ed.), *Singing and Teaching Singing. A Holistic Approach to Classical Voice* (2nd edn.) (pp. 161–90). San Diego, CA: Plural Publishing.

McCoy, S. (2004). *Your Voice: An Inside View*. Princeton, NJ: Inside View Press.

McKinney, J.C. (1982). *The Diagnosis and Correction of Vocal Faults*. Nashville, TN: Broadman Press.

Manén, L. (1987). *Bel Canto: The Teaching of the Classical Italian Song-schools, Its Decline and Restoration*. Oxford: Oxford University Press.

Mendoza, E., Valencia, N., Muñoz, J. & Trujillo, H. (1996). Differences in voice quality between men and women: use of the long-term average spectrum (LTAS). *Journal of Voice*, 10(1), 59–66. doi:10.1016/S0892-1997(96)80019-1

Miller, R. (1986). *The Structure of Singing: System and Art in Vocal Technique*. New York, NY: Schirmer Books.

Miller, R. (1993). *Training Tenor Voices*. New York, NY: Schirmer Books.

Miller, R. (1996). *On the Art of Singing*. New York, NY: Oxford University Press.

Miller, R. (2000). *Training Soprano Voices*. New York, NY: Oxford University Press.

Miller, R. (2004). *Solutions for Singers*. New York, NY: Oxford University Press.

Nair, G. (1999). *Voice Tradition and Technology: A State-of-the-Art Studio*. San Diego, CA: Singular Publishing Group.

Nettl, B. (1964). *Theory and Method in Ethnomusicology*. London: Free Press.

Proctor, D.F. (1980). *Breathing, Speech, and Song*. Vienna: Springer-Verlag.

Rothenberg, M. (1984). Source-tract acoustic interaction and voice quality. In V.L. Lawrence (ed.), *Transcripts of the Twelfth Symposium, Care of the Professional Voice*, 1983, Pt. I (pp. 15–31). New York, NY: The Voice Foundation.

Sataloff, R.T. (ed.) (2005). *Professional Voice: The Science and Art of Clinical Care* (3rd edn.). San Diego, CA: Plural Publishing.

Sataloff, R.T. (1992). The human voice. *Scientific American*, 267(6), 108–15.

Schutte, H.K. & Miller, R. (1984). Resonance balance in register categories of the singing voice: A spectral analysis study. *Folia Phoniatrica et Logopaedica*, 36(6), 289–95. doi:10.1159/000265758

Serafine, M.L. (1988). *Music as Cognition: The Development of Thought in Sound*. New York, NY: Columbia University Press.

Storr, A. (1992). *Music and the Mind*. London: Harper Collins.

Sundberg, J. (1987). *The Science of Singing*. Dekalb, IL: Northern Illinois University Press.

Sundberg, J. (1990). Chest wall vibrations in singers. *Journal of Research in Singing and Applied Vocal Pedagogy*, *13*(2), 25–53.

Sundberg, J. (1994). Perceptual aspects of singing. *Journal of Voice*, *8*(2), 106–22. doi: 10.1016/S0892-1997(05)80303-0

Sundberg, J. (2005). Vocal tract resonance. In R.T. Sataloff (ed.), *Professional Voice: The Science and Art of Clinical Care* (3rd edn.), Vol. I (pp. 275–91). San Diego, CA: Plural Publishing.

Titze, I.R. (1981). Is there a scientific explanation for tone focus and voice placement? *The NATS Bulletin*, *7*(5), 26–27.

Titze, I.R. (1982). Sensory feedback in voice production. *The NATS Bulletin*, *38*(4), 32.

Titze, I.R. (1994). *Principles of Voice Production*. Englewood Cliffs, NJ: Prentice Hall.

Titze, I.R. (1998). Voice research: five ingredients of a physiologically gifted voice. *Journal of Singing*, *54*(3), 45–46.

Titze, I.R. & Verdolini Abbott, K. (2012). *Vocology: The Science and Practice of Voice Habilitation*. Salt Lake City, UT: The National Center for Voice and Speech.

Tomatis, A.A. (1991). *The Conscious Ear: My Life of Transformation through Listening* (S. Lushington, trans., B.M. Thompson, ed.). New York, NY: Station Hill Press.

Vennard, W. (1967). *Singing: The Mechanism and the Technic* (rev. edn.). New York, NY: Carl Fischer.

Welch, G.F. (1994). The assessment of singing. *Psychology of Music*, *22*(1), 3–19. doi: 10.1177/0305735694221001

Chapter 3: Body Alignment and Breath Management

Writers on singing emphasize that efficient breath management is funda-mental to vocal control in expressive singing. As Miller put it, 'any error in vocal technique, or any accomplishment of technical skill in singing, usually can be traced to techniques of breath management; control of the breath is synonymous with control of the singing instrument' (1986, p. 37).

Singers need to control respiration in order to meet musical demands in relation to phrase length, pitch range, loudness, musical articulation, time between phrases, and so on. In addition, breath management must be geared to producing the vocal quality appropriate to the particular style. The bulk of research on breath management has focused on classical singing, but over the last 20 years or so some research on non-classical singing has emerged.

Studies by Hoit, Christie, Watson, and Cleveland (1996) and Cleveland, Stone, Sundberg, and Iwarsson (1997) found the breath management practices of country singers to be similar in singing as in speech. In 1998 Cleveland compared the breath management strategy of classical singers with that of country singers. In most cases, classical singers initiate phrases at approximately 70% of vital capacity and use breath that is beyond the resting expiratory level, whereas country singers, while they also use breath beyond the resting expiratory level, initiate phrases at about 55% of vital capacity, a point close to tidal breathing. Country singers use similar breath strategies for speech and singing, and therefore their singing sounds more like speech, which is stylistically appropriate.

In two studies which used only a single female subject, Broadway music theatre singing was shown to use greater glottal adduction, and therefore higher subglottal pressure than that used in operatic singing, but similar to loud speech (Stone et al., 2003; Sundberg et al., 2012). Björkner's study using five male singers also produced similar results (Björkner, 2008). Zangger Borch and Sundberg found their one baritone subject used higher subglottal pressure in rock singing than he did in Swedish dance band style, and also substantially higher than that typically used in music theatre or opera (2011, p. 536).

According to Hixon and Hoffman (1979, p. 9) breathing for [classical] singing differs from resting breathing in that it uses:

- a far greater range of lung volumes,
- higher expiratory alveolar pressures and lower inspiratory alveolar pressures,
- lower expiratory airflow and higher inspiratory airflow,
- longer expiratory breathing phases and shorter inspiratory breathing phases, and

- torso shapes that depart more from the relaxed configuration of the chest wall.

For classical singers, the transition from inspiration to expiration is characterized by equal and opposite decreases in abdomen volume, and increases in ribcage volume occurring without a change in lung volume, and the transition from expiration to inspiration by rapid decrements in lung volume immediately preceding the onset of inspiration (Cleveland, 1998).

In an investigation into 'supported singing,' Mcdonald, Rubin, Blake, Hirani, and Epstein (2012) measured the recruitment patterns of the transverse abdominis muscle and internal oblique muscle of 25 vocalists (12 male and 13 female) singing in a semi-supine position. The participants, all college vocal students aged 17 to 34 years, sang in three different vocal qualities, labelled 'opera,' 'belt,' and 'normal,' involving different larynx height and different articulatory adjustments. The results relate only to singing at low and medium pitch, since some of the participants found singing at higher pitch difficult. The study showed that the periabdominal muscles play an active role in supported singing, with the transverse abdominis being the preferential muscle recruited. This seems unsurprising given the semi-supine position. It is not clear why that position was chosen. Singing at higher pitch (requiring higher subglottal pressure) while standing upright would provide more meaningful data.

Many researchers (e.g. Allen & Wilder, 1977; McGlone, 1977; Brown et al., 1978; Watson & Hixon, 1985; Sundberg, 1987; Brown et al., 1988; Hoit et al., 1996; Cleveland, 1998) have noted that accomplished trained singers use respiratory strategies different from both those of untrained singers and those that they themselves use in normal speech. Some researchers (e.g. Brown et al., 1988; Sundberg et al., 1995) have suggested that accomplished singers may have superior sensory abilities that help them develop finely tuned control of subglottal pressure and airflow to meet musical demands. The research into respiration in singing suggests that it is training, rather than any particular physiological endowment, that produces this control. An understanding of respiration and of the factors involved in breath management is therefore essential for the efficient teaching of singing.

The role of the diaphragm

Reporting a study of different national approaches to singing technique, Miller asserted that 'national schools of singing clearly indicate a lack of agreement as to how to approach breath management' (1977, p. 20). He attributed this lack of agreement to differing assumptions about the kinds of muscular action that are thought to occur during the breath cycle, particularly in relation to the control of the musculature that regulates or influences the diaphragm:

'Some teachers of singing claim that the diaphragm is an involuntary muscle which can be only indirectly controlled by the action of other controllable muscles; others attempt localized control over its movement' (p. 20).

In extended steady singing, the diaphragm is active at very large volumes, along with the inspiratory component of the ribcage wall and the abdominal wall. Activity of the diaphragm ceases at a large lung volume, with the ribcage wall providing the required braking action against the relaxation pressure (Hixon, 2006, p. 82). With the diaphragm quiescent, both the ribcage wall and abdominal wall are subjected to identical pressure changes across each wall. However, the continuous singing of phrases of various lengths required by a musical composition require rapidly changing adjustments of the respiratory apparatus (Hixon, 2006, p. 102), with the diaphragm remaining generally inactive (p. 117).

A 1985 study by Watson and Hixon and a 1987 study by Leanderson, Sundberg, and von Euler (Leanderson et al., 1987a) reached contradictory conclusions about the role of the diaphragm in breath management for singing. The Watson and Hixon study recorded anteroposterior diameter changes of the ribcage and abdomen in six baritones during four respiratory, four speaking, and four singing activities. The respiratory activities were vital-capacity manoeuvres, muscular relaxations of the respiratory apparatus at different lung volumes, and isovolume shape changes of the respiratory apparatus at a single lung volume. The speaking activities were two minutes of spontaneous conversation, reading aloud a declarative passage, reading the same passage at what the singer judged to be twice his normal volume, and reading aloud the words of the first verse of 'The Star Spangled Banner.' The participants sang 'The Star Spangled Banner,' two Italian songs, and an aria of the participant's choice, material making contrasting musical and language demands. Data were collected to calculate lung volume, volume displacements of the ribcage and abdomen, and to infer muscular mechanisms.

The singing training of the participants varied from five to 20 years of classical training, their performance experience ranged from largely university or college performances in oratorio and recital to professional opera performance, and their ages ranged from 23 to 38. The researchers made measurements using a noninvasive kinematic procedure requiring little experimental sophistication on the part of the singers and allowing the experimental setup to resemble performance conditions. They described the kinematic procedure as treating the chest wall as a two-part system consisting of the ribcage and abdomen. Relying on the fact that each part displaces volume as it moves (and that together they displace a volume equal to that displaced by the lungs), the procedure enables calculation of the relative volumes displaced by measuring changes in anteroposterior diameter for each part.

These investigators found two principal patterns of inspiration. In one, the volume contribution of the ribcage exceeded that of the abdomen. In the other, the contribution of the abdomen exceeded that of the ribcage during the first part of inspiration, followed by equal ribcage and abdominal displacement, then followed by a predominant ribcage contribution at the end of inspiration. They also found two patterns for the expiratory part of the breath cycle. In one, the volume contribution of the ribcage was greater. In the other, the abdominal contribution was greater for the first part of expiration, followed by equal ribcage and abdominal displacement, and then by predominant ribcage contribution during the last part of expiration. There were also two main types of transition from expiration to inspiration, one in which ribcage displacements predominated and one in which abdominal displacements predominated. Marked changes in relative contributions were associated with musical demands; inward abdominal displacement and outward ribcage displacement were associated with increases in loudness, stress, or high notes, while inward ribcage displacement and outward abdominal displacement were associated with passages involving high flow, as in the case of voiceless fricatives.

Watson and Hixon stated:

> the chest wall was continuously distorted from its relaxed configurations during singing . . . meaning that muscular forces were continuously in operation. The rib cage was found always to be maintained in a more expanded state and the abdomen always to be maintained in a less expanded state than were these two when relaxed at corresponding lung volumes. (1985, p. 116)

They went on to suggest a specific role for the abdomen:

> mainly one of posturing the chest wall in a manner that aids both the rib cage and diaphragm in their primary functions. This role involves the configuration of the chest wall and extends across both phases of the respiratory cycle for singing. (p. 119)

They attributed to the ribcage the major role of pressurization of the pulmonary system in expiration and to the diaphragm the role of inflating the pulmonary system quickly in inspiration.

Taken together, these confusing statements presumably mean that a body posture departing from the usual relaxed state is assumed for classical singing and that the muscles of ribcage and abdomen are active throughout the respiratory cycle. It is not clear exactly what this body posture is, whether it was the same for all six baritones, whether posture related to the different inspiratory patterns observed, and what bearing it had on the finding that all participants used a 'belly-in' strategy. The authors also acknowledged the difficulty, common to many studies of the singing voice, of assessing the contribution of singing training to the differences in data obtained from the singers used in their study.

The attribution to the abdomen of a posturing role seems at odds with the finding of marked abdominal displacement (presumably produced by muscle activity) accompanying increases in loudness, stress, or high notes. Watson and Hixon's assumption that the diaphragm is active during inspiration but plays no role in controlled expiration is common to many recent writings on singing. Doscher, for example, stated:

> Contrary to popular belief, we have little or no voluntary control over diaphragmatic action. The diaphragm has no proprioceptive (stimuli arising within an organism) nerve endings, and therefore it is impossible to experience any sensation of its position or movement. (1994, p. 18)

Control, however, does not only depend on feedback of muscle length or tension, and there are other sources of feedback – for example, the volume receptors in the lungs themselves.

The assumption made in many singing texts that the diaphragm is active only during inspiration has been called into question by a series of experiments conducted by Leanderson and collaborators on the role of the diaphragm in establishing adequate subglottal pressure in singing (1984, 1987a, 1987b). In one study (Leanderson et al., 1987a), the researchers conducted two different experiments. The first experiment investigated diaphragmatic activity during singing tasks requiring rapid changes in subglottal pressure. Four trained singers (one tenor and three baritones) performed tasks demanding rapid changes of subglottal pressure. On the basis that diaphragmatic activity acts to decrease intrathoracic pressure at the same time as it exerts positive pressure on the abdominal contents, pressure above and below the diaphragm was measured to indicate diaphragmatic activity. This required participants to swallow an esophageal catheter with two small pressure transducers. Oral pressure during /p/ occlusion was regarded as a good approximation of subglottal pressure with zero airflow and was measured by a thin catheter in the corner of the mouth. It is not clear whether this rather intrusive procedure affected the singing of the participants. Participants used varying strategies in producing the syllable sequence /paːpaːpaː/ . . ., in singing octave leaps, and in performing *subito forte-piano* tasks; yet all used a similar strategy for performing a trillo and in singing a coloratura passage. However, individual participants used similar strategies to perform some tasks and different strategies to perform others. What the significance of these variations might be is difficult to assess. Despite the variations, evidence for a consistent use of the diaphragm was found in all participants.

In this study the limited number of participants, the facts that they were all men, and that even among four participants there was inter-participant variability, make it difficult to assess the application of these results. From the practitioner point of view, it would be useful to know whether – and, if so, how – the different strategies used by the singers affected the sound quality they produced. Regardless of the variations, it was clear that some singers did activate the diaphragm when there was a need for a rapid decrease of subglottal pressure, such as when singing a falling octave interval, when shifting from a loud to a soft note, to save air during a /p/ explosion, or in performing a trillo involving a repeated switch between glottal adduction and abduction.

The second experiment in the Leanderson et al. (1987a) study investigated the effect of diaphragmatic activity on the voice source. Two female and four male untrained participants and two trained singers were asked to perform tasks first with an active diaphragm and then with a passive diaphragm. The tasks for the trained and untrained participants were different: the singers sang triads, octaves, and sustained tones of different intensity; the untrained participants sang gliding and sustained tones. The method of measurement was the same as in the first experiment, with sound pressure level measured in addition. The trans-diaphragmatic pressure was displayed on an oscilloscope screen as a visual feedback. In some participants, diaphragmatic activity apparently affected vocal fold adduction, producing airflow in the direction of flow phonation (a high amplitude of the flow glottogram combined with a marked closed phase). Again, there was inter-participant variation.

Body posture and breath management

Breath management involves gravity, elastic recoil, and muscular activity. Clearly, body alignment and use affect all these factors: the downward pull of gravity depends on the posture of the singer; the posture of the torso and the alignment of the spine can affect elastic recoil; and the degree of muscular effort and the direction of that effort may be directly influenced by body posture or indirectly by gravity and elastic recoil factors (Cleveland, 1998).

Some singing pedagogies attempt to correct the natural curvature of the spine, mistakenly believing that a perpendicular spine will assist breath management. Hixon (2006, p. 55) pointed out that the spinal cord is a long appendage of the brain that extends down through the vertebral column. Attempting to remove the natural curvature of the spine in fact results in misalignment and rigidity, interfering with breath management. Richard Miller recommended adopting the 'Garcia position': 'that is, placing the back of the hands together dorsally at the sacroiliac region,' a manoeuvre that 'assures the natural curvature of the spine, elevates the thoracic cage, and balances the stance' (1999, p. 45).

As is clear from the earlier discussion, the same subglottal pressure can be generated in different ways. For instance, the abdominal wall may be bulging out or pulled in during phonation, depending on the relative activation of the thoracic and abdominal wall musculature. A bulging out of the abdominal wall would also arise as a consequence of diaphragmatic activation (Leanderson & Sundberg, 1988). A number of researchers (e.g. Hixon & Hoffman, 1979; Miller, 1986; Leanderson & Sundberg, 1988; Carroll & Sataloff, 1991; Sataloff, 1992; Sundberg, 1993; Titze, 1994) have discussed the relative merits of the 'belly-in' and 'belly-out' methods of support. It is not yet clear how these different approaches may affect airflow and other aspects of laryngeal control.

Titze (1994) characterized these two extremes of body posture that position the chest in relation to the abdomen as the 'pear-shape-up' approach ('belly-in' method) and the 'pear-shape-down' approach ('belly-out' method), or the 'up-and-in' and 'down-and-out' methods of support. In the 'belly-in' approach the singer places emphasis on keeping the ribcage high and stable; in the 'belly-out' approach the singer places emphasis on maintaining stable abdominal pressure. While Miller (1977) identified many variations in approach to breath management among national schools of singing pedagogy, it is broadly true to say that the German school favours Titze's

'pear-shape-down' approach, while the English, French, and Italian schools favour the 'pear-shape-up' approach.

In 1979, Hixon and Hoffman analysed the advantages and disadvantages of these diametrically opposed torso shapes and found that neither was clearly superior to the other. In the 'belly-in' method, both the ribcage expiratory muscles and the diaphragm are at near optimum position on their length-tension characteristics, which means that they are capable of producing rapid, forceful expiratory efforts. The disadvantage of this approach is that abdominal wall muscle activity tends to distend the diaphragm so that it comes under progressively greater passive tension in the inspiratory direction on the ribcage wall, which is counterproductive to the overall expiratory task required for singing. This does not happen in the 'belly-out' method, which still has the same ribcage wall advantage as the 'belly-in' configuration. An additional advantage of the abdomen-out configuration is that the abdominal wall musculature is placed at near optimum positions on its length-tension characteristic, which means that it is more capable of producing forceful efforts. However, a major disadvantage of this configuration is that the relatively flat diaphragm is in an unfavorable position to generate inspiratory force, which is a limitation when the music demands quick inspiration. Titze (1994) reserved judgment on the relative merits of the different methods, pointing out that Hoit and Hixon's 1986 study suggested body type may be a factor in determining the optimal approach for different individuals.

A study by Collyer, Kenny, and Archer (2009) studied the effect on breath management of two different directives given to singers. Five female classical singers sang Caccini's 'Ave Maria' three times: once without directive and then under two directives: 'steadily pull the abdomen inward' and 'steadily expand the abdomen' through each phrase. While the directives had a significant effect on chest-wall dimension at initiation of phrase and on excursion, at the end of each phrase the dimension reverted to habitual behaviour. They found that in all singers ribcage dimensional change counteracted abdominal change to maintain consistent lung volumes. It was clear that well-trained classical singers were able to modify their kinematic behaviour, but the return to habitual behaviour raises the question of what factors determine habitual kinematic patterns and lung volumes and what effects these might have on voice function and quality.

In a later study those researchers examined whether changes in abdominal kinematic strategy were perceptible and whether listeners identified a particular strategy with a preferred vocal quality (Collyer et al., 2011). They point out that in the singing studio the teacher aurally monitors changes in the singer's vocal quality and from those observations makes assumptions about the singer's physical behaviour: 'The assumption that change in breathing behaviour has a direct effect on vocal quality is a cornerstone of singing pedagogy and plays a crucial role in singing training' (Collyer et al., 2011, p. e15). Five experienced female classical singers recorded sung examples under three different conditions: their habitual breath management, while drawing the abdomen inward ('belly-in') during each phrase, and while gradually expanding the abdomen ('belly-out') during the phrase. It was taken into consideration the degree of similarity between each directive and singer's habitual abdominal and ribcage behaviour. The 'belly-in' strategy is often recommended since contracting the abdominal wall raises the diaphragm, and, through increasing intrathoracic pressure, contributes to subglottal pressure. In addition, the abdominal wall acts as an antagonist to the diaphragm and ribcage to facilitate subtle, rapid, and precise adjustments in subglottal pressure with changes in vocal demands. The 'belly-out' strategy has often been criticized as having deleterious effects on vocal quality, although there has been little study of this perception.

The results were mixed. The ability of experienced listeners to detect changes in breathing behaviour depended on the individual singer and on the extent to which the directive deviated from the singer's habitual pattern. Findings suggested that the standard of singing was compromised by any directive eliciting breath management behaviour antithetical to habitual behaviour. The results question pedagogical assumptions about the direct relationship between breath management, breathing training directives, and perceptible changes in vocal quality. Plainly certain directives work for some singers and not for others, and training needs to be tailored to individual needs. This may relate to other research findings in relation to gender and body type.

In their 1985 study (discussed above), Watson and Hixon found that regardless of the beliefs held by participants about their breath management strategy, they all employed 'the so-called "belly in" strategy for singing.' They concluded that 'unanimous use of this strategy by the participant group suggests that it may have a collection of advantages for the singer towards which he naturally migrates with performance experience' (p. 120). In view of the small number of participants (six) studied and the fact that all participants were of the same voice type and therefore likely to be of the same body type, these results cannot be regarded as generally conclusive for all singers.

However, in reviewing research studies on chest wall behaviour during singing Hixon asserted that all singers, both trained and untrained, invariably used some variation of belly-in configuration, attributing that to the fact that the belly-in configuration is mechanically advantageous (Hixon, 2006, p. 112). Even in studies where attempts were made to impose a belly-out configuration on some singers, they reverted to a belly-in configuration, suggesting that the latter is easier, more comfortable, and more efficient. I am not aware of any studies of German singers habitually using the belly-out configuration.

In other experiments Leanderson, Sundberg, and von Euler (Leanderson et al., 1987a; Sundberg et al., 1989) found that when participants used a 'belly-out' strategy in conjunction with contracting the diaphragm relatively forcefully throughout the phrase, the trachea exerted an increased pull on the larynx. This tracheal pull increased the need for cricothyroid contraction – that is, the breathing strategy affected the voice control mechanism. Tracheal pull also appeared to reduce glottal adduction, increasing the amplitude of the lowest partial of the voice spectrum. Such a strategy may not be effective for singing at very high pitches, where some larynx elevation is necessary. This may be another area where male-female differences need to be clarified for the purposes of pedagogy.

Iwarsson (2001) investigated the effect of inhalatory abdominal wall movement on vertical laryngeal position, using 34 (17 male, 17 female) untrained participants. No instructions were given in relation to body alignment or movement of the ribcage. Vertical laryngeal position is influenced by respiration and provides the link to the phonatory system, with a lower larynx being linked to high lung volumes, and higher larynx to lower lung volumes. This could be an effect of tracheal pull, 'a mechanical linkage between the breathing apparatus and the larynx. The tracheal pull means that when the diaphragm contracts and descends for inhalation, it exerts a downward directed force on the larynx because of the elastic structure of the trachea' (Iwarsson, 2001, p. 386). The study aimed to test the hypothesis that inhalation with an expanding abdominal wall induces a lower position of the larynx during the subsequent phonation. The surprising finding of this study was that an abdominal expansion strategy tends to induce an *ascending* rather than a descending movement of the larynx. This finding probably related to the postures and lung volumes of the naive subjects. For singers and singing teachers the relationship between body use, head alignment, respiration, and larynx position are pivotal in producing the vocal qualities appropriate to different genres and styles – an issue needing further detailed study.

Appoggio technique

In his 1986 book, *The Structure of Singing*, Miller commented that 'widely disseminated techniques of singing have been based on assumed muscle relationships that are patently absurd' and, on the basis of functional efficiency, advocated the *appoggio* technique of the historic Italian school, 'a system for combining and balancing muscles and organs of the trunk and neck, controlling their relationships to the supraglottal resonators, so that no exaggerated function of any one of them upsets the whole' (p. 24). In *appoggio* technique

> the sternum must initially find a moderately high position; this position is then retained throughout the inspiration-expiration cycle. . . . Both the epigastric and umbilical regions should be stabilized so that a feeling of internal-external muscular balance is present. This sensation directly influences the diaphragm. . . . Although the lower abdomen (hypogastric, or pubic, region) does not distend, there is a feeling of muscular connection from sternum to pelvis. . . . However, to move out the lower abdomen either during inspiration or during the execution of a phrase, as some singers are taught to do, is foreign to *appoggio* technique. Equally alien is the practice of pulling inward on the pubic area as a means of 'supporting' the voice. (p. 24)

While this approach fits Titze's (1994) 'pear-shape-up' posture, its emphasis on flexibility seems not to fit either the 'belly-out' or 'belly-in' methods of support as advocated by many practitioners. Indeed, Miller preferred the term 'breath management' to 'support.' The flexible approach of *appoggio* seems to answer the need for dynamic breath management strategies to meet different musical demands and to suit different body types.

The concept of support
As Hixon observed:

> Support is generally recognized as important in singing. Teachers teach it. Singers feel it. Listeners think they can identify it. And scientists are trying to determine what it is. (Hixon, 2006, p. 113)

Sand and Sundberg (2005) point out that the usefulness of a term depends on the extent to which it means the same thing to different people. They investigated the term 'support.' Co-author Sand gave singing lessons to five students at varying stages, recorded them, and selected 42 examples, each a few seconds long, that she judged representative of different degrees of support. Nine expert listeners, all with a professional involvement in singing, then evaluated them. The experts' ratings of support tended to agree. Thus, the term support seems meaningful and useful, but as yet its physiological and acoustic correlates aren't known.

'Support' may be difficult for scientists to investigate because, while it may relate primarily to respiratory strategies, it involves whole-body use in controlling air pressure and airflow in meeting changing musical demands. The historic technique of *appoggio* described above is a flexible, holistic approach that probably best answers these demands.

Singers and teachers of singing often use the term 'support' to refer to the coordinations required to control the interrelated parameters of subglottal pressure and airflow and implying aspects of posture. McKinney defined support as 'the dynamic relationship between the breathing-in muscles and the breathing-out muscles whose purpose is to supply adequate breath pressure to the vocal cords for the sustaining of any desired pitch or dynamic level' (1982, pp. 55–56). Thus, breath management for singing also implies control of laryngeal function. What is involved in this, and how the appropriate co-ordinations can best be taught, are matters of some contention.

In recent years some experimental research has been directed to clarifying what support means in physical terms. A preliminary study by Griffin, Woo, Colton, Casper, and Brewer (1995) aimed to develop an objective definition of the supported singing voice based on physiological characteristics. Other studies relating to subglottal pressure, airflow, and the role of the diaphragm in singing are also relevant to pedagogical approaches to support. Some of these studies are discussed below. Unfortunately, the range of methods used from one study to another, the small number of participants used, and the range of training and performance experience of participants from one study to another – and in some cases within the one study – make evaluation of the experimental evidence and its application to pedagogy difficult.

In the Griffin et al. (1995) study, the participants were eight classically trained singers – four male and four female – having a minimum of a bach-elor's degree in vocal performance or five years of private voice study and at least five years of professional solo singing experience in opera, oratorio, or both. They wrote definitions of supported singing voice and descriptions of how it is produced, as well as singing samples of the sustained vowel /ɛ/ (at low, medium, and high pitches defined for each voice) and repetitions of the syllable /bɛp/. Participants defined the supported singing voice as being characterized by resonance, clarity, and extended vocal range produced by correct adjustment of the breathing muscles. The researchers found 'supported voice' to be louder and to be more efficient in terms of having increased peak flow and a longer glottal closed phase.

This preliminary study found that breathing patterns were highly variable among participants, but no significant differences in breathing activity were found when the participants produced supported, as opposed to unsupported, voice. It is not stated whether breathing patterns varied for individual singers performing different tasks, at different pitches, or in different registers. There is no information on whether breathing patterns were related to larynx height or whether there were differences in the accuracy of intonation between sup-ported and unsupported voice. The study did find that ribcage activity was greater than abdominal activity during the singing tasks in supported voice.

Given the isolated nature of the tasks, however, it is difficult to draw any conclusions in relation to patterns of respiration and breath management; that would require the study of respiratory strategies used in connected song, both within whole phrases making different musical demands and between phrases.

The Griffin et al. study reported the majority of participants as referring only to breath management when describing production of the supported singing voice, while the experimental findings indicated that changes in laryngeal and glottal configuration, such as lowering the larynx and closing the glottis more tightly, played an important role in voice support. The study does, however, mention that six of the eight participants also included descriptions of inhalation (details are not given); three participants also referred specifically to posture and laryngeal or vocal tract involvement. Common pedagogical directions associated with inhalation, such as 'breathing the start of the yawn,' involve laryngeal and vocal tract adjustments, as do matters of posture. The fact that the majority of singers referred to these considerations and the fact that they were able to produce at will differences in voice quality between supported and unsupported voice, suggest that they were aware of factors other than respiration, even though they may have been unable to articulate this knowledge.

Another question raised by the study, which needs extended investigation, is the differences between male and female voices, both in terms of anatomical and physiological characteristics and management strategies. The study found significant differences in many variables for gender, or pitch, or both. One finding was that subglottal pressure was higher in supported singing than unsupported singing for all voices except female low pitch. Since it is likely that the female low pitch (presumably sung in 'chest register') had some overlap with the male high pitch (sung in 'head register'), it would be interesting to know how this finding relates to register rather than to fundamental frequency in isolation. A marked difference was found between the amplitudes of the singer's formant in the supported and unsupported male voice. (The singer's formant is defined and discussed in Chapter 5.) It is not clear how this relates to the finding that men used more 'compression of the larynx' and lowered the larynx more markedly than women, nor is it clear what this term means. If men used a lowered larynx high in their range, how did this affect laryngeal and respiratory strategies used to achieve the pitch and how did this compare with those adopted by women singing higher and with a higher larynx? Singing low in their range, did the women adopt similar strategies to those of the men singing high in their range?

Because of its importance in singing, subglottal pressure has been the focus of much research in recent years. Subglottal pressure may affect both loudness and pitch. In order to control intonation, particularly in loud singing, a singer needs fine control of subglottal pressure (Leanderson & Sundberg, 1988) because an increase in subglottal pressure may also, as a secondary effect, raise pitch (Sundberg, 1987). Many musical demands made of singers (for example, *messa di voce*, staccato, coordinated onset of phonation, leaps, and coloratura) require synchronized control between breathing muscles and pitch muscles (Astraquillo et al., 1976; Proctor, 1980; Miller, 1986; Leanderson & Sundberg, 1988; Titze, 1992, 1996; Sundberg, 1993; Cleveland, 1994). Control of these coordinations is therefore of basic importance in singing, and understanding the factors involved and their interrelationship is important for voice teachers.

Subglottal pressure depends on a complex system of passive recoil forces and active muscular forces. The demands on muscular forces to supply the required air pressure for phonation continuously change during singing as the music makes varying demands and as the recoil forces change with the lung volume. If the pressure generated by the recoil forces is too high for the intended phonation, then the inspiratory muscles must be contracted to reduce the pressure. The need for this activity then gradually decreases as the lung volume decreases until a volume is reached at which the passive recoil forces generate no pressure. Beyond this point, the muscles of exhalation must take over more and more to compensate for the increasing passive recoil force caused by the continuous compression of the ribcage (Leanderson & Sundberg, 1988).

A study by Leanderson, Sundberg, and von Euler (1987b) concluded that abdominal musculature contributes to the fast and dynamic control of subglottal pressure that is required for voice production. They reported this finding as being in contrast to the finding of Watson and Hixon (1985) (discussed further below) that the role of the abdominal muscles was 'mainly one of posturing the chest wall,' while 'pressurization of the pulmonary system for singing, by contrast, appears to be the major role of the ribcage' (p. 119).

In a 1989 report, Watson, Hoit, Lansing, and Hixon described abdominal muscle activity during singing. They used electromyography at upper lateral, lower lateral, and midline sites of the abdomen to measure muscle activity during singing by four classical singers (bass, baritone, and ass-baritone). Muscle activity was found to be regional: The lateral region of the abdomen was highly active, whereas the middle region was not. Differential activation of the upper and lower portions of the lateral abdomen was also found, with the most common pattern showing greater activation of the lower portion than of the upper portion. Brief decrements in lateral abdominal activity often occurred in association with the onset of the inspiratory side of the breathing cycle. However, the investigators interpreted these findings on abdominal muscle activity as evidence that the abdominal muscles play an important role in the posturing of the chest wall for singing. The investigators were in turn critical of the fact that the Leanderson et al. (1987a) study used only single-site recordings.

Regardless of the conflicting interpretations the researchers put on the findings of these studies, from a practitioner point of view it seems that there is at least agreement that the abdominal muscles are important in controlling subglottal pressure. Since these studies used only male singers, the question arises whether the same breath management strategies apply to female singers.

The 1985 Watson and Hixon study used six male participants. In 1990, Watson, Hixon, Stathopoulos, and Sullivan reported a similar study using four female participants. That investigation found no difference in kind between the kinematic behaviour of the respiratory apparatus during the performance of these trained female classical singers and the comparable group of male classical singers studied earlier. This suggests that the same approach to respiratory training is appropriate for both male and female singers.

While both loudness and pitch are dependent on subglottal pressure, these factors are also influenced by airflow: similar loudness can be achieved from a sound with reduced subglottal pressure and increased airflow, or from a sound with increased subglottal pressure and decreased airflow (Leanderson & Sundberg, 1988). As Cleveland put it, 'The tradeoff between airflow and subglottal pressure is one directly related to the adductory force of the vocal folds' (1992, p. 26). He observed that trained classical singers seem to derive a louder sound with less subglottal pressure than untrained singers, which suggests that trained singers sing with less adductory force in the vocal folds than untrained singers. Efficiency of airflow in relation to vocal fold adduction results in flow phonation, rather than the breathy voice resulting from excessive airflow or the pressed voice resulting from insufficient airflow (Sundberg, 1987; Titze, 1994).

Breath management and laryngeal control

While it is sometimes useful to examine the component parts of the vocal mechanism (i.e., breath management, phonation, and resonance), I have already emphasized that for teachers of singing, whole-body use is of paramount importance. Issues of breath management are fundamental because of their influence on the whole of the vocal instrument. Movement approaches that facilitate whole body/breath use are discussed in greater detail in Chapter 8. Some scientific studies involving respiration and other aspects of voice have been discussed above. In addition, four studies examining the influence of lung volume on laryngeal control are now considered.

A 1999 study of *messa di voce* is of immediate interest because it studied the physiological and acoustic characteristics of a vocal figure that many teachers prescribe as an exercise. The reason *messa di voce* is prescribed as an exercise is that the gradual increase in loudness (crescendo) and then gradual decrease in loudness (decrescendo) on the one note is quite common in vocal litera-ture, and for a singer to execute it competently throughout the range requires practised coordination. The gradual transition from pianissimo to fortissimo and back is a challenge to the singer's ability to change loudness while keep-ing constant pitch, vowel and timbre. Ideally, the crescendo and decrescendo halves of the figure are symmetrical. Titze, Long, Shirley, Stathopoulos, Ramig, Carroll, and Riley (1999) investigated whether the singers in their study were able to achieve this and, if there was an asymmetry in intensity whether it could be attributed to a non-uniform depletion of lung volume. They also looked at whether there were problems at register transitions.

The participants were three male and three female singers covering a wide age range (25 to 61 years) and with varying performing experience (graduate student to ex-Metropolitan Opera soloist). The experimenters employed a method followed in earlier experiments, collecting data from a combination of transducers and electroglottograph. Each participant produced 27 tokens of the *messa di voce* over a range of about 1.5 octaves, each targeted to last 10 seconds – five seconds for the crescendo and five seconds for the diminuendo.

Ribcage displacement generally mirrored the lung volume rather closely, with abdomen displacement more variable. Sound pressure level was typically asymmetrical, with a delayed rise followed by an accelerated fall. Since the lung volume changes were generally quite linear throughout the exercise, this could not be attributed to a non-uniform expulsion of air. Variations in lung pressure and flow were seen in conjunction with variations in abdomen and ribcage displacement, suggesting that some differences in respiratory strategy seem to carry over to phonatory control. The participants displayed great vari-ability in approach to 'support,' and there is no indication of which approach might be the most efficient in relation to phonatory control. While difficul-ties were identified in performing the exercise at higher pitches and (for the amateur tenor) at the register transition, stability of pitch, vowel, and timbre were not considered. These aspects of the complex coordinations required to execute a *messa di voce* need further study.

Some years later I was part of a research team pursuing the challenges of understanding the factors involved in *messa di voce* (Collyer et al., 2007). We identified two major challenges for singers: first, the singer should dem-onstrate a smooth transition in all aspects associated with the crescendo; second, the change in dynamic across the crescendo and decrescendo should be symmetrical. We examined to what extent linearity and symmetry are characteristic of *messe di voce* performed by well trained female classical singers.

Five trained female classical singers performed *messe di voce* across their musical pitch range – in total 318 tokens between E_3 and E_6 – to identify acoustic characteristics and the influence of fundamental frequency. The findings generally support the conclusions of the 1999 Titze et al. study with respect to non-linearity of sound pressure level change. There were large differences in the sound pressure level ranges of the crescendo and decrescendo in the same *messa di voce*, with fundamental frequency apparently not being a factor. Sound pressure level range was generally greater during crescendo at higher pitches and during decrescendo at lower pitches. Changes in sound pressure level during the *messa di voce* were predominantly non-linear, and the shape of the sound pressure level traces differed greatly between crescendo and decrescendo. Non-linearity in sound pressure level change was not related to sound pressure level range but did show a fundamental frequency influence in decrescendo. Change in spectral balance with respect to sound pressure level change showed more symmetry than linearity, so that changes in the mode of phonation during the *messa di voce* were dependent upon sound pressure level regardless of whether the singer was in crescendo or decrescendo.

In 1998, Iwarsson and collaborators published two studies. One (Iwarsson et al., 1988) examined the effects of lung volume on the glottal voice source and the other (Iwarsson & Sundberg, 1998) the effects of lung volume on vertical larynx position during phonation. The study on glottal voice source followed up previous research that had raised the possibility that a variation in lung volume induces a variation of an abductive force component in the glottis. Because decreased abduction results in lower vocal fold vibration amplitude and longer closed phase, and hence a smaller amplitude of the airflow pulses through the glottis, it is obviously relevant to singing. Twenty-four untrained participants – 14 men and 10 women – phonated at different pitches and degrees of vocal loudness at different lung volumes. Mean subglottal pressure was measured, and voice source characteristics were analysed by inverse filtering. The investigation demonstrated that lung volume affects phonation: with decreasing lung volume, the closed quotient increased, while subglottal pressure, peak-to-peak flow amplitude, and glottal leakage tended to decrease. Based on these findings, the authors suggest that hyperfunctional voices might profit from phonation at high lung volumes, while for hypofunctional voices it may not be helpful to initiate phonation after a deep inhalation.

The study on vertical larynx position used a multichannel electroglottograph to measure larynx position in 29 healthy, vocally untrained participants – 16 men and 13 women – who phonated at different lung volumes, pitches, and degrees of vocal loudness. High lung volume was found to be clearly associated with a lower larynx position, presumably one reason trained classical singers typically initiate phrases at high lung volumes.

Application to pedagogy

The physiology of respiration is complex, and the many interrelated aspects of breath management in singing are still being investigated. It seems that optimal breath management strategies may vary from singer to singer, depending on body-type, and may also vary from one musical task to another. Indik points out that breath management is not just 'brain to breath to folds to articulation.' Such factors as consonant impedance and tracheal pull also affect breath requirements (Indik, 2009, p. 133). What is essential is flexible, whole-body connection to meet musical demands.

Studies have highlighted the discrepancy between what singers believe they do to manage respiration and what they actually do. Watson and Hixon found that their highly trained and successful participants had 'misconceptions . . . concerning physical principles, some involving cause and effect, associated with respiratory physiology and mechanics' and 'with regard to the function of the respiratory apparatus as a system' (1985, p. 119). They advocated

> additional emphasis in educating singers with regard to the workings of the respiratory apparatus and how such workings translate into performance. It seems reasonable to suppose that singers who have accurate conceptualizations about respiratory function would be in better position to influence their performance product and use the respiratory apparatus more efficiently in performance. (p. 120)

Practitioners do not always agree. For example, Carroll and Sataloff (1991) maintained that the movement of the muscles of the lower abdomen, the upper abdomen and lower thorax, and the back that are involved in support should be inward and slightly upward, but 'if teachers advise a student to bring abdominal muscles in and up, the student will also raise his or her shoulder, chest, and neck muscles' (p. 385). They suggested that the advice to support 'down and out' is a matter of teaching imagery used to counter these unwanted muscular tensions (p. 386). Doscher (1994) was wary of using the term 'support' at all, pointing out that the term suggests an inadvisable rigidity. She mentioned teachers successfully using 'such imagery as feeling a cushion of air around the waist (patently physically impossible), of feeling the buoyancy of treading water, or of balancing lightly on a trampoline' (p. 24). Titze took a similar view in discussing approaches to teaching the coordinations that produce the appropriate airflow. He suggested using images that contain an ample number of the right physiological buzz-words. . . . Thus, we could cushion the air with tone [sic], breathe the sound, connect the tone with the breath, or make the sound more or less airy, hooty, and fluty. The point is, we somehow want to make a connection between the laryngeal, pharyngeal, or oral sensations of airflow and the auditory perception of the sound produced. (Titze, 1994, p. 77)

In an issue of the *Journal of Voice* devoted to respiration and singing, White articulated two major responsibilities of singing teachers:

The first is to achieve a thorough understanding of the physiological-mechanical processes through which the singing voice is produced. . . . The second responsibility for teachers of singing is to formulate concepts based upon their understanding of the physiological-mechanical process and present them to students in terms they can understand and apply toward the development of a singing technique. (1988, p. 26)

Both White (1988) and Emmons (1988) asserted that in the studio most teachers use imagery to convey voice science understandings to students. Emmons argued that

every teacher of singing accepts the fact that the possession of anatomically accurate information does not guarantee an effective *use* of air for singing. Frequently, a working concept (even an anatomically faulty one) is more useful (p. 30)

So may the teacher be led to look about for a way to control the thoracic and abdominal muscle groups *indirectly*, a way that would allow *them* to respond to the task, rather than to the specific controls of the singer. (p. 32)

An indirect approach to control is endorsed by the findings of Swank's 1984 investigation of verbal directives on support used by singing teachers and choral directors. Swank assumed that supported (i.e., well-sustained) tone would enable consistent tone quality from beginning to end, ability to sustain the integrity of the vowel over an extended period, and ability to maintain or increase the level of intensity over a period of time. She found that some directives had superior results at given pitches, while others showed superiority in solving another problem area of voice production. The most generally effective verbal directive was:

Following inhalation, press against the sternum with 2 fingers at the xiphoid process (lowest part of the sternum) and keep the *rib cage responding* to the *pressure* there throughout the sustained tone. Be conscious of the *expansion of the ribs at the sides* as you press with your fingers. (p. 14)

This directive was based upon developing student awareness of raised ribcage, high sternum, and lateral expansion of ribs during the entire line of sustained sound and suggests Titze's (1994) 'pear-shape-up' posture. It was a directive based on physical awareness and was most effective at higher pitches. The next most effective directive was to 'Sing *through* the *line* to end of the count, just as you would sing through the phrase of a song' (Swank, 1984, p. 13). This directive was most often issued with the intent of lessening tensions in singers and developing the concept of 'flow' and 'direction,' while allowing the student to concentrate on the 'end of the count.' It was a directive based on mental control and was effective at lower pitches.

Swank concluded that 'those directives which were most effective in this study encouraged postural aspects necessary to free and balanced respiratory technique for singing . . . and developed the concept of "line" and breath as the carrier of tone' (1984, p. 17). This is an important point often neglected in scientific studies: from the pedagogical point of view, the correlation between body posture and breath management strategies is of primary importance.

While the studies by Watson and Hixon (1985) and Leanderson et al. (1987a) produced conflicting conclusions about the role of the diaphragm in controlled expiration in singing, both these studies demonstrated that singers were able to quickly learn new breath management strategies in response to visual feedback. In the Watson and Hixon study, one participant was able to train himself in the course of the experiment using observation of an oscilloscope. The researchers suggest that this may be a more efficient means of training respiratory behavior:

> Perhaps the use of only verbal instruction, visual example, and imagery in training singers should be discontinued. That is, it may be that in the case of respiratory function, at least, there is a useful role to be played by instrumentation of the type used in this investigation. (p. 120)

Leanderson et al. (1987a) reported that untrained participants were able to develop voluntary control of diaphragmatic activation in response to visual feedback, but point out that the trained participants had, without visual feedback, already developed such voluntary control during the course of their training. Visual feedback may be effective in speeding respiratory training.

The discussion above makes clear that breath management strategies influence phonation; issues of phonation are examined in greater detail in the following chapter.

References

Allen, E. & Wilder, C. (1977). Respiratory patterns in singers: a proposed research design. In V.L. Lawrence (ed.), *Transcripts of the Sixth Symposium on Care of the Professional Voice* (pp. 18–20). New York, NY: The Voice Foundation.

Astraquillo, C.J., Blatt, I.M., Happel, L. & Martinez, R. (1976). Investigation of the relationship between abdominal muscular discipline and the act of singing: an electromyographic study. *Annals of Otology, Rhinology and Laryngology, 84,* 498–519.

Björkner, E. (2008). Musical theater and opera singing: why so different? A study of subglottal pressure, voice source & formant frequency characteristics. *Journal of Voice, 22*(5), 533–40. doi:10.1016/j.jvoice.2006.12.007

Brown, W.S., Hunt, E. & Williams, W.N. (1988). Physiological differences between the trained and untrained speaking and singing voice. *Journal of Voice, 2*(2), 102–10.

Brown, W.S., Rothman, H. & Williams, W. (1978). Physiological differentiation between singers and non-singers. In V.L. Lawrence (ed.), *Transcripts of the Seventh Symposium on Care of the Professional Voice*, Pt. I (pp. 45–47). New York, NY: The Voice Foundation.

Carroll, L.M. & Sataloff, R.T. (1991). The singing voice. In R.T. Sataloff (ed.), *Professional Voice: The Science and Art Of Clinical Care* (pp. 381–401). New York, NY: Raven Press.

Cleveland, T.F. (1992). Voice pedagogy for the twenty-first century: physiological and acoustical basis for vocalises relating to subglottal pressure. *The NATS Journal, 49*(2), 25–26.

Cleveland, T.F. (1994). A clearer view of singing voice production: 25 years of progress. *Journal of Voice, 8*(1), 18–23.

Cleveland, T.F. (1998). A comparison of breath management strategies in classical and nonclassical singers. *Journal of Singing*, Part 1, *54*(5), 47–49; Part 2, *55*(1), 45–46; Part 3, *55*(2), 53–55.

Cleveland, T.F., Stone, R., Sundberg, J. & Iwarsson, J. (1997). Estimated subglottal pressure in six professional country singers. *Journal of Voice, 11*(4), 403–9.

Collyer, S., Davis, P.J., Thorpe, C.W. & Callaghan, J. (2007). Sound pressure level and spectral balance linearity and symmetry in the *messa di voce* of female classical singers. *Journal of the Acoustical Society of America, 121*(3), 1728–36. doi: 10.1121/1.2436639

Collyer, S., Kenny, D.T. & Archer, M. (2009). The effect of abdominal kinematic directives on respiratory behaviour in female classical singing. *Logopedics Phoniatrics Vocology, 34*(3), 100–10. doi:10.1080/14015430903008780

Collyer, S., Kenny, D.T. & Archer, M. (2011). Listener perception of the effect of abdominal kinematic directives on respiratory behavior in female classical singing. *Journal of Voice, 25*(1), e15–e24. doi:10.1016/j.vice.2009.10.006.

Doscher, B. (1994). *The Functional Unity of the Singing Voice* (2nd edn.). Metuchen, NJ: Scarecrow Press.

Emmons, S. (1988). Breathing for singing. *Journal of Voice*, 2(1), 30–35.

Griffin, B., Woo, P., Colton, R., Casper, J. & Brewer, D. (1995). Physiological characteristics of the supported singing voice: a preliminary study. *Journal of Voice*, 9(1), 45–56.

Hixon, T.J. (2006). *Respiratory Function in Singing: A Primer for Singers and Singing Teachers*. Tucson, AZ: Redington Brown.

Hixon, T.J. & Hoffman, C. (1979). Chest wall shape in singing. In V.L. Lawrence (ed.), *Transcripts of the Seventh Symposium on Care of the Professional Voice*, Pt. I (pp. 9–10). New York, NY: The Voice Foundation.

Hoit, J.D., Christie, L.J., Watson, P.J. & Cleveland, T.F. (1996). Respiratory function during speaking and singing in professional country singers. *Journal of Voice*, 10(1), 39–49.

Hoit, J.D. & Hixon, T.J. (1986). Body type and speech breathing. *Journal of Speech and Hearing Research*, 29, 313–24.

Indik, L. (2009). The end of breath for singing: exhalation and the control of breath at the end of the phrase. *Journal of Singing*, 66(2), 131–40.

Iwarsson, J. (2001). Effects of inhalatory abdominal wall movement on vertical laryngeal position during phonation. *Journal of Voice*, 15(3), 384–94. doi:10.1016/S0892-1997(01)00040-6

Iwarsson, J. & Sundberg, J. (1998). Effects of lung volume on vertical larynx position during phonation. *Journal of Voice*, 12(2), 159–65.

Iwarsson, J., Thomasson, M. & Sundberg, J. (1998). Effects of lung volume on the glottal voice source. *Journal of Voice*, 12(4), 424–33.

Leanderson, R. & Sundberg, J. (1988). Breathing for singing. *Journal of Voice*, 2(1), 2–12.

Leanderson, R., Sundberg, J. & von Euler, C. (1987a). Role of diaphragmatic activity during singing: a study of transdiaphragmatic pressures. *Journal of Applied Physiology*, 62(1), 259–70.

Leanderson, R., Sundberg, J. & von Euler, C. (1987b). Breathing muscle activity and subglottal pressure dynamics in singing and speech. *Journal of Voice*, 1(3), 258–61.

Leanderson, R., Sundberg, J., von Euler, C. & Lagercrantz, H. (1984). Diaphragmatic control of the subglottic pressure during singing. In V.L. Lawrence (ed.), *Transcripts of the Twelfth Symposium, Care of the Professional Voice, 1983*, Part II (pp. 216–20). New York, NY: The Voice Foundation.

Mcdonald, I., Rubin, J.S., Blake, E., Hirani, S. & Epstein, R. (2012). An investigation of abdominal muscle recruitment for sustained phonation in 25 healthy singers. *Journal of Voice*, 26(6), 815e.9–815.e16. doi:10.1016/j.voice.2012.04.006.

McGlone, R. (1977). Supraglottal air pressure variation from trained singers while speaking and singing. In V.L. Lawrence (ed.), *Transcripts of the Sixth Symposium on Care of the Professional Voice* (pp. 48–49). New York, NY: The Voice Foundation.

McKinney, J.C. (1982). *The Diagnosis and Correction of Vocal Faults.* Nashville, TN: Broadman Press.

Miller, R. (1977). *English, French, German and Italian Techniques of Singing: A Study in National Tonal Preferences and How they Relate to Functional Efficiency.* Metuchen, NJ: Scarecrow Press.

Miller, R. (1986). *The Structure of Singing: System and Art in Vocal Technique.* New York, NY: Schirmer Books.

Miller, R. (1999). The 'Sway-Back' Singer: Sotto Voce. *Journal of Singing, 55*(3), 45–46.

Proctor, D.F. (1980). *Breathing, Speech, and Song.* Vienna: Springer-Verlag.

Sand, S. & Sundberg, J. (2005). Reliability of the term 'support' in singing. *Logopedics Phoniatrics Vocology, 30*(2), 51–54. doi:10.1080/14015430510006712

Sataloff, R.T. (1992). The human voice. *Scientific American, 267*(6), 108–15.

Stone, R.E., Cleveland, T.F., Sundberg, P.J. & Prokop, J. (2003). Aerodynamic and acoustical measures of speech, operatic & broadway vocal styles in a professional female singer. *Journal of Voice, 17*(3), 283–97. doi: 10.1067/S0892-1997(03)00074-2

Sundberg, J. (1987). *The Science of Singing.* Dekalb, IL: Northern Illinois University Press.

Sundberg, J. (1993). Breathing behavior during singing. *The NATS Journal, 49*(3), 4–51.

Sundberg, J., Iwarsson, J. & Billström, A.-M. (1995). Significance of mechanoreceptors in the subglottal mucosa for subglottal pressure control in singers. *Journal of Voice, 9*(1), 20–26.

Sundberg, J., Leanderson, R. & von Euler, C. (1989). Activity relationship between diaphragm and cricothyroid muscles. *Journal of Voice, 3*(3), 225–32.

Sundberg, J., Thalen, M. & Popeil, L. (2012). Substyles of belting: phonatory and resonatory characteristics. *Journal of Voice, 26*(1), 44–50. doi:10.1016/jvoice2010.10.007

Swank, H. (1984). Some verbal directives regarding support concepts and their effects upon resultant sung tone. *The NATS Journal, 40*(3), 12–18.

Titze, I.R. (1992). Voice research: *Messa di voce. The NATS Journal, 48*(3), 24.

Titze, I.R. (1994). *Principles of Voice Production.* Englewood Cliffs, NJ: Prentice Hall.

Titze, I.R. (1996). Voice research: More on *messa di voce. Journal of Singing, 52*(4), 31–32.

Titze, I., Long, R., Shirley, G.I., Stathopoulos, E., Ramig, L., Carroll, L. M. & Riley, W.D. (1999). *Messa di voce*: an investigation of the symmetry of crescendo and decrescendo in a singing exercise. *Journal of the Acoustic Society of America, 105,* 2933–40. doi: 10.1121/1.426906

Watson, P.J. & Hixon, T.J. (1985). Respiratory kinematics in classical (opera) singers. *Journal of Speech and Hearing Research, 28,* 104–22. doi:10.1044/jshr.2801.104

Watson, P.J., Hixon, T.J., Stathopoulos, E.T. & Sullivan, D.R. (1990). Respiratory kinematics in female classical singers. *Journal of Voice, 4*(2), 120–28.

Watson, P.J., Hoit, J.D., Lansing, R.W. & Hixon, T.J. (1989). Abdominal muscle activity during classical singing. *Journal of Voice*, *3*(1), 24–31.

White, R.C. (1988). On the teaching of breathing for the singing voice. *Journal of Voice*, *2*(1), 26–29.

Zangger Borch, D. & Sundberg, J. (2011). Some phonatory and resonatory characteristics of the rock, pop, soul & Swedish dance band styles of singing. *Journal of Voice*, *25*(5), 532–37. doi:10.1016/j.jvoice.2010.07.014

Chapter 4: Phonation

The quality of the singing voice can only be as good as the voice source, the complex sound produced by the larynx. The vocal folds of the larynx open and close hundreds of times each second, chopping the air stream from the trachea into a stream of pressure pulses. Vocal folds rely on a steady subglottal pressure to open and close, as moving air drives the vocal fold tissue into motion. The frequency of this valving at the larynx is expressed in Hertz, or pitch (e.g. A_4 equals 440 Hz). As the singer increases air pressure against adducted vocal folds kept at a constant length, the pitch rises, and the loudness (volume or amplitude) increases. Increased volume means a wider excursion of the vocal folds, lower volume a narrower excursion. By modifying vocal fold length, stiffness, and thickness, singers can increase subglottal pressure without raising pitch. Skilled singers accomplish this complex task using primarily acoustic and kinesthetic feedback.

The operation of the larynx is affected by air pressure in the tube below (the trachea), the air column in the tube above (the vocal tract), the actions of the intrinsic muscles, the support provided by the extrinsic muscles, and the alignment of head and spine. This means that 'countless varieties of sounds and voice qualities can be obtained depending on the muscular, aerodynamic, and acoustical conditions in the glottis and in the vocal tract' (Björkner & Sundberg, 2006).

The multilayered structure of the vocal folds is peculiarly suited to the delicate demands of phonation, with the cover and body acting as a double-structured vibrator. These small folds are, however, susceptible to strain through overuse, or through poor use due to inefficiencies in the larger system, respiratory infection, or dehydration. These factors, and possibly on-going repair of vocal fold tissue, account for the variability of ease of voice onset experienced by singers (Titze, 1998). (Issues of vocal health are examined in Chapter 7.)

Over the last 40 years or so, technological developments have stimulated research into phonation. While laryngoscopy has facilitated examination of the larynx in action, it is still the case that theories about human laryngeal function are often of necessity extrapolated from research carried out on excised canine and feline larynges or inferred from mathematical models.

As the least accessible part of the human vocal mechanism, the larynx still presents many puzzles. In 1988, Hirano admitted that

> the science is far behind the art. In spite of many investigations conducted by many researchers throughout the world, our knowledge of the vocal mechanism in singing is quite limited. There are two major

bottlenecks: limitation in subjects and limitation in techniques. (Hirano, 1988, p. 69)

There has been some change since then: researchers have developed more precise instrumentation and less invasive techniques, and therefore more singers are now willing to act as research subjects.

Effect of factors external to the larynx

It is apparent that body alignment and use affect all aspects of singing. This is very clear in relation to laryngeal function. Given that the larynx, the hyoid bone, and the base of the tongue work as a physiological entity, anything that alters their relationship to each other and to the sternum, spinal column, and skull affects phonation (Vilkman et al., 1996). The head needs to be positioned so that the sternocleidomastoid and scalene muscles can do their job of stabilizing the neck and thorax, and the external muscles contributing to voice production (the strap muscles, cricopharyngeal, and stylopharyngeal) can work efficiently. With the exception of the cricopharyngeal muscle, the forces produced by the extrinsic laryngeal muscles act directly on the thyroid cartilage (Vilkman et al., 1996).

In Chapter 3, I mentioned that the posturing of the ribcage in relation to the abdomen adopted in different breath management strategies affects vocal control, partly through tracheal pull. Tracheal pull may increase the need for cricothyroid contraction and also reduce glottal adduction.

Then there is the unruly tongue. Because the tongue is attached to the hyoid bone, from which the larynx is suspended, tongue position affects the larynx: extending the tongue raises the larynx, and depressing the tongue lowers it. Tension in the jaw is undesirable in classical style, as it affects laryngeal position through the muscles connected to the hyoid bone (the digastric, stylohyoid, mylohyoid, and geniohyoid). In some other nonclassical styles, the jaw may be more firmly positioned by muscular activity.

Onset

As a physical skill closely related to the musical aesthetics of singing, the onset of phonation is an aspect of vocal control that receives attention in most books on singing addressed to teachers and performers (see, for example, Vennard, 1967; Husler & Rodd-Marling, 1976; Miller, 1977, 1986; McKinney, 1982; Salaman, 1989; Estill, 1996; Bunch Dayme, 2009; Chapman, 2012; Callaghan et al., 2012). Estill's model of voice training (1995, 1996) differs from many in addressing laryngeal skills in a quite mechanical way, through what she termed 'compulsory figures' to achieve different modes of onset, retraction of the false vocal folds, vocal fold plane and mass, and laryngeal tilt.

Airflow at the glottis is determined by the interrelationship of subglottal pressure and vocal fold resistance, with phonation onset important for both musical aesthetics and vocal efficiency (Callaghan et al., 2012, p. 562). There is a continuum of possible vocal onsets, with most breathy at one extreme and most pressed (hard) at the other. In the centre of that continuum is balanced onset, which achieves an optimal airflow to adduction ratio and is more favourable in establishing flow phonation. While some degree of breathiness or some degree of hardness may sometimes be appropriate for aesthetic effect, neither breathy nor pressed phonation is efficient, and continued use of either extreme may lead to vocal problems.

Despite the practitioner's concern with onset, little experimental research has been centred on this aspect of the singing voice. Following Vennard's (1967) advocacy of the imaginary-aspirate onset as a technique to achieve balance between airflow and vocal fold adduction, Hirano (1971) investigated the muscular activity of three singers producing the 'imaginary H' onset and three other types of onset: soft, hard, and breathy. For the 'imaginary H' onset, in the lead-up to phonation, gradually increasing activity was observed in crico-thyroid, lateral cricoarytenoid, and vocalis muscles, with that activity reaching its maximum level around the vocal onset. The vocal initiation was not as slow as in the soft onset and not as abrupt as in the hard onset. There was no audible aspiration before onset. This mode of onset has been described by many practitioners as 'simultaneous onset' (Doscher, 1994; Estill, 1996) or 'balanced onset' (Miller, 1986; Chapman, 2012; Callaghan et al., 2012); for classical styles, it is often advocated as being aesthetically pleasing and functionally more efficient than the extremes of breathy onset or glottal (hard) onset.

As mentioned in the previous chapter, airflow at the glottis is determined by the interrelationship of subglottal pressure and vocal fold resistance. Efficient coordination of these aspects of phonation produces maximum aerodynamic-to-acoustic energy conversion and minimum disturbance of the natural vibratory patterns of the vocal folds (flow phonation) (Titze, 1994). Flow phonation lessens mechanical stress on the laryngeal tissues and enables the production of vocal intensity with economical breath use (Gauffin & Sundberg, 1980; Sundberg, 1991).

The rate at which the airflow across the glottis decreases from maximum to minimum sets the overtone content of the voice source spectrum and also affects the overall amplitude of the sound (Sundberg, 1981; Sundberg et al., 1993). (The influence of laryngeal position on resonance factors is discussed further in Chapter 5.) When increased loudness, brightness, or excitement is called for, many singers tend toward pressed phonation. In this mode of phonation, the vocal processes are pressed together, reducing the average glottal aperture. The amplitude of vibration is relatively small and airflow is interrupted suddenly upon vocal fold collision and may produce irregularity in vocal fold vibration (Titze, 1992). A slightly spread posture of the vocal folds actually produces more power (Titze, 1994), with a convergent or near rectangular glottal configuration reducing the phonation threshold pressure to a minimum (Lucero, 1998). It is not intuitively obvious that this posture is advantageous; it is a learned skill (Titze, 1994).

While pressed phonation is not vocally efficient, neither is breathy phonation. The degree of acoustic interaction between the glottal source and the vocal tract is reduced when there is not a fairly complete glottal closure following the glottal flow pulse. Therefore, a voice that is breathy (in the sense that complete glottal closure is not attained during voicing) cannot develop the added carrying power that 'inertive vocal tract loading' brings (Rothenberg, 1981). A longer closed phase means less acoustic energy is lost to the listener due to the coupling in of the subglottal cavities; less stored lung air is vented in each cycle, improving the efficiency of energy usage and enabling notes to be held for a longer time; and creating less breathiness of the voice quality (Howard et al., 1990). Research by Howard et al. (1990) and Howard (1995) found a positive correlation between the number of years of singing training and experience and the closed quotient. In men, closed quotient remained essentially constant with fundamental frequency, whereas in women closed quotient was reduced for pitches below D_4 and increased, with training, for pitches higher than B_4.

Research is beginning to explain the interactions between the form of the glottal flow pulses and the shape of the vocal tract (Ananthapadmanabha & Fant, 1982). Rothenberg (1981, 1983, 1984, 1987) suggests that the acoustic interaction between the glottal source and the vocal tract depends on an inertive force actualized by a momentary, inertia-induced increase in pressure in the trachea and a decrease in pressure in the pharynx caused by the inertia of the supraglottal air pulling it away from the closing glottis. Björkner et al. pointed out that 'to gain information about the voice source, the acoustic filtering effect of the vocal tract resonances must be eliminated' (2006, p. 157).

Two studies (Sundberg & Högset, 2001; Björkner et al., 2006) investigated subglottal pressure in male singers. Since it is generally agreed that vocal registers are associated with the vibrational characteristics of the vocal folds, the Sundberg and Högset study measured transglottal airflow in professional singers – four countertenors, five tenors, and four baritones – to clarify differences across registers. They sang the syllable /pæ:/ in soft, middle, and loud voice in modal and falsetto/countertenor register. Subglottal pressure, closed quotient, relative glottal leakage, and the relative level of the fundamental were analysed. Unfortunately the use of the terms 'modal' and 'falsetto' makes it difficult for practitioners to assess the results of such studies. Both terms seem to have been adopted from speech science; how they apply to singing is not clear. While the report acknowledges that 'registers are important to singing, particularly in countertenors, who use a special register that is commonly regarded as falsetto. On the other hand, many voice pedagogues regard the register used by countertenors as different from the typical falsetto register' there is no clarification of what is meant by 'modal' or 'falsetto.' The pitches used go across the primary register change for countertenors (approx. C_4–E_4), tenors (approx. D_4–F_4), and baritones (usually B_4). Since countertenors are falsettists, presumably they used their usual production for notes above the register change, but it is not clear whether the tenors, baritones, and countertenors used their habitual production for the higher pitches, or whether, for the purpose of this experiment, the tenors and baritones sang in what in singing is usually termed 'falsetto' in the pitch range where they would normally sing in 'head voice,' 'light registration,' or 'cricothyroid-dominant registration.' And there is no recording of the sound to clarify just what 'falsetto' meant in this study! These issues of terminology are discussed below and, in more detail, in Chapter 6.

Unsurprisingly, the highest pressures were used for the loudest production and within a given degree of vocal loudness the pressures tended to increase with fundamental frequency in both registers. The range of pressure used by countertenors for a given pitch was narrow, presumably because of the need to maintain the countertenor default of falsetto production for higher pitches, and a matching vocal tone for lower pitches. There were several voice source differences between modal and falsetto register, with the differences varying somewhat between the three voice classifications.

Björkner et al. (2006) had five professional Swedish baritones, aged 29 to 65 years, sing a diminuendo at a constant pitch while repeating the syllable /pæː/. The singers repeated the sequence three times at each of three pitches located at approximately 25%, 50%, and 75% of their professional pitch range measured in semitones. Whilst the individual singers were consistent in their use of subglottal pressure, there was considerable difference between singers. The pressure used by one singer was almost twice as high as the pressure used by another singer. This difference applied at different pitches and differing loudness. This can probably be attributed to different breathing strategies.

Different styles, different phonation

Recent research is investigating the different approach to phonation required to produce the different vocal aesthetics of different genres and styles. While it has long been clear that the vocal quality used in classical singing requires a low larynx and the initiation of phrases at high lung volume, what is required to produce the loud, brassy sound termed 'belting' used in such styles as pop, rock, R&B, jazz, country, world music, and music theatre is gradually being clarified.

As early as 1991, Schutte and Miller pointed out that in the pitch range G_4–D_5 in female voices belting required larynx elevation to match the first formant with the second harmonic on open (high first formant) vowels (Schutte & Miller, 1993). Presumably this would have implications for breath management strategies; as mentioned in Chapter 3, body alignment and breath management affect lung volume and larynx height.

A study by Lovetri et al. (1999) on the ability of trained music theatre singers to control laryngeal musculature to achieve the qualities of belt ('a powerful chest or modal register'), mix ('a lighter sound, as might be imagined by combining modal register with loft register, or *belt* with *head register*'), and legit ('a strong head voice such as might be produced by an opera singer') (p. 219) confirmed some earlier observations . . . tension and find the most efficient individual coordination.

The bulk of the scientific research has been conducted on classical singers, where flow phonation, characterized by the lowest degree of glottal adduction that still produces glottal closure, is the norm. However, country singers have been found to sing with pressed phonation (Cleveland et al., 1997; Sundberg et al., 1999) and belting is associated with a high degree of glottal adduction (Sundberg et al., 1993; Bestebreurtje & Schutte, 2000).

Thalén and Sundberg's study of different phonation modes for different genres (2001) examined differences in the voice source produced by laryngeal muscle adjustment combined with subglottal pressure. An important factor was glottal adduction, by which a singer can change the mode of phonation within a wide range. The subject was one professional female singer, who sang a triadic melody in classical, pop, jazz, and blues styles in soft, middle, and loud phonation. An expert panel then identified the triads as examples of those styles. The classical singing used flow phonation. The phonatory characteristics of blues singing were similar to that of pressed phonation, with high subglottal pressure, high closed quotient, and a weak fundamental, similar to that used in country singing. The phonatory characteristics of pop and jazz were similar to that for neutral (such as used in speech), and in these genres singers tend to select keys that allow them to use a more speech-like range than that typically used in classical singing.

In 2012 Sundberg et al. published the results of a study on belting substyles that found the voice source to be the main factor distinguishing the styles. While the belting substyles all differed from classical style in formant frequencies, the substyles they labelled 'ringy' and 'brassy' were similar to 'classical' in terms of subglottal pressure. They found 'heavy' belting required high subglottal pressure, modal (thyroarytenoid-dominant) register, and a higher contact quotient. Use of modal register implies thick vocal folds, requiring more driving pressures, and the voice source contributing substantially to vocal loudness. While this experiment used only one singer, the recorded material was tested by an expert panel and does reinforce earlier findings by Estill (1988), Schutte and Miller (1993), and Bestebreurtje and Schutte (2000).

An interesting study examined the 'dist' tones used as a timbral ornament in rock singing (Zangger Borch et al., 2004). While, again, the data was provided by only one singer, the findings are important and will hopefully inspire further investigations. Two vibrations were found: one at the glottis and one, at a lower frequency, in the supraglottal mucosa. The slower vibration included the ventricular folds, and to some extent also the aryepiglottic folds and the anterior part of the mucosa covering the arytenoid structures. The two different vibrations showed a regular $2 + 1 + 2 + 1 + 2 + 1$ pattern. Each low amplitude pulse is preceded and followed by a pair of pulses with greater and similar amplitudes. The low amplitude pulses were synchronous with the approximation of the supraglottic mucosa, suggesting that the reduction of the pulse amplitude was the result of a narrowing of the supraglottal airway caused by the approximation of the supraglottal mucosa. When the vocal folds vibrated at 480 Hz the supraglottal mucosa vibrated at 160 Hz, indicating some coupling between the two. However, this harmonic relationship did not characterize all 'dist' tones. The authors point out that the vibratory pattern in 'dist' tones is similar to that observed in Mongolian 'throat singing,' although in that style the vibrations are usually harmonically related.

The Zangger Borch and Sundberg (2011) study discussed in Chapter 3 found variation in subglottal pressure in the different styles of singing (rock, pop, soul, and Swedish dance band), depending on whether phonation was neutral or pressed, soft or loud, high or low. However, the closed quotient varied much less systematically with subglottal pressure than has been found in operatic baritone voice; it was particularly great in the softest phonations in rock and pressed styles. The Björkner study (2008) discussed in Chapter 3 found higher closed quotients in music theatre singers, which they attributed to lower values for the relationship between first and second formant, indicating a weaker fundamental frequency.

Vibrato

It was previously thought that vocal vibrato was a phenomenon of the respiratory mechanism; recent studies have clarified that it is largely a phenomenon of the phonatory mechanism. Vibrato is, however, associated with movements of the articulatory apparatus and is perceived as an aspect of timbre.

I have therefore chosen to discuss it in the following chapter, which deals with resonance.

Control of pitch

Pitch control rarely receives specific attention in texts on singing technique (Proctor, 1980 and Bunch Dayme, 2009 are exceptions). The implicit assumption is that if posture, audiation, breath management, onset, and registration factors are under control, then the intended pitch will be produced.

There are three primary ways of regulating fundamental frequency: by contracting the cricothyroid muscles; by contracting the thyroarytenoid muscles; or by changing lung pressure to change the length, stiffness, and mass of the vocal folds (Titze, 1991). These mechanisms may, however, be interdependent. Frequency control may also involve vertical larynx position and larynx tilt, achieved by extrinsic laryngeal muscular activity.

Controlling either pitch or volume by lung pressure alone is inefficient, because these factors are interdependent. Fant (1985) maintained that the relative role of lung pressure as a determinant of voice output intensity has been overestimated and that 'the abduction-adduction and other vocal cord activities carry the major part of the source dynamics, whilst lung pressure variations are slower and carry less information' (pp. 24–25). Hirano (1988) pointed out that the mechanism of intensity control is somewhat different in different registers and is also affected by fundamental frequency. More recently, studies discussed above support these views. These factors are further discussed in Chapter 6 in relation to registration.

Hirano's experiments have demonstrated that the activity of the cricothyroid, lateral cricoarytenoid, and vocalis muscles is positively related to fundamental frequency. The cricothyroid stretches and tenses the vocal fold, increasing fundamental frequency directly. The lateral cricoarytenoid stretches and tenses the vocal fold. The vocalis shortens the vocal fold and loosens the mucosa, which could be expected to decrease fundamental frequency, but when the vocalis contracts simultaneously with the cricothyroid, it may contribute to an increase in fundamental frequency (Hirano, 1988).

Further investigations into the regulation of fundamental frequency suggest that both positive and negative changes in fundamental frequency can occur with increased thyroarytenoid activity. At lower fundamental frequencies and lower vocal intensities, fundamental frequency correlates positively with thyroarytenoid activity, but at higher fundamental frequencies and low intensity (especially in falsetto voice), an increase in thyroarytenoid activity tends to lower fundamental frequency (Titze et al., 1989).

Larynx height and tilt may also affect fundamental frequency control. The extrinsic laryngeal muscles are capable of changing the configuration of

the structures important for fundamental frequency: the cricoid cartilage, the thyroid cartilage, and the hyoid bone (Erickson et al., 1983). Investigations by Erickson et al. (1983) of the role of the strap muscles (extrinsic laryngeal muscles) in pitch-lowering in speech found that a fall from high to low pitch was initiated by relaxation of the cricothyroid, with the strap muscles involved well after initiation of the frequency fall. A fall from mid to low pitch, however, was initiated by the strap muscles, with the cricothyroid playing a relatively small role.

In 1975, Shipp and Izdebski found that inexperienced singers used an upward (from rest) larynx position for higher voice frequency, presumably to accomplish an increase in vocal fold stretching in a vertical plane to supplement the horizontal pulling forces provided by dorsocaudal tilting of the cricoid cartilage. Experienced singers, on the other hand, tended to maintain larynx position near or well below the physiological resting level as they raised frequency, presumably utilizing almost exclusively the horizontal pulling forces provided by cricothyroid muscle contraction. This latter strategy maintains supraglottal resonator configuration. A further investigation by Shipp (1977) concluded that while it may require less effort to produce high frequencies by elevating the larynx, voice quality suffers. Sundberg and Askenfelt's 1981 study supported this finding. They found larynx rise to be associated with an upward shift in the formant frequencies but, generally, also a decrease in the amplitude of the source spectrum fundamental and in the amplitude of the vibrato undulations. Thus, vertical laryngeal position affects both phonation and resonance.

Pitch matching

Experiments in vocal matching of pitch patterns (Leonard & Ringel, 1979; Leonard et al., 1988) have found a direct relationship between interval size and speed of matching. Leonard and collaborators (1979, 1988) also found pitch lowering to be faster than pitch raising, with singers faster and more accurate than nonsingers. The participants in these experiments were all men with baritone or bass voices, singing in modal register. Sundberg's 1979 investigation of speed of pitch change used equal numbers of male and female participants. His results confirmed the findings of Leonard and collaborators: trained singers were able to change pitch faster than untrained subjects; the greater the pitch rise, the slower the response time; and pitch drops were performed faster than pitch elevations (at least by untrained subjects). He also found that women tended to perform pitch changes faster than men. Untrained subjects used larynx height to achieve pitch changes, whereas trained subjects maintained a relatively stable larynx position in order to maintain the singer's formant. (The influence of laryngeal position on resonance factors is discussed further in Chapter 5.) The results did not support the view that larynx height alterations increase the speed of pitch changes.

The usual assumption is that singers' superior pitch-matching ability is associated with superior auditory awareness. Sundberg (1979) proposed that it may also depend on the fact that singers have developed more precise cricothyroid muscle control and a 'muscle memory' appropriate to the task. Among singers in this investigation, pitch changes of a given direction tended to be synchronized with the phase of the vibrato cycle that changed the frequency in the same direction, probably controlled at least in part by the auditory feedback system.

Intrinsic pitch of vowels

Another issue involved in fundamental frequency is what has been called the intrinsic pitch of vowels. Sapir (1989) pointed out that high vowels, such as /i/ and /u/, tend to be produced with higher fundamental frequency than low vowels, such as /ɑ/, even in the same phonetic context and that this effect has been demonstrated in normal speech, in singing, and in the speech of deaf speakers. Knowledge of singing technique and articulatory and acoustic phonetics would lead to the assumption that such a phenomenon is related to tongue position. Sapir also reported several rival hypotheses, however, based on different types of coupling between the articulatory and the phonatory systems: acoustic coupling, mechanical coupling, and neural coupling. In his assessment of the then-available data, Sapir concluded that the evidence was insufficient to establish which mechanism or combination of mechanisms is responsible for the intrinsic pitch of vowels.

Vilkman et al. (1996) suggested the longitudinal tension of the vocal folds is changed by the cricothyroid muscle as a reflex-like compensation to vertical articulatory movements such as tongue and palate heightening and lowering of the larynx.

For practitioners, the important consideration is how to compensate for the intrinsic pitch of vowels. Sapir (1989) postulated that singers may achieve better fundamental frequency control by adopting strategies that decouple the articulatory and phonatory systems. He suggested restricting vertical laryngeal movements for vowel production and assuming the oral postures least likely to affect laryngeal tension. Sapir's research, and that on pitch matching described above, support the received wisdom of singing pedagogy that articulatory manoeuvres should not be allowed to interfere with the phonatory mechanism.

Singers' superior control of fundamental frequency seems to result at least in part from training and experience (Murry, 1990), although it is not clear what innate abilities may be involved (Murry & Zwirner, 1991). No doubt training and experience contribute to singers' ability to achieve the balance between subglottal pressure and vocal fold stiffening involved in pitch and dynamic changes. Practitioners use the traditional *messa di voce* exercise to cultivate this coordination (Cleveland, 1992; Titze, 1996).

Music psychologists suggest that pitch-matching accuracy relates to the perceived musical relevance of the task and the quality of feedback available. In teaching, an indirect approach that addresses posture, audiation (auditory imagery), breath management, onset, and registration factors usually ensures that the intended pitches will be produced.

As in other aspects of vocal development, real-time visual feedback has been shown to be effective in improving pitch matching (Welch et al., 1989; Howard & Welch, 1993; Howard et al., 2004; Wilson et al., 2008).

Application to pedagogy

Much of the research reviewed above examines only one or two factors involved in phonation; an accumulation of such studies clarifies the elements involved. However, for practitioners, the concern is the interrelationship of these elements: how changing one may affect the others and change the voice source. For practitioners, the concern is to master the coordinations that produce the basic phonation to generate the required vocal sound.

The singer must develop fine control of the interaction between breath management, glottal valving, and voicing – what Titze and Verdolini Abbott

(2012) call the 'union of breathing, valving and voicing' (2012, pp. 252–83). In the past the elements of voicing – the breath pressure produced by the lungs, the vocal fold vibration at the larynx, and the vocal tract – have often been discussed as separate elements. However, these elements are part of an interactive system, where one component affects the others. 'Vocal tract pressure . . . can affect vocal fold vibration and glottal flow, which in turn can affect the intraglottal pressure and tracheal airflow. Epilarynx tube pressure can even reach back and affect tracheal airflow. Hence, the whole system of components is technically the sound source' (Titze & Verdolini Abbott, 2012, p. 254). This is the major concern in interpreting the results of experiments for application to singing.

For example, several studies have identified consistent use of subglottal pressure by individual singers, but considerable variation across singers undertaking the same task. Unfortunately, there is no audio data, so it is difficult for singing teachers to interpret these results: do they produce different vocal sounds? Might one be more desirable than the other? And in what context?

For practitioners, another difficulty in interpreting scientific studies is the use of terminology different from that used in singing. Register terminology, seemingly adopted from speech science, is a particular difficulty. 'Modal' is not a term in common use in singing pedagogy, and 'falsetto' applies to that particular vocal quality produced when the thyroarytenoid muscles release completely so that vocal fold length is determined entirely by action of the cricothyroids, assisted by some of the external laryngeal muscles at the highest and lowest pitches (Thurman et al., 2000). The resulting voice quality has in singing historically been called falsetto. This is a very different sound from the 'full voice' sound of 'head voice' commonly used by trained male classical singers above the primary register change. In Western music the use of falsetto is unremarkable in folk music, jazz, music theatre, and many popular styles from rock to country-and-western. It is heard in pantomime, comedy and drag acts where a man portrays a woman. In many scientific studies using the term 'falsetto,' it is not clear whether what is intended is what singers would call head voice or falsetto. Issues of register terminology are discussed further in Chapter 6.

The studies on different strategies for different phonations for different vocal styles are of particular interest to practitioners. The insights they provide into subglottal pressure, contact quotient, and larynx height are illuminating. Of particular interest is the study of 'dist' tones in rock singing (Zangger Borch et al., 2004), providing an insight into how these timbral ornaments are produced, and how they might be safely articulated.

It is clear that pitch control requires overall coordination of the system with refining audiation. While it is possible to control pitch or volume by lung volume alone, this is inefficient, and it is important for the singer to gain control of the interdependent coordination of breath and laryngeal operation, including laryngeal height and tilt, and vocal onset. Vertical laryngeal position affects not only phonation, but also resonance, which is discussed in detail in Chapter 5.

References

Ananthapadmanabha, T.V. & Fant, G. (1982). Calculation of true glottal flow and its components. *Speech Communication*, *1*(3–4), 167–84. doi:10.1016/0167-6393(82)90015-2

Bestebreurtje, M. & Schutte, H. (2000). Resonance strategies for the belting style: results of a single female subject study. *Journal of Voice*, *14*(2), 194–204.

Björkner, E. (2008). Musical theater and opera singing: why so different? A study of subglottal pressure, voice source & formant frequency characteristics. *Journal of Voice*, *22*(5), 533–40. doi:10.1016/j.jvoice.2006.12.007

Björkner, E., Sundberg, J. & Alku, P. (2006). Subglottal pressure and normalized amplitude quotient variation in classically trained baritone singers. *Logopedics Phoniatrics Vocology*, *31*(4), 157–65. doi:10.1080/14015430600576055

Bunch Dayme, M. (2009). *Dynamics of the Singing Voice* (5th edn.). Vienna: Springer-Verlag.

Callaghan, J., Emmons, S. & Popeil, L. (2012). Solo voice pedagogy. In G.E. McPherson & G.F. Welch (eds.), *The Oxford Handbook of Music Education*, Vol. I (pp. 559–80). New York, NY: Oxford University Press.

Chapman, J.L. (2012). *Singing and Teaching Singing: A Holistic Approach to Classical Voice* (2nd edn.). San Diego, CA: Plural Publishing.

Cleveland, T.F. (1992). Voice pedagogy for the twenty-first century: physiological and acoustic basis for vocalises relating to subglottal pressure. *The NATS Journal*, *49*(2), 25–26.

Cleveland, T.F., Stone, R.E., Sundberg, J. & Iwarsson, J. (1997). Estimated subglottal pressure in six professional country singers. *Journal of Voice*, *11*(4), 403–9.

Doscher, B. (1994). *The Functional Unity of the Singing Voice* (2nd edn.). Metuchen, NJ: Scarecrow Press.

Erickson, D., Baer, T. & Harris, K.S. (1983). The role of the strap muscles in pitch lowering. In D.M. Bless & J.H. Abbs (eds.), *Vocal Fold Physiology: Contemporary Research and Clinical Issues* (pp. 279–85). San Diego, CA: College-Hill Press.

Estill, J. (1988). Belting and classic voice quality: Some physiological differences. *Medical Problems of Performing Artists*, *3*(1), 37–43.

Estill, J. (1995). *Voice Craft: A User's Guide to Voice Quality*. Vol. 2: *Some Basic Voice Qualities*. Santa Rosa, CA: Estill Voice Training Systems.

Estill, J. (1996). *Voice Craft: A User's Guide to Voice Quality*. Level One: *Primer of Compulsory Figures*. Santa Rosa, CA: Estill Voice Training Systems.

Fant, G. (1985). Acoustic parameters of the voice source. In A. Askenfelt, S. Felicetti, E. Jansson & J. Sundberg (eds.), *Proceedings of the Stockholm Music Acoustics Conference, 1983*, Vol. 1 (pp. 11–26). Stockholm: Royal Swedish Academy of Music.

Gauffin, J. & Sundberg, J. (1980). Data on the glottal source behavior in vowel production. *Speech Transmission Laboratory Quarterly Progress Status Report* (KTH, Stockholm), *2-3*, 61–70.

Hirano, M. (1971). Laryngeal adjustment for different vocal onset. *Journal of Otolaryngology of Japan*, *74*, 1572–79.

Hirano, M. (1988). Vocal mechanisms in singing: laryngological and phoniatric aspects. *Journal of Voice*, *2*(1), 51–69. doi:10.1016/S0892-1997(88)80058-4

Howard, D.M. (1995). Variation of electrolaryngographically derived closed quotient for trained and untrained adult female singers. *Journal of Voice*, *9*(2), 163–72.

Howard, D.M., Lindsey, G.A. & Allen, B. (1990). Toward the quantification of vocal efficiency. *Journal of Voice*, *4*(3), 205–12.

Howard, D.M. & Welch, G.F. (1993). Visual displays for assessment of vocal pitch matching development. *Applied Acoustics*, *39*(4), 235–52. doi: 10.1016/0003-682X (93)90008-T

Howard, D.M., Welch, G.F., Brereton, J., et al. (2004). WinSingad: a real-time display for the singing studio. *Logopedics Phoniatrics Vocology*, *29*(3), 135–44. doi:10.1080/14015430410000728

Husler, F. & Rodd-Marling, Y. (1976). *Singing: The Physical Nature of the Vocal Organ*. London: Hutchinson.

Leonard, R.J. & Ringel, R.L. (1979). Vocal shadowing under conditions of normal and altered laryngeal sensation. *Journal of Speech and Hearing Research*, *22*(4), 794–817. doi:10.1044/jshr.2204.794

Leonard, R.J., Ringel, R., Horii, Y. & Daniloff, R. (1988). Vocal shadowing in singers and nonsingers. *Journal of Speech and Hearing Research*, *31*, 54–61. doi:10.1044/jshr.3101.54

Lovetri, J., Lesh, S. & Woo, P. (1999). Preliminary study on the ability of trained singers to control the intrinsic and extrinsic laryngeal musculature. *Journal of Voice*, *13*(2), 219–26.

Lucero, J. (1998). Optimal glottal configuration for ease of phonation. *Journal of Voice*, *12*(2), 151–58.

McKinney, J.C. (1982). *The Diagnosis and Correction of Vocal Faults*. Nashville, TN: Broadman Press.

Miller, R. (1977). *English, French, German and Italian Techniques of Singing: A Study in National Tonal Preferences and How they Relate to Functional Efficiency*. Metuchen, NJ: Scarecrow Press.

Miller, R. (1986). *The Structure of Singing: System and Art in Vocal Technique*. New York, NY: Schirmer Books.

Murry, T. (1990). Pitch-matching accuracy in singers and nonsingers. *Journal of Voice*, *4*(4), 317–21.

Murry, T. & Zwirner, P. (1991). Pitch matching ability of experienced and inexperienced singers. *Journal of Voice*, *5*(3), 197–202.

Proctor, D. F. (1980). *Breathing, Speech, and Song*. Vienna: Springer-Verlag.

Rothenberg, M. (1981). The voice source in singing. In J. Sundberg (ed.), *Research Aspects on Singing* (pp. 15–28). Stockholm: The Royal Swedish Academy of Music.

Rothenberg, M. (1983). An interactive model for the voice source. In D. M. Bless & J. H. Abbs (eds.), *Vocal Fold Physiology: Contemporary Research and Clinical Issues* (pp. 155–65). San Diego, CA: College-Hill Press.

Rothenberg, M. (1984). Source-tract acoustic interaction and voice quality. In V. L. Lawrence (ed.), *Transcripts of the Twelfth Symposium, Care of the Professional Voice, 1983*, Pt. I (pp. 15–31). New York, NY: The Voice Foundation.

Rothenberg, M. (1987). Così fan tutte and what it means, or Nonlinear source-tract acoustic interaction in the soprano voice and some implications for the definition of vocal efficiency. In T. Baer, C. Sasaki & K. S. Harris (eds.), *Laryngeal Function in Phonation and Respiration* (pp. 254–67). Boston, MA: College-Hill Press.

Salaman, E. (1989). *Unlocking Your Voice: Freedom to Sing*. London: Victor Gollancz.

Sapir, S. (1989). The intrinsic pitch of vowels: theoretical, physiological, and clinical considerations. *Journal of Voice*, *3*(1), 44–51.

Schutte, H. K. & Miller, D. G. (1993). Belting and pop, nonclassical approaches to the female middle voice: some preliminary considerations. *Journal of Voice*, *7*(2), 142–50.

Shipp, T. (1977). Vertical laryngeal position in singing. *Journal of Research in Singing*, *1*(1), 16–24.

Shipp, T. & Izdebski, K. (1975). Vocal frequency and vertical larynx positioning by singers and nonsingers. *Journal of the Acoustical Society of America*, *58*(5), 1104–6. doi: 10.1121/1.380776

Sundberg, J. (1979). Maximum speed of pitch changes in singers and untrained subjects. *Journal of Phonetics*, *7*(2), 71–79.

Sundberg, J. (1981). The voice as a sound generator. In J. Sundberg (ed.), *Research Aspects on Singing* (pp. 6–14). Stockholm: The Royal Swedish Academy of Music.

Sundberg, J. (1991). Comparisons of pharynx, source, formant and pressure characteristics in operatic and musical theatre singing. *Speech Transmission Laboratory Quarterly Progress Status Report* (KTH, Stockholm), 2–3, 51–62.

Sundberg, J. & Askenfelt, A. (1981). Larynx height and voice source: a relationship? *Speech Transmission Laboratory Quarterly Progress Status Report* (KTH, Stockholm), *2-3*, 23–36.

Sundberg, J., Cleveland, T., Stone, R. E. & Iwarsson, J. (1999). Voice source characteristics in six premier country singers. *Journal of Voice*, *13*(2), 168–83.

Sundberg, J., Gramming, P. & Lovetri, J. (1993). Comparisons of pharynx, source, formant, and pressure characteristics in operatic and musical theatre singing. *Journal of Voice*, 7(4), 301–10.

Sundberg, J. & Högset, C. (2001). Voice source differences between falsetto and modal registers in counter tenors, tenors and baritones. *Logopedics Phoniatrics Vocology*, 26(1), 26–36. doi:10.1080/14015430116949

Sundberg, J., Thalén, M. & Popeil, L. (2012). Substyles of belting: phonatory and resonatory characteristics. *Journal of Voice*, 26(1), 44–50. doi:10.1016/jvoice2010.10.007

Sundberg, J., Titze, I. & Scherer, R. (1993). Phonatory control in male singing: a study of the effects of subglottal pressure, fundamental frequency & mode of phonation on the voice source. *Journal of Voice*, 7(1), 15–29.

Thalén, M. & Sundberg, J. (2001). Describing different styles of singing: a comparison of a female singer's voice source in 'Classical,' 'Pop,' 'Jazz' and 'Blues.' *Logopedics Phoniatrics Vocology*, 26(2), 82–93. doi:10.1080/140154301753207458

Thurman, L., Welch, G., Theimer, A., Grefsheim, E. & Feit, P. (2000). The voice qualities that are referred to as 'vocal registers.' In L. Thurman and G. Welch (eds.), *Bodymind and Voice: Foundations of Voice Education* (rev. edn.), Vol. 3 (pp. 421–48). Collegeville, MN: The VoiceCare Network.

Titze, I.R. (1991). Mechanisms underlying the control of fundamental frequency. In J. Gauffin and B. Hammarberg (eds.), *Vocal Fold Physiology: Acoustic, Perceptual and Physiological Aspects of Voice Mechanisms* (pp. 129–38). San Diego, CA: Singular Publishing Group.

Titze, I.R. (1992). Voice research: voice quality: Part 1. *The NATS Journal*, 48(5), 21, 45.

Titze, I.R. (1994). *Principles of Voice Production*. Englewood Cliffs, NJ: Prentice Hall.

Titze, I.R. (1996). Voice research: more on *messa di voce*. *Journal of Singing*, 52(4), 31–32.

Titze, I.R. (1998). Voice research: on the springiness and stickiness of vocal fold tissues. *Journal of Singing*, 54(5), 35–36.

Titze, I.R., Luschei, E.S. & Hirano, M. (1989). Role of the thyroarytenoid muscle in regulation of fundamental frequency. *Journal of Voice*, 3(3), 213–24.

Titze, I.R. & Verdolini Abbott, K. (2012). *Vocology: The Science and Practice of Voice Habilitation*. Salt Lake City, UT: National Center for Voice and Speech.

Vennard, W. (1967). *Singing: The Mechanism and the Technic* (rev. edn.). New York, NY: Carl Fischer.

Vilkman, E., Sonninen, A., Hurme, P. & Körkkö, P. (1996). External laryngeal frame function in voice production revisited: A review. *Journal of Voice*, 10(1), 78–92.

Welch, G.F., Howard, D.M. & Rush, C. (1989). Real-time visual feedback in the development of vocal pitch accuracy in singing. *Psychology of Music*, 17(2), 146–57. doi:10.1177/0305735689172005

Wilson, P., Lee, K., Callaghan, J. & Thorpe, W. (2008). Learning to sing in tune: does real-time visual feedback help? *Journal of Interdisciplinary Music Studies*, *2*(1–2), 157–72.

Zangger Borch, D. & Sundberg, J. (2011). Some phonatory and resonatory characteristics of the rock, pop, soul & Swedish dance band styles of singing. *Journal of Voice*, *25*(5), 532–37. doi:10.1016/j.jvoice.2010.07.014

Zangger Borch, D., Sundberg, J., Lindestad, P.-Å. & Thalén, M. (2004). Vocal fold vibration and voice source aperiodicity in 'dist' tones: a study of a timbral ornament in rock singing. *Logopedics Phoniatrics Vocology*, *29*(4), 147–53. doi:10.1080/14015430410016073

Chapter 5: Resonance

As I emphasized in Chapter 4, the quality of the voice depends essentially on the voice source. It also depends on how that spectrum of sound is filtered by the vocal tract. Even the level of the fundamental is dependent not only on the voice source, but also on the vocal tract filtering and the characteristics of the sound radiation from the lip opening (Gauffin & Sundberg, 1989). As discussed in the previous chapter, however, articulatory adjustments (for both timbre and word articulation) need to be achieved without compromising the voice source: voice source and vocal tract filter are interdependent, just as subglottal pressure and laryngeal adjustment are interdependent.

Pedagogical concerns about resonance and articulation include production of the timbre appropriate to the musical context, vowel quality, vibrato, and articulation of text. Vocal resonance and word articulation are interdependent parameters reliant on the movements of the articulators. It is with respect to these interdependent parameters that an understanding of the relationship between physical manoeuvres and acoustic results is vital for pedagogy.

The traditional identification of different vowels with particular emotions and vocal colour (as discussed, for example, in Vennard, 1967 and Manén, 1987) is supported by acoustic findings. Each vowel sound corresponds to a characteristic pattern of articulator adjustment. Each articulation also corresponds to a combination of formant frequencies characteristic of that vowel.

Vowels and resonance

Vowel production for speech involves the shape of the lips, the opening between the jaws, the position of the soft palate, and the shape of the tongue. Classification of vowels, however, has usually been done by reference only to the position of the main body of the tongue in the oral cavity: high-low and front-back (O'Connor, 1973; Denes & Pinson, 1993). In the traditional vowel triangle, /i/ is at the high front corner, /u/ at the high back corner, and /ɑ/ at the low back corner. Titze (1997) likened these vowels to primary colours, in that the articulatory space defined by these 'corner vowels' defines that required for the vowels in many (if not all) languages. Other vowels, such as the neutral /ʌ/ and /ə/ vowels, are classified as central. Vowels may also be classified as 'closed' (the tongue near the palate) or 'open' (the tongue low, at the bottom of the mouth) (Denes & Pinson, 1993).

> The tongue position in effect produces two acoustic chambers through which sound passes, and regulates conductivity between the chambers. Each chamber can be considered an acoustic resonator, amplifying acoustic energy near its resonances and reducing energy at frequencies

far from those resonances. Those frequencies that are amplified can be thought of as resonance peaks, and are called formants. The fundamental frequency (musical pitch) is labeled F_0, and the formants F_1, F_2, F_3, and so on, from lowest to highest. It is the relationship between F_1 and F_2 that defines a vowel. (Callaghan et al., 2012, pp. 563–64)

In moving from speaking to singing, vowels are modified to produce a wider dynamic range (for both artistry and audibility), to maintain a balance in loudness across phonemes, and in order to produce particular vocal timbres (Titze, 1995). In this modification, many combinations of articulatory adjustment may be involved, allowing shifts in formant frequencies and subtle adjustments to timbre and vowel quality. Unfortunately, the adjustments required to achieve power and matching timbre throughout the range (an aesthetic assumption in classical singing) mean that at high pitches intelligibility is compromised (Westerman Gregg & Scherer, 2006; Dromey et al., 2010).

Recent research has increased understanding of how articulatory adjustments are used in formant tracking and in production of the singer's formant.

Control of formant frequencies

The first formant is particularly affected by the mandible, the second formant by the tongue shape, and the third formant by the position of the tip of the tongue or, when the tongue is retracted, to the size of the cavity between the lower incisors and the tongue (Sundberg, 2005).

These principles have been elaborated by Pickett (1980) as rules for the modification of formant frequencies by specific articulatory manoeuvres. Pickett's first rule is that all formant frequencies decrease uniformly as the length of the vocal tract increases. The second rule is that all formant frequencies decrease uniformly with lip rounding and increase with lip spreading. In combination with larynx height adjustments, lip rounding or spreading can be effective in darkening or brightening the vowels.

Pickett lays down two additional rules for when either the front half of the vocal tract (the mouth) or the back half (the pharynx) is narrowed in relation to the other half. His third rule is this: a front constriction (e.g. raising the tongue towards the roof of the mouth (as in the phoneme /i/) lowers the first formant and raises the second formant. This creates a more diffuse sound across the frequency spectrum. More acoustic energy is spread out over both low and high frequencies. The fourth rule states that a back constriction raises the first formant and lowers the second formant, making the overall sound more compact in the middle part of the frequency spectrum, as in the case of an /ɑ/ vowel. A constriction in the centre of the vocal tract, as in /u/, does not affect the formant frequencies, but the large degree of lip rounding lowers both first and second formant for /u/.

Titze (1998) pointed out that widening the pharynx produces a darker, stronger sound quality. The first formant frequency is lowered, and the vocal tract emphasizes lower partials. For the vowel to be identified, the location and degree of constriction of the vocal tract characteristic of the vowel must remain relative to the mouth configuration. For example, for a vowel to be perceived as /ɑ/, the vocal tract must be more constricted in the pharynx than in the mouth.

Vocal intensity can be significantly increased by tuning formants of the vocal tract to harmonics of the source (Titze, 1991). When one of the lowest formant frequencies coincides with the frequency of a source spectrum partial this resonance adjustment is usually termed 'formant tuning.' A singer may use what Titze (1995) called the 'megaphone effect' produced by lowering the jaw and moving the lips forward and inward at the corners of the lips. This manoeuvre both widens and lengthens the vocal tract, producing a louder sound.

Increasing acoustic output power with formant tuning is very sensitive to fundamental frequency (Titze, 1984). In a landmark investigation of the pitch-dependent changes in lip and jaw opening made in a professional soprano, Sundberg (1975) found that the formant frequencies were similar to those of normal speech only when the fundamental was lower in frequency than the first formant. When the fundamental rose to a higher value, dropping and retracting the jaw and spreading the lips shifted the frequency of the first formant upwards close to the fundamental. This manoeuvre achieves an amplification of the vocal source far more economically than would be possible using subglottal pressure. Using this strategy, however, causes the formant frequency differences between the vowels to gradually disappear as the fundamental frequency increases, resulting in the well-known phenomenon of words being difficult to distinguish when sung at high pitch in operatic style.

Subsequent studies (Bloothooft & Plomp, 1984, 1985; Scotto di Carlo & Rutherford, 1990; Gottfried & Chew, 1992; Johansson et al., 1992; Smith & Scott, 1992) confirmed the finding of decreasing intelligibility with rising pitch. Both Gottfried and Chew (1992) and Smith and Scott (1992) found that intelligibility was improved by the presence of consonantal transitions. Smith and Scott (1992) suggested that the generally accepted notion that vowel sounds are largely unintelligible on higher notes pertains only to a restricted manner of production (i.e. operatic voice quality). They found isolated vowels sung with a raised larynx to be more intelligible than isolated vowels sung in operatic quality, and vowels sung with a high larynx and consonantal transitions to be even more intelligible.

In a study reported in 2000, Hollien et al. examined the intelligibility of vowels sung at high fundamental frequencies. They recorded 18 classical singers, 13 females and five males, drawn from a single studio in order to use relatively homogeneous stimuli. Some singers were professional singers, some were advanced students. Subjects sang three steady-state vowels, /i/, /ɑ/, and /u/, at moderately low and extremely high pitches of their range, and at loudness levels as soft and as loud as they could. Four groups of listeners, in total 50, consisting of voice teachers, phoneticians, speech-language pathology students, and 12 controls (undergraduate students) listened to the recordings to determine the identity of vowels and the nature of the confusions with other vowels. Acoustical analysis identified the fundamental frequencies sung, plus those defining the first two vowel formants. It was found that fundamental frequency change had a profound effect on vowel perception, with the greatest degradation of vowel intelligibility occurring when the fundamental frequency exceeds the usual first formant. This was particularly evident in females singing /ɑ/ at high pitches. The intelligibility of vowels sung at high pitch depends on the context within which the vowel is produced and its general co-articulatory environment. Incorrectly identified vowels tend to be confused with centre vowels.

Barnes et al. (2004) investigated how, in the absence of a singer's formant, professional operatic sopranos shape the vocal tract to achieve vocal energy through formant tuning at high fundamental frequencies. The voices of six operatic sopranos of national and international standard were recorded performing arpeggios and song tasks. The arpeggios were sung on the Italian vowels /ɑ/, /i/, and /o/, beginning on A_4. The song tasks were the first verse of the Australian national anthem, 'Advance Australia Fair,' and an excerpt of at least 30 seconds duration of an aria in their regular repertoire. Acoustic analyses of vowel data were compared with song task data to assess the consistency of the approaches. Comparisons were also made with regard to two conditions of intended vocal projection (maximal and comfortable), the two song tasks, two recording environments (studio and anechoic room), and between subjects. The results were consistent across conditions.

The singers produced high frequency energy levels on /ɑ/ and /o/ vowels, with the /ɑ/ vowel exhibiting the greatest high frequency energy. In contrast, no /i/ vowel exhibited high frequency energy, suggesting that the normal articulation for this vowel is probably sufficient for good audibility. Those /ɑ/ and /o/ vowels with L_{HF} between 6 and 10 dB had HF energy equivalent to vowels with singers' formant.

This study emphasized the importance of identifying the performance rank of singers in interpreting results. The investigators used singers rated (on the taxonomy of Bunch & Chapman, 2000) as of national or international level. The subject with the highest position in the taxonomy ranked first for HF energy and the lowest rank for HF energy corresponded to the subject with lowest taxonomic position. The investigators suggested that enhanced HF energy is something that develops through both experience and practice. It may involve epilaryngeal narrowing.

Sundberg (2009) revisited the issue of the strategies adopted by classical singers to achieve consistent power and timbre throughout the range. Articulation of a professional soprano singing an ascending triad pattern from C_4 to G_5 on the vowels /i, e, u, o, ɑ/ was analysed using magnetic resonance imaging. Lip and jaw opening and tongue dorsum height were measured and analysed as a function of pitch. Considerable systematic articulatory changes were observed, presumably to increase first formant frequency so as always to keep it above fundamental frequency. The soprano started to modify lip opening, jaw opening, or the height of tongue dorsum at a pitch between four and five semitones below the frequency that equalled her normal first formant value in low-pitched singing. The changes in jaw opening varied between 8 and 19 mm, depending on pitch and vowel. The associated changes of lip opening were either counteracted or amplified depending on pitch and vowel. The tongue dorsum relative to the lower jaw was reduced in the vowels /i, e, u/ and remained more constant in the vowels /ɑ, o/.

Lindestad and Södersten (1988) found that in singing at high pitch their four countertenor subjects employed a different strategy from that reported for sopranos. Using countertenor voice, the subjects sang fundamental frequencies of 662, 524, and 494 Hz (roughly E_5, C_5, and B_4), all frequencies higher than the normal value of the first formant frequency in men. Rather than using jaw opening to raise the first formant, they achieved this effect by shortening the vocal tract by means of larynx raising and lower pharynx narrowing. The researchers noted a great deal more pharyngeal activity in connection with variations in pitch and intensity in the countertenor than in the baritone singing of the subjects, notably a clear change in the configuration of the laryngeal tube when changing from modal voice to countertenor phonation, with a widening at the level of the ventricular folds. This may have been because the countertenors were not as accomplished in the baritone range of the voice, or because they did not cultivate the singer's formant in the baritone range in order to achieve a better match in timbre with the countertenor sound.

Austin (2007) also investigated jaw opening. He looked at two groups of singers, those with fewer than four years of training (novice) and those with more than eight years of training (experienced) in the Western tradition of opera and art song. Using the carrier phrase 'I say b(v)p' where (v) was each of three vowels, /ɑ/, /i/, and /u/, the subjects first spoke, then sang on a repeated pitch at three notes of low, medium, and high range. He found no statistically significant difference in jaw opening between the novices and the experienced singers. However, the vowel was significant for jaw opening in both groups, with /ɑ/ being produced with more jaw opening than /i/ or /u/. There was greater jaw opening as pitch increased. Most typically, the jaw opening was less in low singing than in speech, then increased for both medium and high singing. Decreasing jaw opening lowers the frequency of the first formant, which would be helpful in increasing intensity at lower pitches.

Several researchers (e.g., Miller & Schutte, 1990; Carlsson & Sundberg, 1992) have noted Coffin's system of singing training based on tuning the vocal tract. Coffin's *Sounds of Singing* (1987) and *Overtones of Bel Canto* (1980), and the 'Chromatic vowel chart for voice building and tone placing' in the later publication, were built on the premise that 'while spoken vowel values vary according to languages and dialects, in singing they cannot depart from the coincidence of a vowel pitch and an harmonic of the sung pitch. This is an absolute of singing' (1987, p. 4). Coffin's system is essentially a documentation of traditional pedagogies (he quotes Lamperti, Mancini, Tosi, Garcia, Marchesi, Lilli Lehmann, and Nicolai Gedda's teacher, Paola Novikova) with the purpose of showing 'how to bring the frequencies of the vocal cords and the vocal tract into concord on the various notes and vowels' (1987, p. 45). The vowel chart is a system of 'vowel shading' (i.e., modification expressed in terms of colour) 'for louder resonance.' It shows quite specific vowel modifications for specific pitches, related to vocal registration for a range of voice types, and notes the general rule that 'low notes should be brightened to accentuate the high harmonics so the voice can be heard . . . High notes should be rounded in all voices to place energy in the lower harmonics' (Coffin, 1987, Chromatic Vowel Chart). An essential aspect of the system is identification of *passaggi* (register transitions) for the different voice types and an interpretation of 'high notes' and 'low notes' in relation to these voice types.

Dromey et al. (2011) analysed the acoustic effects of vowel equalization training in singers. In aiming for vocal projection and resonance with a balance of bright and dark timbres, classically trained singers make adjustments to tongue and jaw position. In Hopkin's method of vowel equalization the jaw position for the closed vowels /i/ and /u/ remains constant while the tongue moves, meaning these opposite (front–back) vowels are closely related by their similar height. Likewise, an equivalent relationship exists between /e/ and /o/. Higher and lower vowels are also equalized using this approach, with the extent of tongue raising and lowering reduced for the vowel pairs /i-ɑ/, /i-e/ and /e-ɑ/. When producing the /i-e/ pair, singers are encouraged to hold a relatively stable lingual posture while relying on jaw motion to move between the vowels.

In this experiment, 16 amateur singers – seven males and nine females – ranging in age from 18 to 25 years were recorded singing 'Somewhere Over the Rainbow' three times at a comfortable pitch. The passage was chosen because it contained the vowels /ɑ/, /e/, /i/, /o/, and /u/. Each singer then sustained those vowels three times each. After training in vowel equalization, the singers then sang the passage three times and sustained the isolated vowels three times. Following training, the frequency of both first and second formants decreased significantly for the vowel /ɑ/. The frequency of the second formant also decreased significantly for /e/, /i/ and /u/, indicating a more neutral placement for vowels /e/ and /i/. A formal perceptual evaluation was not conducted, so it is not clear whether the vowels could still be clearly distinguished and whether they were perceived as of appropriate timbre.

Miller and Schutte (1990) examined the amplifying power of formant tuning employed by a baritone in the range 230–380 Hz (roughly $B\flat_3$ to F_4), a range traversing the *primo passaggio.* (main register transition). The baritone used different strategies, depending on the musical context. In a rising arpeggio spanning the octave from $B\flat_3$, sung on /bi- bi- bi- bi-/, the singer produced notes of considerable intensity by tuning the formants to match one of the low harmonics. In singing a descending scale passage from F_4 to $B\flat_3$ on the vowel /i/ after a /b/ onset, there was little vowel modification and the first formant stayed close to the fundamental. Presumably the combination of rising pitch and plosives required increasing subglottal pressure for the rising arpeggio, causing formant tuning to be employed to maintain uniform intensity. This, as well as the fact that it traversed the *passaggio*, required vowel modification. In the descending scale passage, on the other hand, subglottal pressure was not an issue, and the closeness of the intervals with no intervening consonant would make vowel distortion obvious.

Carlsson and Sundberg (1992) had a similar finding in relation to synthesized 'singing' of a descending chromatic scale. They found that an expert panel preferred constant formant frequencies to formant tuning, presumably because of the shifts in vowel quality between adjacent notes that formant tuning causes.

Different styles, different resonance

As in other areas of voice production, 21st-century research studies on resonance in singing are beginning to clarify the differences between the vocal tract coordinations required by singers in classical and nonclassical styles. The 1993 Sundberg et al. study discussed in Chapter 4 showed marked differences between operatic singing and belting in relation to the voice source. The resonatory differences were not so marked, with classical singing having a moderate degree of jaw opening and a lowered larynx. In belting the larynx was high and there was wide variation in pharyngeal shape with vowel and pitch. The side walls of the pharynx were advanced and the sinus piriformes were small in many vowels.

In the Zangger Borch and Sundberg (2011) study already referred to in Chapters 3 and 4, in the rock, pop, soul, and Swedish dance band styles of singing differences of both phonation and resonance were identified. Differences in larynx height and jaw opening produced differences of timbre, with soul showing low values for both first and second formant, probably reflecting a low larynx position. Swedish dance band showed low values for the first formant, and pop and rock had high first formant values.

The Sundberg et al. (2012) study on the substyles of belting showed phonatory differences, but few systematic resonance differences between the substyles. There was, however, a clear difference between belting and classical singing in that in the classical examples the first formant was markedly lower across all vowels than in the belting substyles.

In a 2011 study, Sundberg et al. examined the formant tuning strategies of professional male singers. Many singing teachers and classically trained singers use formant tuning to achieve maximum vocal output without compromising vocal health or evenness of timbre. The researchers pointed out that, although there have been several studies on formant tuning, some questions remain: whether there are specific benefits of using this technique; how it would be applied to different vowels throughout the range; and how it would apply to the *passaggio*. They had eight professional male singers (three tenors and five baritones, in the age range 23 to 42 years) sing both ascending and descending scales, firstly using a classical strategy, then a nonclassical one. The scales were sung across the *passaggio* range and on different vowels – /æ/, /ɑ/, /u/, and /i/. They found that the classical and nonclassical formant tuning strategies differed in a consistent way that was clearly perceptible. There were four results common to the classical versions: first, the first and second formant tended to be lower; second, the first formant was between 1.5 and 5 semitones lower than the second harmonic; third, the highest notes showed a rising spectrum envelope over the three lowest partials; and fourth, in the highest notes, the first formant coincided with the second harmonic at some scale tones. In the nonclassical versions, the first and second formant coincided with a lower spectrum partial for some tones in the scale, without being preceded or followed by a clear change in their frequencies.

The relationship of formant tuning (vowel modification) to the singer's formant and to vocal registration is discussed below.

The singer's formant

There has long been interest in what produces the exciting ringing quality of the professional singing voice, the quality that gives an arresting 'edge' to the voice. This quality – the singer's formant – assists register blending and legato line and is essential for singers to be heard clearly over large orchestras, electronic instruments, or background noise. For these reasons, much of the literature on vocal technique in singing contains directions on how to achieve brilliance or 'ring' (e.g. Vennard, 1967).

In his pioneering work in the 1960s, Vennard (1967, p. 166) stated that the singer's formant results when 'the resonators are in tune with the vibrator,' that is, when the resonators are shaped to reinforce vowel formants that are harmonics of the fundamental. The most common way of tuning formant frequencies is to adjust the vocal tract shape by moving the articulators.

Constricting the vocal tract in the glottal region also leads to an increase of the formant frequencies. If the third, fourth, and fifth formants are close in frequency, thus forming a formant cluster, the singer's formant peak can be explained as an articulatory phenomenon that can be produced with a normal voice source. Clustering of formants can be attained if the pharynx is wide in comparison with the entrance to the larynx tube. This tube, immediately above the vocal folds, is about 2 cm long, with its anterior wall formed by the epiglottis and the posterior wall by the arytenoid cartilages (Sundberg, 1995a).

Since the invention of instrumentation for objective voice analysis, voice science has been able to offer some explanations of the singer's formant. A series of investigations by Sundberg found that the singer's formant is resonated by a complex cavity produced by the expansion of the laryngeal ventricle, pyriform sinuses, and laryngopharyx. Sundberg found that this cavity requires a low larynx and a wide pharynx leading to a narrowed larynx tube, with the widened pharynx being six times the area of the opening to the larynx tube (Sundberg, 1974, 1977, 1981, 1983, 1987, 1991, 1995a, 2001).

Sundberg (2005) has identified the singer's formant as an exceptionally high spectrum envelope peak appearing in the vicinity of 3 kHz in all vowel spectra. The acoustic effect may be reinforced by the fact that the frequencies in the 3 kHz range are those most easily perceived by the human ear. The centre frequency of the singer's formant is around 2.2 kHz for basses, around 2.7 kHz for baritones, around 2.8 kHz for tenors, and around 3.2 kHz for altos. Sundberg suggested that in sopranos it is nothing but a perfectly normal third and fourth formant. Nevertheless, the perceptual effect of clear, ringing quality, independent of vowel or pitch, is certainly present in accomplished soprano singing. In his 2001 article, Sundberg suggested that when the high frequency range (2–4 kHz) reaches 6 dB, the excess energy is sufficient to say that there may be a singer's formant.

Detweiler (1994) tested Sundberg's hypothesis on three classically trained professional male singers. The singers did produce the singer's formant, but without achieving the laryngopharygeal/laryngeal outlet cross-sectional area ratio requisite to Sundberg's model. They also sang with varying laryngeal height. Detweiler pointed out that these data on larynx height are consistent with the data of Shipp and Izdebski (1975) (discussed in Chapter 4), Wang (1985), Sengupta (1990), and Dmitriev and Kiselev (1979). She maintained that the laryngeal system as modelled by Sundberg is not the resonance source of the singer's formant in these subjects, and postulates that the singer's formant is an aggregate formant constituted by the combined resonances of two component formants. This position is similar to that taken by Simonson (1987), who investigated the acoustic effects on the singer's formant of tuning the first formant with the fundamental. He found effective increases in intensity of both the first formant and the singer's formant by placing the fundamental and the first formant in a harmonic relationship.

Responding to Detweiler's work, Sundberg (1995a) measured the formant frequency changes due to a doubling of the cross-sectional area at each 0.5 cm interval along the vocal tract length axis, in order to test the assumption that the fourth formant is strongly dependent on the larynx tube. He found that the fourth and fifth formants were very sensitive to the details of the area function of the larynx tube. His results supported the assumption that the singer's formant is strongly, though not entirely, associated with the larynx tube. He made the point that more accurate assessment requires sweep frequency measurements of high fidelity, three-dimensional models of the vocal tract.

A study by Sundberg (1995a) study also attempted to quantify how prominent the spectrum envelope peak at the level near 3 kHz needs to be to qualify as a singer's formant. The formant levels were mathematically predicted, and these predictions were compared with data collected from singers in an anechoic chamber. Four tenors and four baritones or basses, all professional opera singers, sang a vowel sequence with the consonant /v/ interspersed between the vowels. Three sopranos sang the solo part of Mendelssohn's motet *Hear My Prayer*.

All male singers showed a clear singer's formant. For the sopranos, the result was varied. In some cases a given vowel showed a strong singer's formant, and in other cases the singer's formant was absent. The singer's formant is said to be a phenomenon of the operatic voice; Sundberg does not explain why singing tasks so different in kind were set for men and women, nor why the repertoire selected for the sopranos was from oratorio rather than opera and from a piece frequently performed by the boy treble voice. It is likely that such a choice would have affected the vocal quality employed by the subjects.

Most work on the singer's formant has assumed a 'classical' Western timbre. Wang (1985), however, studied larynx position in 10 tenors singing in three different styles, Western operatic, Chinese, and that used for Western early music, all showing 'bright timbre.' He found the singer's formant in conjunction with low larynx in the Western operatic style, and in conjunction with high larynx in Chinese and early music singers. Sengupta's investigation of some acoustic features of North Indian classical singing identified the singer's formant in both male and female singers. He found that the centre frequency of the singer's formant increased with rising pitch, as has been found in other vocal qualities (Sengupta, 1990).

Perceptually, the vocal quality of these styles has much in common with that loud, 'twangy' sound usually labelled 'belting' by Western practitioners.

'Twang' is one aspect of a number of vocal qualities. Yanagisawa et al. (1989) attributed 'twang' to constriction of the aryepiglottic sphincter. They found that when the aryepiglottic sphincter is constricted, it creates an extra reso-nator between the aryepiglottic rim and the vocal folds, raising the partials in the 3 kHz area of the spectrum. This resembles Sundberg's theory (1987, 1995a) that a wide pharynx and narrowed larynx tube are prerequisites for production of the singer's formant.

For a voice to have a strong ringing quality, there must also be a stronger than average distribution of high frequency energy in the glottal airflow pulses entering the vocal tract from the glottis; this energy is generated by the acoustic interaction between the glottal source and the inertance present in the subglottal and supraglottal airflow (Rothenberg, 1984). The sharp cutoff of airflow that is characteristic of the glottal wave is an important source of the high-frequency components of the glottal source spectrum. It is also possible to sharpen the cutoff by adjusting the mechanical properties of the vocal folds (Baken, 2005). The creation of the high-frequency components

of the voice source is thus dependent on both transglottal flow and laryngeal adjustment.

Howard et al. (1990) found that if the closed phase of the vocal fold vibratory cycle is increased, due to the coupling in of the subglottal cavities, less acoustic energy is lost to the listener. By increasing the closed quotient, the professional singer increases overall system efficiency: an increase in output acoustic energy associated with a decrease in the expenditure of stored input energy is a natural acoustic consequence of adjusting how the folds vibrate. Titze (1986) pointed out that not only does a constriction above the vocal folds followed by an expansion in the pharynx resonate the partials around 3 kHz, but the constriction itself causes the larynx to produce more energy in the higher partials, producing a kind of feedback effect. It also achieves an acoustic decoupling of the vocal folds from the influence of changing vowels (Titze & Story, 1977). Reid (1990) emphasized the interrelationship between 'close cavity coupling,' in which resonance at larynx level is reinforced by pharyngeal configuration, and the importance of the larynx as a regulator of the amplitude of sound waves introduced into the vocal tract. He identified narrowing of the ventricular folds as an essential element in creating a build-up of supraglottal pressure and regulating the amount of energy introduced into adjacent resonators.

In summary, current research indicates that production of the singer's formant is associated with a long closed phase in the vocal fold vibratory cycle, narrowing of the vocal tract immediately above the larynx; a wide pharynx, and adjustment of the articulators to maximize close cavity coupling. It may also involve aryepiglottic constriction and narrowing of the ventricular folds.

A study by Teie (1976) confirmed the assumption that for the majority of singers, the ability to produce the singer's formant is learned. He compared the characteristics of the singer's formant in the voice spectra of male and female singers at four levels: untrained singers, first year college voice students, fourth year college voice students, and mature singers (voice faculty). The only statistically significant differences in the intensity peaks of the singer's formant among groups were found between the untrained singers and the trained singers. No statistically significant differences were found among the trained singer groups. Findings on the centre frequency of the singer's formant in the different voice types suggest the possibility of classifying voices by objective formant analysis.

Nasal resonance versus brilliance

Many pedagogies associate cultivation of brilliance with either a particular 'placement' or with sinus or nasal resonance. In English, Italian, and German, vowels and most consonants are oral-resonant, that is they are produced with the velum raised. However, it has often been asserted by singers and teachers of singing in the Western art tradition that resonance in the nasal passages and sinuses of the head plays an important part in tone production (Austin, 1995, 1997). Husler and Rodd-Marling (1976), for instance, claimed that different vocal functions are stimulated by different 'placements' of the voice by which 'the singer rouses (innervates) the inner and outer muscles of the throat' (p. 69). 'Placing the tone in the forehead (often with the fictive idea of the sinuses as resonators)' (p. 71) is said to draw the larynx slightly upwards.

> The chief result of what is often termed 'singing in the mask,' usually practised by placing the tone at the root of the nose, is to bring into action the main body of the muscle that lies in the vocal folds, the vocal *lip* (vocalis), i.e. the specific *Tensor*. (p. 70)

In 1987, Scotto di Carlo and Autesserre wrote:

> To sing, one must necessarily lower the velum, or at least use velar positions as close to the lowered position as possible. (p. 7)
>
> In speech, when the velum is raised to its highest point, it touches the rear pharyngeal wall, totally cutting off the nasal pharynx from the buccal cavity. This never occurs in singing where the nasal cavity always remains open, as we can see on the telexeroradiographic documents taken of various professional singers. (p. 12)

Troup et al. (1989) replied:

> While not denying the validity of their research as applied to the group of singers studied, and to the language [French] sung by the subjects, we believe that velum closure in singing depends on many factors: the instructor, the language, the singer and the style of singing. (1989, p. 35)

In 1993, Alderson asserted:

> directing a portion of the sound waves through the nasal cavity adds a more brilliant ring to the tone, while it is largely the responsibility of the oral cavity to turn sound waves into vowel colors. (p. 26)

Related to theories about the role of the nasal cavity in resonance are theories about the role of the sinuses, either as sound producers or sound modifiers. E.G. White's sinus tone theory of voice production maintains that voice is created in the skull sinuses. In addition, it emphasizes the role of the nasal cavity. According to this theory,

> a well developed voice blends the activity of all the sinuses, variations in pitch and quality being determined by the extent to which the frontal sinuses are supplemented by the other cavities. In the highest notes the

frontal sinuses, lying immediately above the eye-brow ridge, are predominant; they remain active throughout the compass but as the pitch is lowered vibrations spread more strongly to the ethmoid cells and sphenoid sinuses. Tone created in these sinuses is amplified in the larger volumes of air in the nasal cavity, the mouth, and the maxillary sinuses. (Hewlett, 1981, p. 13)

By contrast Wooldridge (1956), in a much-quoted study, compared the vowels produced by six professional singers under normal conditions and when the nasal passages had been filled with cotton gauze. A jury of expert listeners was unable to distinguish any difference. A repetition of the experiment by Vennard in 1964 (cited in Vennard, 1967) confirmed the original findings.

Austin (1997) compared the action of the velopharyngeal port in normal speech and Western operatic singers. He had four highly trained female singers read sentences containing nasal consonants at a normal conversational rate and then sing the sentences in recitative style in low, medium, and high singing ranges. For these singers, the velopharyngeal port was closed significantly longer in singing than in speaking. He found that the amount of time the velopharyngeal port was opened was greatest in speech and diminished as the singer ascended in pitch.

Confusion about the role of the velum and the sinuses of the skull may stem from the singer's sensations of resonance, aural perceptions of 'nasal resonance,' and traditional exercises using the nasal continuants /m/, /n/, and /ŋ/. Miller (1993) attributed the confusion of 'nasality with brilliance' to the 'vocal tract adjustment that conducts sensations of balanced resonance to the bony and cartilaginous portions of the face, including the nasal cartilages, through sympathetic vibration' (p. 121). The 'considerable controversy over whether vocal timbre, which is perceived by some singers and listeners as being marked by "nasal resonance" but free of "nasality," may also depend on laryngeal configuration as well as on internal vocal tract impedance' (Miller, 1986, p. 295).

For centuries, singers have used exercises based on /m/, /n/, and /ŋ/ for 'improving resonance balance in vowels that follow them' (Miller, 1986, p. 80). The different nasals serve to stimulate different vibratory sensations in different areas. In /m/, for example,

> because the lips are closed, and because the mouth, pharynx, and the nostrils are now connected cavities, distinct vibratory sensations are felt in regions of the pharynx, the nose, the mouth, and the area of the sinuses. (Miller, 1986, p. 81)

In /n/ the vibrations are located higher, 'in the region of the upper jaw and maxillary sinuses.' In /ŋ/ 'vibratory sensations in the frontal area of the face are often intense' (p. 85). Miller directed that in moving from the nasal to the vowel

> no continuance of actual nasality should be present in the tone, but the same sensation should pertain in the nasal and sinusal areas (sympathetic resonance experienced by the singer largely through bone and cartilage conduction). (p. 81)

Titze (1987) pointed out that confusion may arise when a singer's perception is linked to production without careful scrutiny of the acoustic signal. Different productions may lead to similar spectral patterns and hence similar perceptions. The ratio of the peak energy in the high-frequency portion of the spectrum (2–4 kHz) to the peak energy in the low-frequency portion (0–1 kHz) is increased both when the singer's formant (brilliance) is produced, or when a vowel is nasalized. In the case of the singer's formant, the high-frequency prominence of the oral and pharyngeal resonance is increased by creating an additional resonator in the larynx. In the case of nasalization, the low-frequency prominence of the oral and pharyngeal resonance is lowered by creating an acoustic leakage through the nose. Lowering the velum and coupling the nasal cavity to the rest of the vocal tract introduces anti-resonances into the formant envelope. Nasalization reduces the intensity at and near the frequency of any of a number of anti-resonances, including between 2 and 3 kHz, the range in which the singer's formant occurs (Austin, 1995).

Birch et al. (2002) analysed the velopharyngeal opening in 17 professional operatic singers – three high sopranos, three sopranos, two mezzo-sopranos, three tenors, two baritones, two bass-baritones, and two basses – singing the vowels /ɒ, i, u/ at medium volume at different pitches throughout their range. The velopharyngeal opening was measured by three means: nasofibroscopy; recording nasal and oral airflow by means of a divided flow mask; and comparison of the level of the fundamental in the nasal and oral airflow signals. An expert panel then assessed the tokens produced by the singers for nasality. Clear evidence of velopharyngeal opening was found for all singer classifications, at least under some conditions. It was observed for the vowels /a/ and /u/ and, for one tenor, on /i/. All tenors showed velopharyngeal opening near their *passaggio*. Since the listening test revealed no correlation with perceived nasality in the vowel /a/, it was suggested that singers may use a velopharyngeal opening to fine-tune vocal timbre. The researchers suggest that further investigation of a well-controlled velopharyngeal opening for vocal timbre is needed.

A further study (Sundberg et al., 2007) analysed the resonatory effects of velopharyngeal opening used by professional opera singers. The investigators constructed acoustic epoxy models based on CAT scan imaging of a professional baritone singer's vocal tract and nasal cavities, including the maxillary sinuses. A velopharyngeal opening was found to attenuate the first formant in /a/, so that the relative level of the singer's formant increased. They found a similar effect for /u/ and /i/, although it also showed a substantial widening of the first formant bandwidth, which would probably produce a nasal quality. While these results were derived from a model, and that from a single subject, it does seem likely that singers can enhance higher spectrum partials by a careful tuning of a velopharyngeal opening.

The difference between brilliance and nasality was clarified by a study conducted by Yanagisawa et al. (1990). By means of simultaneous velolaryngeal videoendoscopy, the study examined the role of the soft palate in normal laryngeal functions, as well as in its contribution to nasal and oral voice qualities. Singers executed a five-part task, beginning with a totally nasalized /n/ and progressing to a nasalized /i/, a nasalized /i/ in twang quality, an oral /i/ in twang quality, and an /i/ in which the oral twang quality was modified by lowering the larynx. The sequential changes in quality were noted, from a completely nasal to a rather loud oral tone. The endoscopy verified that the first three conditions were indeed nasal, as judged by an open velopharyngeal port, while in the last two conditions, in which the velopharyngeal port was closed, the qualities were oral. The authors contrasted the dull quality, produced by nasality, with the bright quality of twang, produced by aryepiglottic constriction, qualities that have often been termed 'nasal.'

In 2010, Sundberg and Thalén published a study on the voice quality often labelled 'twang' and commonly used in pop, rock, country, and music theatre. A single female professional vocalist and pedagogue sang examples of twang and neutral voice quality, which a panel of experts classified in almost complete agreement with the singer's intentions. While there were differences in the voice source (discussed in Chapter 4), the formant differences were more important for the perception of 'twanginess': the first and second formant frequencies tended to be higher, and the third and fifth formant frequencies lower, in twang. The researchers noted that as resonatory effects occur independently of the voice source, the formant frequencies in twang may reflect a strategy advantageous to vocal health.

Experimental studies have thus clearly demonstrated that the production of brilliance in the voice is unrelated to the nasal passages or sinuses of the head.

Vibrato

The vibrato used in Western classical singing is an undulation of the fundamental frequency. It seems that this is produced by the phonatory mechanism rather than the respiratory mechanism (Cleveland, 1994). Vibrato can be described in terms of four parameters: the rate (number of undulations per second), the extent (how far phonation frequency departs up and down from its average during a vibrato cycle), the regularity (how similar the frequency excursions are to one another), and the waveform of the undulations (Sundberg, 1995b). Rate and extent are the two parameters most often studied.

Researchers have suggested that the periodic undulation of the fundamental frequency involved in vibrato may be a stabilized tremor of the cricothyroid and thyroarytenoid muscles (Titze, 1994; Hsiao et al., 1994). How the stabilization is achieved is not yet certain. Many structures in the vocal tract, such as the velum, the tongue, and the side walls of the pharynx, may be engaged in a rhythmic pulsation synchronous with the vibrato; sometimes the tongue and lower jaw shake with the vibrator (Sundberg, 1987). Estill et al. (1984) found vibrato in the 5–6 Hz range in the suprahyoid muscles. Also, a natural resonance in the breathing system occurs at about 6 Hz, which is almost identical to the normal vibrato rate (Sundberg, 1987).

Shipp et al. (1980) found a significantly slower vibrato rate in male singers than in female singers; vibrato rate was uninfluenced by vocal pitch or by vocal effort. However, skillful singers vary the pitch oscillation and rate of vibrato in response to artistic judgement informed by the musical style. Shipp et al. (1983) suggested that the extent of the oscillation is monitored by the singer principally through the auditory pathways, and the rate is mainly a function of the autonomic nervous system's influence on the vibrato generator. The acceptable rate of vibrato in classical Western singing styles has changed since the early 20th century, when it varied from 6–7 Hz, to the 5.5 Hz more common today (Shipp et al., 1980; Titze, 1994). The pitch modulation varies by approximately one semitone (Shipp et al., 1980, 1988).

Siegwart and Scherer (1995) used commercial recordings to compare the judgements of experienced listeners with the acoustic measurements of spectral characteristics of voice quality. They used two extracts from the cadenza to the aria 'Ardon gl'incensi' from Donizetti's *Lucia di Lammermoor*. While Siegwart and Scherer suggested that vibrato might be a feature of the voice that contributes to the emotional communication of the music, they did not study that aspect of voice.

Howes et al. (2004) followed up on the Siegwart and Scherer study to investigate whether vibrato influenced listeners' perceptions. There were three related studies. The first used commercial recordings of the same five singers and the same cadenza examined by Siegwart and Scherer, measuring vibrato rate and extent in each performance, and tested that against the judges' preference for singers. The two singers rated by Siegwart and Scherer's judges as most successful in expressing 'fear of death' had the fastest rate of vibrato. One of the two least preferred singers had the slowest vibrato rate, a wide vibrato extent, and less stability in rate and extent than the others singers.

In the second and third studies recordings of different singers and a different cadenza were used. Vibrato onset, rate, and extent were measured and compared with perceptual assessments to assess the singer's degree of success in communicating emotion. In the second study the perceptual assessments were made by 14 highly regarded professional singing teachers with national and international reputations, who also were experienced adjudicators of major singing competitions. In the third study the judges were 24 opera-lovers. In neither Study 2 nor Study 3 did the perception of vibrato features show a clear relationship to the measurement of vibrato. 'However, a comparison of the acoustic measurements with the preference and emotion judgments suggested that some elements of vibrato may affect listeners' perception of the voice, their preference for a particular singer, and assist the communication of emotion between singer and audience' (Howes et al., 2004, p. 216).

In order for vibrato not to interfere with the melody, its extent needs to decrease when rapid pitch changes occur. A study by Michel and Myers (1991) found that vibrato width increased with increasing crescendo, but remained constant in decrescendo. The greatest vibrato width occurred at the middle frequencies. Baken and Orlikoff (1987) suggested that the regular pitch variation of vibrato disguises the pitch fluctuations produced by articulation. Some researchers have distinguished between 'frequency vibrato,' 'amplitude vibrato,' and 'timbre vibrato,' although it is likely that they have a common origin (Schutte & Miller, 1991). Schutte and Miller found that 'amplitude vibrato' and 'timbre vibrato' were largely the result of the shifting prominence of the various partials and formants as fundamental frequency modulated.

Acoustic characteristics and perceptual judgement

A valuable study by Ekholm et al. (1998) identified perceptual criteria used by voice experts for the assessment of voice quality in classical singing and related them to objective measurements taken from acoustic analysis of the voice signal. This study is helpful to singing teachers (and to scientists) in linking perceptual features with acoustic features and, by implication, with physical coordinations.

Sixteen male singers – four countertenors, seven tenors, and five baritones – were recorded in a medium-sized concert hall singing an excerpt from Mozart's concert aria 'Ch'io mi scordi di te' with piano accompaniment. Samples of vowels /a/, /i/, and /o/ demanding constant pitch and loudness in the singer's mid range were then extracted from the recordings and submitted to spectral analysis. A panel of seven expert voice teachers evaluated the 16 audiotaped performances in terms of the perceptual categories 'appropriate vibrato,' 'resonance/ring,' 'colour/warmth,' and 'intensity.' These criteria were four of 12 generally accepted perceptual criteria that had been established in a previous study (Wapnick & Eckholm, 1997).

The investigators identified the standard for vibrato in professional Western classical singing as an ever-present, smooth, and fairly even undulation of the fundamental frequency of about 5–7 Hz, with an average excursion from the average frequency of less than ±1 semitone. The singers all produced data within a 'normal' range: for baritones a rate of 5.1 to 6.8 Hz and extent of 3.6 to 5.1%; for tenors a rate of 5.1 to 6.4 Hz and extent of 4.3 to 8.0%; and for countertenors a rate of 5.1 to 6.2 Hz and extent of 3.5 to 7.5%. A delayed onset of vibrato or a lack of vibrato resulted in a low rating from the judges. Of the two countertenors who sang with vibrato, the judges gave a higher ranking to the singer having an average vibrato rate of 6.0 Hz (closer to the usual rate for female voices than for baritones) and extent of 3.5%. While the countertenor who ranked lower had the more regular vibrato of the two, his average vibrato rate was lower at 5.4 Hz and the extent was much higher at 7.5%. Of the two baritones ranked either first or second in all criteria, the sample segment ranked lower for appropriate vibrato had an amplitude modulation of approximately 90%, as compared to 22% for the other segment.

'Resonance/ring' was acoustically identified by presence of the singer's formant. It has been shown that the auditory system serves as a band of filters, with the critical band (that bandwidth at which subjective responses of listeners change abruptly) varying as a function of frequency (Lieberman & Blumstein, 1988). Following Bloothooft and Plomp (1986), who used two critical bands of hearing in their study of the sound level of the singer's formant in professional singing, the Ekholm et al. study measured spectral energy distribution and the mean spectral amplitude in two one-third octave frequency bands, one centred at 2540 Hz and the other at 3140 Hz. As would be expected, the singer's formant range was lower in baritones than in tenors. Results for countertenors were similar to that for baritones.

There was a strong correlation of the perceptual ratings for 'resonance/ring' and mean amplitude of sound level within the lower band for baritones, and within the upper band for tenors. A baritone with most of the spectral energy in the singer's formant above 2800 Hz, the upper critical band of hearing in that range, received clearly lower 'resonance/ring' ratings than other baritones. Not surprisingly, countertenors (singing in falsetto) received low ratings on this criterion. One countertenor, however, had a singer's formant comparable to that found in baritones and was rated consistently higher. Laryngoscopic examination of this singer revealed that the cartilaginous part of the vocal folds was notably longer than expected, effectively decreasing the length of the membranous vibrating vocal fold to a size expected in females.

The perceptual quality of 'colour/warmth' is associated with a strengthening of the fundamental frequency, lower formant frequencies, and a less pronounced singer's formant. It is consistent with a voice production using a lowered larynx. This study found strong correlations between ratings for 'colour/warmth' and 'appropriate vibrato' and a higher spectral energy in the singer's formant range. A high positive correlation with mean 'vowel formant' frequency was observed in baritones, and a significant negative correlation was observed in countertenors and tenors. The 'colour/warmth' rating for baritones was higher than that for countertenors and tenors. These last two findings can presumably be attributed to register and vowel-modification factors in those voices singing at higher pitches.

The perceptual criterion 'clarity/focus' relates to the degree of nonharmonic noise in the vocal tone. The judges rated vowel segments with elevated levels of nonharmonic spectral energy lower on this criterion. Two singers displayed subharmonic components in the spectrogram. 'Clarity/focus' showed a significant positive correlation with vowel formant frequency.

Application to pedagogy

Pedagogical concerns about resonance and articulation include production of an aesthetically appropriate timbre, vowel quality, vibrato, and text articulation. Recent research is clarifying the different resonant configurations needed to produce the vocal qualities required in different styles, for example, in classical styles and belting.

The Ekholm et al. study clarified the attributes of good voice quality appropriate for Western classical singing. Such voice quality needs a balance of vibrato rate and extent, a low rate of amplitude vibrato, and a vibrato present throughout each note. It needs good vowel definition and the warmth of tone conferred by a lowered larynx, balanced by the 'ring' of the singer's formant with its spectral location within the appropriate bandwidth for the voice classification. While intonation accuracy was not a perceptual criterion in this study, poor intonation negatively affected the perception of all other qualities.

Taken in conjunction with findings on the centre frequency of the singer's formant in different voice types, the findings of the Ekholm et al. (1998) study on the perception of 'ring' are significant for the teaching of singing. Voice classification is a subtle and complex matter, involving a number of parameters. I mentioned earlier in this chapter that formant analysis is one factor that could be used as a guide in voice classification; in Chapter 6 other factors are discussed. Given appropriate classification according to register changes, range, and optimal tessitura, it then needs to be borne in mind that the perceptual qualities of the voice should align with expectations for that voice type. The centre frequency of the singer's formant needs to be appropriate for the voice type: tenors sound like tenors if the centre frequency is around 2.8 kHz, baritones like baritones if it is around 2.7 kHz, and altos like altos if it is around 3.2 kHz. While an expert musical ear is invaluable, acoustic analysis and computer-assisted visual feedback can assist student and teacher in achieving the articulatory adjustments necessary to effect the appropriate changes in voice quality.

In the teaching studio, the singer does much tuning of formant frequencies intuitively by attention to vowel quality and the emotional motivation of a text, with the teacher supplying the analytical ear able to identify articulatory problems causing acoustic distortion. The danger is that one fixed configuration of articulators may be seen as correct, militating against the subtle adjustments necessary to maintain acoustic balance while the relative dimensions of the vocal tract resonators change in response to phonetic articulation (Miller, 1986).

References

Alderson, A. (1993). Positioning the velum. *Journal of Research in Singing and Applied Vocal Pedagogy*, *16*(2), 25–32.

Austin, S.F. (1995). Nasal resonance: dispelling the myth. *Australian Voice*, *1*, 18–23.

Austin, S.F. (1997). Movement of the velum during speech and singing in classically trained singers. *Journal of Voice*, *11*(2), 212–21.

Austin, S.F. (2007). Jaw opening in novice and experienced classically trained singers. *Journal of Voice*, *21*(1), 72–79. doi:10.1016/j.jvoice.2005.08.013

Baken, R.J. (2005). An overview of laryngeal function for voice production. In R.T. Sataloff (ed.), *Professional Voice: The Science and Art of Clinical Care* (3rd edn.) (pp. 237–55). San Diego, CA: Plural Publishing.

Baken, R.J. & Orlikoff, R.F. (1987). The effect of articulation on fundamental frequency in singers and speakers. *Journal of Voice*, *1*(1), 68–76.

Barnes, J.J., Davis, P., Oates, J. & Chapman, J. (2004). The relationship between professional operatic soprano voice and high range spectral energy. *Journal of the Acoustic Society of America*, *116*, 530–38. doi:10.1121/1.1710505

Birch, P., Gümoes, B., Stavad, H., Prytz, S., Björkner & Sundberg, J. (2002). Velum behavior in professional classic operatic singing. *Journal of Voice*, *16*(1), 61–71. doi: 10.1016/S0892-1997(02)00073-5

Bloothooft, G. & Plomp, R. (1984). Spectral analysis of sung vowels. I. Variation due to differences between vowels, singers & modes of singing. *Journal of the Acoustical Society of America*, *75*(4), 1259–64. doi:10.1121/1.390732

Bloothooft, G. & Plomp, R. (1985). Spectral analysis of sung vowels. II. The effect of fundamental frequency on vowel spectra. *Journal of the Acoustical Society of America*, *77*(4), 1580–88. doi:10.1121/1.392001

Bloothooft, G. & Plomp, R. (1986). The sound level of the singer's formant in professional singing. *Journal of the Acoustic Society of America*, *79*, 2028–33. doi: 10.1121/1.393211

Bunch, M. & Chapman, J. (2000). Taxonomy of singers used as subjects in research. *Journal of Voice*, *14*(3), 363–69.

Callaghan, J., Emmons, S. & Popeil, L. (2012). Solo voice pedagogy. In G. E. McPherson & G. F. Welch (eds.), *The Oxford Handbook of Music Education*, Vol. I (pp. 559–80). New York, NY: Oxford University Press.

Carlsson, G. & Sundberg, J. (1992). Formant frequency tuning in singing. *Journal of Voice*, *6*(3):256–60.

Cleveland, T. F. (1994). A clearer view of singing voice production: 25 years of progress. *Journal of Voice*, *8*(1), 18–23.

Coffin, B. (1980). *Overtones of Bel Canto: The Phonetic Basis of Artistic Singing*. Metuchen, NJ: Scarecrow Press.

Coffin, B. (1987). *Coffin's Sounds of Singing: Principles and Applications of Vocal Techniques with Chromatic Vowel Chart* (B. Coffin, ed.). Metuchen, NJ: Scarecrow Press.

Denes, P. B. & Pinson, E. N. (1993). *The Speech Chain: The Physics and Biology of Spoken Language* (2nd edn.). New York, NY: Freeman.

Detweiler, R. F. (1994). An investigation of the laryngeal system as the resonance source of the singer's formant. *Journal of Voice*, *8*(4), 303–13.

Dmitriev, L. & Kiselev, A. (1979). Relationship between the formant structure of different types of singing voices and the dimensions of supraglottic cavities. *Folia Phoniatrica et Logopaedica*, *31*, 238–41. doi:10.1159/000264170

Dromey, C., Heaton, E. & Hopkin, J. A. (2011). The acoustic effects of vowel equalization training in singers. *Journal of Voice*, *25*(6), 678–82. doi:10.1016/j.jvoice.2010.09.003

Ekholm, E., Papagiannis, G. & Chagnon, F. (1998). Relating objective measurements to expert evaluation of voice quality in Western classical singing: critical perceptual parameters. *Journal of Voice*, *12*(2), 182–96.

Estill, J., Baer, T., Honda, K. & Harris, K. S. (1984). The control of pitch and quality, Part I: an EMG study of supralaryngeal activity in six voice qualities. In V. L. Lawrence (ed.), *Transcripts of the Twelfth Symposium, Care of the Professional Voice, 1983*, Pt. I (pp. 86–91). New York, NY: The Voice Foundation.

Gauffin, J. & Sundberg, J. (1989). Spectral correlates of glottal voice source waveform characteristics. *Journal of Speech and Hearing Research*, *32*, 556–65. doi:10.1044/jshr.3203.556

Gottfried, T. L. & Chew, S. L. (1992). Intelligibility of vowels sung by a countertenor. *Journal of Research in Singing and Applied Vocal Pedagogy*, *16*(1), 13–28.

Hewlett, A.D. (1981). *Think Afresh About the Voice* (3rd edn.). London: Classical Music Consultants.

Hollien, H., Mendes-Schwartz, A.P. & Nielsen, K. (2000). Perceptual confusions of high-pitched sung vowels. *Journal of Voice, 14*(2), 287–98.

Howard, D.M., Lindsey, G.A. & Allen, B. (1990). Toward the quantification of vocal efficiency. *Journal of Voice, 4*(3), 205–12.

Howes, P., Callaghan, J., Davis, P., Kenny, D. & Thorpe, W. (2004). The relationship between measured vibrato characteristics and perception in Western operatic singing. *Journal of Voice, 18*(2), 216–30. doi:10.1016/j.jvoice.2003.09.003

Hsiao, T.Y., Solomon, N.P., Luschei, E.S. & Titze, I.R. (1994). Modulation of fundamental frequency by laryngeal muscles during vibrato. *Journal of Voice, 8*(3), 224–29.

Husler, F. & Rodd-Marling, Y. (1976). *Singing: The Physical Nature of the Vocal Organ*. London: Hutchinson.

Johansson, C., Sundberg, J. & Wilbrand, H. (1992). X-ray study of articulation and formant frequencies in two female singers. *Journal of Research in Singing and Applied Vocal Pedagogy, 16*(1), 30–41.

Lieberman, P. & Blumstein, S.E. (1988). *Speech Physiology, Speech Perception, and Acoustic Phonetics*. Cambridge: Cambridge University Press.

Lindestad, P.-Å. & Södersten, M. (1988). Laryngeal and pharyngeal behavior in countertenor and baritone singing: a videofiberscopic study. *Journal of Voice, 2*(2), 132–39.

Manén, L. (1987). *Bel Canto: The Teaching of the Classical Italian Song-schools, Its Decline and Restoration*. Oxford: Oxford University Press.

Michel, J.F. & Myers, R.D. (1991). The effects of crescendo on vocal vibrato. *Journal of Voice, 5*(4), 292–98.

Miller, D.G. & Schutte, H.K. (1990). Formant tuning in a professional baritone. *Journal of Voice, 4*(3), 231–37.

Miller, R. (1986). *The Structure of Singing: System and Art in Vocal Technique*. New York, NY: Schirmer Books.

Miller, R. (1993). *Training Tenor Voices*. New York, NY: Schirmer Books.

O'Connor, J.D. (1973). *Phonetics*. Harmondsworth, UK: Penguin.

Pickett, J.M. (1980). *The Sounds of Speech Communication*. Baltimore, MD: University Park Press.

Reid, C.L. (1990). The nature of resonance. *Journal of Research in Singing and Applied Vocal Pedagogy, 14*(1), 1–25.

Rothenberg, M. (1984). Source-tract acoustic interaction and voice quality. In V.L. Lawrence (ed.), *Transcripts of the Twelfth Symposium, Care of the Professional Voice, 1983*, Pt. I (pp. 25–31). New York, NY: The Voice Foundation.

Schutte, H.K. & Miller, D.G. (1991). Acoustic details of vibrato cycle in tenor high notes. *Journal of Voice, 5*(3), 217–23.

Scotto di Carlo, N. & Autesserre, D. (1987). Movements of the velum in singing. *Journal of Research in Singing and Applied Vocal Pedagogy, 6*(1), 3–13.

Scotto di Carlo, N. & Rutherford, A. (1990). The effect of pitch on the perception of a coloratura soprano's vocalic system. *Journal of Research in Singing and Applied Vocal Pedagogy, 13*(2), 11–23.

Sengupta, R. (1990). Study on some aspects of the 'singer's formant' in North Indian classical singing. *Journal of Voice, 4*(2), 129–34.

Shipp, T. & Izdebski, K. (1975). Vocal frequency and vertical larynx positioning by singers and nonsingers. *Journal of the Acoustical Society of America, 58*(5), 1104–6.

Shipp, T., Leanderson, R. & Haglund, S. (1983). Contribution of the circothyroid muscle to vocal vibrato. In V.L. Lawrence (ed.), *Transcripts of the Eleventh Eymposium on Care of the Professional Voice, 1982* (pp.131–33). New York, NY: The Voice Foundation.

Shipp, T., Leanderson, R. & Sundberg, J.S. (1980). Some acoustic characteristics of vocal vibrato. *Journal of Research in Singing, 4*, 18–25.

Shipp, T., Sundberg, J. & Doherty, E. T. (1988). The effect of delayed auditory feedback on vocal vibrato. *Journal of Voice, 2*(3), 195–99.

Siegwart, H. & Scherer, K.R. (1995). Acoustic concomitants of emotional expression in operatic singing: the case of Lucia in *Ardi gli incensi. Journal of Voice, 9*(3), 249–60.

Simonson, D.R. (1987). The relationship between the fundamental pitch, the first vowel formant and the singing formant: An acoustical experiment. Unpublished doctoral dissertation, Northwestern University, Evanston, IL.

Smith, L.A. & Scott, B.L. (1992). Increasing the intelligibility of sung vowels. *Journal of Research in Singing and Applied Vocal Pedagogy, 15*(2), 13–18.

Sundberg, J. (1974). Articulatory interpretation of the 'singing formant.' *Journal of the Acoustical Society of America, 55*, 838–44. doi:10.1121/1.1914609

Sundberg, J. (1975). Formant technique in a professional female singer. *Acustica, 32*(2), 89–96.

Sundberg, J. (1977). The acoustics of the singing voice. *Scientific American, 236*(3), 82–91.

Sundberg, J. (ed.) (1981). *Research Aspects on Singing*. Stockholm: The Royal Swedish Academy of Music.

Sundberg, J. (1983). Raised and lowered larynx: the effect on vowel formant frequencies. *Journal of Research in Singing, 6*, 7–15.

Sundberg, J. (1987). *The Science of Singing*. Dekalb, IL: Northern Illinois University Press.

Sundberg, J. (1991). Comparisons of pharynx, source, formant and pressure characteristics in operatic and musical theatre singing. *Speech Transmission Laboratory Quarterly Progress Status Report* (KTH, Stockholm), *2-3*, 51–62.

Sundberg, J. (1995a). The singer's formant revisited, *Voice, 4*, 106–9.

Sundberg, J. (1995b). Acoustic and psychoacoustic aspects of vocal vibrato. In P. Dejonckere, M. Hirano & J. Sundberg (eds.), *Vibrato* (pp. 35–62). San Diego, CA: Singular Publishing Group.

Sundberg, J. (2001). Level and center frequency of the singer's formant. *Journal of Voice*, *15*(2), 176–86. doi:10.1016/S0892-1997(01)00019-4

Sundberg, J. (2005). Vocal tract resonance. In R.T. Sataloff (ed.), *Professional Voice: The Science and Art of Clinical Care* (3rd edn.) (pp. 275–91). San Diego, CA: Plural Publishing.

Sundberg, J. (2009). Articulatory configuration and pitch in a classically trained soprano singer. *Journal of Voice*, *23*(5), 546–51. doi:10.1016/j.jvoice.2008.02.003

Sundberg, J. & Thalen, M. (2010). What is 'twang.' *Journal of Voice*, *24*(6), 654–60. doi: 10.1016/j.jvoice.2009.03.003

Sundberg, J., Birch, P., Gümoes, Stavad, H., Prytz, S. & Karle, A. (2007). Experimental findings on the nasal tract resonator in singing. *Journal of Voice*, *21*(2), 127–37. doi: doi:10.1016/j.jvoice.2005.11.005

Sundberg, J., Gramming, P. & Lovetri, J. (1993). Comparisons of pharynx, source, formant, and pressure characteristics in operatic and musical theatre singing. *Journal of Voice*, *7*(4), 301–10.

Sundberg, J., Lã, F.M.B. & Gill, B.P. (2011). Professional male singers' formant tuning strategies for the vowel /a/. *Logopedics Phoniatrics Vocology*, *36*(4), 156–67. doi: 10.3109/14015439.2011.587448

Sundberg, J., Thalén, M. & Popeil, L. (2012). Substyles of belting: Phonatory and resonatory characteristics. *Journal of Voice*, *26*(1), 44–50. doi:10.1016/jvoice2010.10.007

Teie, E.W. (1976). A comparative study of the development of the third formant in trained and untrained voices. Unpublished doctoral dissertation, University of Minnesota, Minneapolis, MN.

Titze, I.R. (1984). Rules for modifying vowels. *The NATS Bulletin*, *40*(3), 30–31.

Titze, I.R. (1986). Voice research: voice qualities governed by the velum and the epiglottis. *The NATS Journal*, *42*(3), 24–25.

Titze, I.R. (1987). Voice research: nasality in vowels. *The NATS Journal*, *34*(4), 34–35, 37.

Titze, I.R. (1991). Voice research: relations between acoustic power, intensity, loudness & sound pressure level. *The NATS Journal*, *47*(3), 31.

Titze, I.R. (1994). *Principles of Voice Production*. Englewood Cliffs, NJ: Prentice Hall.

Titze, I.R. (1995). Voice research: speaking vowels versus singing vowels, *Journal of Singing*, *52*(1), 41–42.

Titze, I.R. (1997). Voice research: are the corner vowels like primary colors? *Journal of Singing*, *54*(2), 35–38.

Titze, I.R. (1998). Voice research: the wide pharynx. *Journal of Singing*, *55*(1), 27–28.

Titze, I.R. & Story, B. (1977). Acoustic interactions of the voice source with the lower vocal tract. *Journal of the Acoustical Society of America*, *101*(4), 2234–43. doi: 10.1121/1.418246

Troup, G.J., Welch, G., Volo, M., Tronconi, A., Ferrero, F. & Farnetani, E. (1989). On velum opening in singing. *Journal of Research in Singing and Applied Vocal Pedagogy*, *12*(1), 35–39.

Vennard, W. (1967). *Singing: The Mechanism and the Technic* (rev. edn.). New York, NY: Carl Fischer.

Wang, S-q. (1985). The relationship between bright timbre, singer's formants and larynx position. *The NATS Bulletin*, *41*(3), 20–22.

Wapnick, J. & Eckholm, E. (1997). Expert consensus in solo voice performance evaluation. *Journal of Voice*, *11*(4), 429–36.

Westerman Gregg, J. & Scherer, R.C. (2006). Vowel intelligibility in classical singing. *Journal of Voice*, *20*(2), 198–210. doi:10.1016/j.jvoice.2005.01.007

Wooldridge, W.B. (1956). Is there nasal resonance? *The NATS Bulletin*, *13*(1), 28–29.

Yanagisawa, E., Estill, J., Kmucha, S.T. & Leder, S.B. (1989). The contribution of aryepiglottic constriction to 'ringing' voice quality: a videolaryngoscopic study with acoustic analysis. *Journal of Voice*, *3*(4), 342–50.

Yanagisawa, E., Kmucha, S.T. & Estill, J. (1990). Role of the soft palate in laryngeal functions and selected voice qualities: simultaneous velolaryngeal videoendoscopy, *Annals of Otology, Rhinology and Laryngology*, *99*(1), 18–28.

Zangger Borch, D. & Sundberg, J. (2011). Some phonatory and resonatory characteristics of the rock, pop, soul & Swedish dance band styles of singing. *Journal of Voice*, *25*(5), 532–37. doi:10.1016/j.jvoice.2010.07.014

Chapter 6: Registration

Singing teachers are interested in vocal registers in order to facilitate use of the whole range of the voice. Skill in negotiating register transitions also offers the ability to sing a gradually modulating quality through that range, avoiding sudden 'breaks' in quality and loudness if that is aesthetically appropriate. McKinney identified registration as an area of vocal instruction 'shrouded with mystery, semantic confusion, and controversy' (1982, p. 97). Over centuries there has been debate about whether vocal registers exist in the well-produced voice or whether they are evidence of a vocal fault and, if registers do exist, how many there are, what terms should be used for them, and at which pitches the transitions between registers occur (e.g. McKinney, 1982; Doscher, 1994; David, 1995; Callaghan, 1996; Bunch Dayme, 2009).

The subject of vocal registers is a controversial one. Despite occasional minority support for a one-register, or no-register, position (e.g. Lehmann, 1902/1952), there is broad agreement among voice scientists, phoneticians, and voice teachers that registers do exist. There is, however, disagreement on the number of registers normal in the singing voice, the names to be given them, the physiological factors involved, the pitches at which register changes occur, and how the teacher should deal with register changes to teach control of quality and intensity. Schoenhard et al. (1984) maintained that singers' registers constitute entities that are different in many respects from speakers' registers. There is disagreement not only across voice professions but also among singing teachers on the theory of register events and incorporation of this theory into an overall pedagogy.

Definition of registers

The term 'register' refers to a range of pitch having a consistent timbre. It is probably borrowed from the terminology of organ registration, referring to perceptually distinct regions of sound quality. The classic 19th-century definition of singer/teacher/researcher Manuel Garcia is significant in linking the sound with the mechanism, the perceptual with the physiological:

> A register is a series of consecutive homogeneous sounds produced by one mechanism, differing essentially from another series of sounds equally homogeneous produced by another mechanism. (Garcia, 1894/ 1982, p. 8)

Since the 1970s, registers have been recognized as the result of interactions between laryngeal and acoustical events, occurring at predictable frequencies in different voice types. Because these interactions alter the voice source, they also produce changes in voice quality. These different qualities have been labelled 'registers.' A complete operational definition of the phenomenon of vocal registration requires reference to perceptual, acoustic, physiological, and aerodynamic data. As yet, these data are far from complete.

In singing, the concept of register is concerned mainly with a change in voice quality at particular pitches due to changes in the action of the inter-dependent cricothyroid and the lateral and vocalis muscles of the larynx. Register transitions are more identifiable than registers themselves. Although vocal registers are commonly conceptualized as being regions of relatively constant quality in which pitch, loudness, and vowel can be adjusted some-what at will, the identification of one register without reference to adjacent registers is difficult. Registers become more distinct as transitions become more abrupt (Titze, 1983).

There are two primary register categories: those where thyroarytenoid activity is dominant and those where cricothyroid activity is dominant. The thyroarytenoid is largely a thickener/shortener of the vocal folds, the crico-thyroid a thinner/lengthener. Changes in muscle activation affect vocal fold oscillation, including the closed versus open time ratio (closed quotient) and vocal fold thickness, producing changes in voice source. However, because pitch and resonance changes are also involved, within those two main cat-egories there are subdivisions (Callaghan et al. 2012, p. 565). Singing teachers often refer to the 'middle' register, of a range of an octave to a tenth in the middle of the voice, where there is a smooth transition from primarily thyro-arytenoid activity to primarily cricothyroid activity.

Register terminology

One of the most vexed areas with regard to registers is the different ter-minologies employed by scientists, voice pathologists, spoken voice teachers, and singing teachers. Mörner et al. (1964) list 107 different names that have been used to identify registers. Each group conceptualizes registers in terms of its particular professional paradigm, adversely affecting interdisciplinary communication. As with many other areas of vocal terminology, performers and teachers of performers tend to use terms based on perception and body sensation, while scientists use terms related to observable, measurable physi-cal phenomena. Much confusion arises from the fact that registration relates to a complex of factors concerned with pitch and timbre. McKinney (1982) ascribed the confusion to the use of the term 'register' to describe many dif-ferent things: (1) a particular part of the vocal range, (2) a resonance area, (3) a phonatory process, (4) a certain timbre, and (5) a region of the voice that is defined or delimited by vocal breaks.

Even among singing teachers there has been substantial variation in reg-ister terminology. Timberlake's 1990 discussion of 'terminological turmoil' presented a table of terms used since the 13th century. At that time singing – or at least the church and secular art singing that was the subject of theoretical writings – was a male preserve, and it continued to be dominated by men, including falsettists and castrati, into the 18th century. In the 20th century, male researchers and male subjects dominated voice research. It is likely that these considerations have influenced the approach to registration. The vocal range used by the repertoire of different periods is also a relevant factor. For example, the fact that Caccini (1602/1970) identified only two registers may relate to the limited range of his *nuove musiche* (new music).

While the circumstances of performance and composition have changed greatly over the centuries, the same terms are current, often with changed meanings. In our time, how these historical terms apply to the vocal qualities demanded by particular genres and styles, such as rock, pop, R & B, country, music theatre, and so on, is a puzzle. It is also becoming clearer that what applies to male singers may not be appropriate for female singers.

In 1981, the Collegium Medicorum Theatri (CoMeT) formed a committee of physicians, scientists, engineers, and voice pedagogues to review the position on vocal registers. In 1983, Hollien reported for CoMeT to the Voice Foundation's Twelfth Symposium, Care of the Professional Voice, stating that the committee had rejected the 'old terms' and proposed using numbers to define the registers, as follows:

1. The very lowest register, probably used only in speaking (old terms: pulse, vocal fry, creak).
2. That (low) register, which is used for most speaking and singing (old terms: modal, chest, normal, heavy).
3. A high register used primarily in singing (old terms: falsetto, light, head).
4. A very high register usually found only in some women and children and not particularly relevant to singing (old terms: flute, whistle). (Hollien, 1984, p. 5; also referred to by Doscher, 1994).

The committee characterized the traditional terms 'chest' and 'head,' which are based on the singer's sensation rather than on laryngeal mechanism, as 'illogical if not absurd.' These, and other traditional terms, are quite logical, however, in identifying either the kinesthetic or perceptual characteristic of a particular register – for example, the very lowest register is felt as a growl, perceived more as a pulse than as a continuous sound. But as a system of labelling, these terms have no internal consistency – for example, while 'pulse' might be a logical perceptual term for the very lowest register, neither 'modal' nor 'heavy' seems a logical perceptual term for the next register. The term 'chest register' is appropriate in light of recent scientific findings. Given that tracheal resonances carry energy into the upper thoracic region (Titze, 1985), there should be little objection to labelling the phenomenon according to the sensation identified by singers as characteristic of this register.

The CoMeT committee found it difficult to scientifically define the additional register in the middle of the frequency range (numbered 2A), but concluded that 'it receives so much (subjective) support, it cannot be ignored' (Hollien, 1984, p. 5). The old terms identified for this register were 'head,' 'mid,' 'middle,' and 'upper.' It is this middle register that is of vital concern to singers and their teachers because it is in this area that most vocal repertoire lies. The committee was also comfortable with a heavy/light or lower/upper distinction.

Speech-voice scientist Harry Hollien in 1974 proposed the terms: 'pulse' for the lowest register; 'modal' for the heavier quality produced at low pitch range; 'loft' for the lighter, thinner produced at the pitch range above modal; and 'flute' for the highest pitch range. While these terms are often used in voice research, many are not common in singing pedagogy. 'Modal' in particular causes confusion because it often seems to include 'middle' register.

The registers defined by Thurman, Welch, Theimer, Grefsheim, and Feit (2000) are similar to those identified by the CoMeT, except that Thurman et al. separate the falsetto/flute from the whistle register, thus yielding five registers: pulse, lower, upper, falsetto/flute, and whistle (2000, p. 436). 'Pulse register is produced when the cricothyroid muscles (lengtheners) have completely released so that the vocal fold length is determined solely by increases and decreases in the contraction of the thyroarytenoids (shorteners)' (p. 436). 'Lower register voice qualities are produced when both the thyroarytenoid and the cricothyroid muscles are simultaneously contracted, but the thyroarytenoids are more prominently contracted than the cricothyroids' (p. 437). 'Upper register voice qualities are produced when both the thyroarytenoid and the cricothyroid muscles are simultaneously contracted, but the cricothyroids are more prominently contracted than the thyroarytenoids' (p. 438). Falsetto is the 'voice quality produced by adult males but is female-like and is produced within the female pitch range'. Thurman et al. identify this quality as being produced in the same way as female flute register, with the thyroarytenoid muscles releasing completely so that vocal fold length is determined entirely by action of the cricothyroids (p. 439). Some have suggested that the sound is produced by air turbulence in the glottis, without significant vocal fold vibration (Titze, 1994). Whistle register is produced in a similar way, but it seems that only the front of the vocal folds vibrate, producing a very high, thin, whistle-like sound (p. 441). Use of 'flute'/'flageolet' and 'whistle' is what allows extension of the upper pitch range of the coloratura soprano.

A study by Walker (1988) compared what the participants believed to be whistle register with what they believed to be head register. He found changes in spectra and airflow associated with an identifiable difference in voice quality, supporting the hypothesis that a change in source function is involved. What that change may be remains unclear.

More refined technology has enabled examination of the interrelated voice source and resonance factors involved in registers. Some of these studies are reviewed below. The recent *Oxford Handbook of Music Education* has a table of comprehensive register terminology for adult singers (Nix, 2012, pp. 552–53), which brings together the interrelated factors of vocal tract properties, laryngeal properties, acoustic properties, perceptual descriptors, and pitch range.

Vennard's (1967) terminology for the two main registers has gained some acceptance; he used 'heavy mechanism' and 'light mechanism,' referring to laryngeal function. Miller (1986) preferred the traditional Italian terms *voce di petto* and *voce di testa*, with the overlapping area called *voce mista*.

Many other writers and teachers use 'chest,' 'middle,' and 'head.' Referring to register events in terms of laryngeal function is logical and does imply other considerations, since the vocal folds react both to the subglottal air pressure and to the conformation of the supraglottic vocal tract. Many singing teachers subscribe to the realistic pedagogical approach of three registers, whatever the terminology used. Because much of the singing range of the female voice is above the usual pitch range of speaking, the 'middle' voice comprises the largest part of the singing voice.

Estill's teaching and research (1991, 1995, 1996a, 1996b) deal with the problem in a logical way by referring to voice qualities defined in physiological, acoustic, and perceptual terms. For example, 'speech quality' is defined as having: a neutral and relaxed vocal tract, with effort at the larynx (physiology); a decreasing amplitude as frequency increases (acoustics); and the sound having 'a certain presence' in the lower range and being easy to hear (perception) (Estill, 1995).

Register change

Vocal register change is regulated mainly by the ratio of vocalis and cricothyroid activities (Hirano, 1988). If the ratio is changed abruptly, the register change is also abrupt and clearly heard. If the ratio is changed gradually, the register change is also gradual and less perceptible. If the change is also associated with a discontinuity of vocal fold vibrations, a 'break' results. The mechanism of fundamental frequency control is different between the heavy or modal register and the light or falsetto register (Hirano, 1988). In the modal register, the activities of the cricothyroid, lateral cricoarytenoid, and vocalis are always positively related to fundamental frequency – that is, the activity increases with rising frequency and decreases with falling frequency. However, the vocalis muscle is antagonistic to the cricothyroid in register control; if vocalis activity is not increased when cricothyroid activity increases to raise fundamental frequency, the balance between the two muscles will result in a shift to a lighter register. For the same register to be maintained, simultaneous increase in vocalis activity is necessary. In the light register, the activity of cricothyroid, lateral cricoarytenoid, and vocalis is not always positively related to fundamental frequency. Hirano (1988) maintained that the cricothyroid, which plays the most important role in fundamental frequency control in the modal register, is not always active in the light register.

In some instances singers decide that an abrupt timbre change serves aesthetic demands. In other instances a blended tone is required, and singers need to work on the relationship between laryngeal action, breath pressure, airflow, and resonance to achieve this.

Schoenhard et al. (1984) made a perceptual study of registers in eight female singers. They found two perceptually recognizable registers that could also be differentiated on the basis of spectral contrasts. The 'light register' exhibited more energy in the fundamental or first harmonic overtone; the 'heavy register' exhibited more energy in the harmonic overtones above 5 kHz.

Keidar et al. (1987) also took a perceptual approach to identification of the primary registers, which they termed 'chest' and 'falsetto.' Ten trained listeners were able to clearly perceive register boundaries and entities, with both male and female shift points identified at ~337 Hz and an average difference of less than two semitones between and within genders for different vowels. Listeners made discriminations more on the basis of quality than of pitch. Studies of vocal fry ('pulse register') have, however, found that register to be perceived primarily as a function of fundamental frequency (Keidar, 1986; Titze, 1988).

Control of registration

Resonance adjustments are achieved by vowel modification. Modification involves the adjustment of vowels to achieve an optimal alignment of source harmonics with vocal tract resonances. While subtle adjustments occur in skilled singers throughout the entire range, precise adjustments are particularly critical at register changes.

Abrupt changes in register may occur voluntarily or involuntarily. Titze (1988) suggested that involuntary timbre transitions result from resonances in the subglottal system (the trachea), and voluntary timbre transitions result from regulating vocal fold adduction. Transitions are less apparent in some voices than in others. If a voice is noticeably registered, a stair-step effect in quality is perceived. To avoid this, a singer should be able to change vocal quality continuously and gradually over some significant range. Some teachers maintain that the voice exists only as a unity, and that if register changes exist, they are the result of poor technique rather than physiological factors. Good technique, however, rests on physiological efficiency, and if register changes are apparent in vocal production where aesthetic judgement determines they should not be, then the issue of vocal registers needs to be dealt with. The singer needs to be able to choose, not to have the instrument dictate what happens.

A major issue in the study of registers is the consistency with which involuntary timbre transitions can be located at specific fundamental frequencies (Titze, 1988). For example, a major involuntary timbre transition is consistently found in the region of 300 to 350 Hz for both men and women. This passaggio seems to reflect the phenomenon of breaking into or out of the chest register. The transition can be smoothed out by training, as in the traditional approach to classical singing, or it can be accentuated and employed artistically as in yodelling, some country-western styles, and some contemporary music theatre and classical repertoire.

There appear to be at least two ways in which timbre transitions can be executed voluntarily: (i) by changing adduction or (ii) by changing lung pressure

(Titze, 1988). An increase in lung pressure will increase the amplitude of vibration, thereby reducing the abduction quotient and enriching the timbre. The vocal processes would be spread apart slightly to offset the increasing amplitude of vibration as the pitch is raised. Alternatively, or additionally, the vocalis muscle could be relaxed gradually to allow the inferior part of the vocal fold to abduct. The adjustment could begin to take place somewhere around C_4, for example, and continue in varying amounts through F_4, with maximum equalization at D_4. If these mechanical factors are not finely coordinated, a change in timbre may be apparent.

A study by Roubeau et al. (1987) identified a succession of phenomena in the shift from one laryngeal mechanism to another in register change. First, there is an adjustment of the glottal configuration tied to variations in the tension of the muscles. This brings about a change in the shape of the glottal wave. This mechanical adaptation is followed by reestablishment of a balance between the tensions of the vibrator and the subglottal pressure, which may occasion a temporary loss of control of fundamental frequency. Hill (1986) postulated airflow as the critical factor in assisting register shift. Subglottal pressure and airflow increase as pitch increases, until the highest pitch of a given register is encountered. At this point, the mechanism shifts to a new and lower subglottal pressure and airflow. Increasing airflow over the *passaggio* facilitates the coordination of the two registers. Several researchers have also found that there is a time delay between the readjustment and stabilization of pitch in the new register (e.g.Roubeau et al., 1991).

At higher pitches, the singer needs both subglottal pressure increase and vowel modification to boost the output power and tune out the undesirable subglottal resonances. Supraglottal resonances, unlike the subglottal resonances, are highly adjustable by articulatory changes. Even within a given vowel category, the first and second formant frequencies can vary by as much as 50 to 100% (Titze, 1988). This makes formant tuning a sensible way to equalize the subglottal resonances.

Studying the singing of octave displacements, MacCurtain and Welch (1985) found differences in vocal tract configurations between different registers as well as between bass and soprano singers. Both bass and soprano progressively widened the vocal tract in moving from 'chest' to 'head' register. While the basses tilted the larynx and lengthened the vocal tract in 'head' register, the sopranos did neither. When the sopranos moved from 'chest' (660 Hz) to 'little' (1320 Hz), they narrowed and shortened the vocal tract. As discussed above, Lindestad and Södersten (1988) observed the same vocal tract configuration in countertenor singing at high pitch. These vocal tract gestures were not found in the baritone or bass in either study. Such gestures seem to cover the register transition by boosting the acoustic output through formant tuning.

Sundberg and Skoog (1996) measured the jaw opening in 10 professional male and female singers of different voice types as they sang an ascending two-octave scale on different vowels after determining the normal first formant frequency at a relatively low pitch. Each of the singers (one bass, two baritones, two tenors, one mezzo-soprano/alto, two mezzo-sopranos, and one soprano) sang six vowels (/a/, /a/, /o/, /u/, /i/, /e/) at 25 pitches. They found that only for the vowels /a/ and /a/ did the singers widen the jaw opening when the fundamental frequency approached that of the first formant. For the other vowels, the jaw was widened at higher pitches. In those vowels, the singer can increase the first formant by reducing tongue constriction.

Echternach et al. (2008) conducted a pilot study using dynamic magnetic resonance imaging to investigate changes of vocal tract shape across the major register change in a baritone and a tenor classical singer. The aim was to test whether MRI can reveal vocal tract modifications (i) during the register transition, and (ii) when singers maintain the 'modal' register through the pitch range E_4 to $F\sharp_4$. The pitch range covered was B_3 to $G\sharp_4$. Surprisingly, the results showed very few vocal tract modifications when the singers changed register, but clear modifications when they maintained the register throughout that pitch range. A similar study of four professional classical female singers was published in 2010 (Echternach, et al, 2010). As would be expected, strong vocal tract modifications occurred when the fundamental frequency reached the vicinity of the first formant, including widening of the lip and jaw openings, as well as elevation of the tongue dorsum. As with the male singers, little vocal tract modification was observed in the major register change. This is a somewhat surprising result that bears further investigation.

A study by Echternach et al. (2011) revealed what appears to be important information about the vocal tract changes made by countertenors traversing the register change between modal and falsetto. However, since all the data were collected with singers in a supine position (presumably to facilitate real-time magnetic resonance imaging), it is unclear whether the results would apply to singing in a standing position. A study by Traser et al., published in 2013, examined the differences in vocal tract shape in professional tenors between supine and upright positions, finding that articulators such as lip opening, jaw opening, tongue position, and uvula position were not affected by the singers' body position. However, the larynx was found to be higher and the jaw more protruded for the supine position.

In the 2011 Echternach et al. study, seven professional male altos, of an age range of 24 to 35 years, sang an ascending and descending major scale from G_3 to E_4, thus traversing their register transition. One set of data was collected with the singers performing the register shift between B_3 and C_4 to what the researchers labelled 'stage falsetto,' for the habitual countertenor upper register. Another set of data was collected for a register shift from modal to what was labelled 'naïve falsetto,' as in an untrained falsetto. In the third condition, all subjects sang the same scale avoiding a register shift. After the ascending scales, the singers were asked to perform the same scale with and without register shifts descending from E_4 to G_3. All scales were sung on /a/. MRI profiles showed clear modifications of vocal tract shape in transitions between modal and stage falsetto. Ascending and descending sequences in all three conditions showed similar tendencies, with modifications stronger for ascending sequences.

The researchers found a significant sudden increase of lip opening between modal and stage falsetto, whereas when maintaining modal register, the singers showed a slower continuous increase of lip opening for the higher pitches. Jaw opening was also increased for stage falsetto, with lip opening and jaw opening strongly correlated. For a given jaw opening, the lip opening was larger for the stage falsetto compared with modal register and naïve falsetto. Stage falsetto was also associated with strong modifications in tongue shape; the jaw was retracted, the tongue lifted and slightly positioned in the back of the mouth, meaning that the pharynx was narrowed. In modal register at high pitches the jaw was protruded and pharynx widened. In both stage falsetto and modal register the uvula lifted at high pitches. In the shift from modal to stage falsetto this lift was more sudden than when maintaining modal register. High pitches in modal register were achieved through continuous elevation of the larynx. For both kinds of falsetto the larynx was lowered and tilted. To summarize, for professional countertenors the register shift from modal to falsetto requires major modifications to vocal tract shape in order to produce a stronger sound spectrum appropriate for use on stage.

Another investigation of the *passaggio* in professional tenors (Echternach & Richter, 2012) investigated perturbation, since regularity of vocal fold oscillation should mean no increase in perturbation measures. Eight professional tenors were tested over the pitch range A_3–A_4 on vowels /a/, /e/, /i/, /o/, and /æ/. The researchers found an increase in frequency perturbation values in the register transition and upper pitch in ascending tasks, but not descending tasks. It was hypothesized that using descending exercises could be more helpful in achieving stable vocal function above the *passaggio*, a common practice in most singing studios.

In singing, the combination of rising pitch and high formant vowel results in an 'open' or 'white' quality. To counteract this tendency, front vowels may be modified in rising pitch so as to reduce the incidence of higher harmonic partials. Traditional pedagogies usually refer to this technique as vowel

modification (Miller, 1986). 'Covering' is another term used for this procedure, but since it is also used in other contexts it can be confusing (Miller,
1989).

Systematic vowel modification requires a knowledge of the phonetic cat-
egorization of vowels on the front–back/open–closed dimensions discussed
above under resonance and articulation. Modification to an adjacent vowel
(from back vowels to more central, from front vowels to more central, from
closed vowels to more open) is employed at the *passaggio* as pitch rises. (See
Miller's 'Systematic Vowel Modification Chart,' 1986, p. 157.)

Acoustically, this modification implies a change of formant frequencies
and an elevated sound pressure level of the fundamental, resulting from an
increased transglottal airflow. Hertegård et al. (1990) pointed out that 'covered' singing near the *passaggio* shows similarities to flow phonation and is
probably preferable from the point of view of vocal hygiene. Aesthetic judgements about word clarity and voice quality will affect the singer's decision
about whether to use vowel modification, what type to use, and how much of
it. Register equalization by adductory control is still an option.

The three factors involved in register control, identified both by scientific
studies and writings on singing technique, are: subglottal air pressure, vocal
fold adduction, and formant tuning. Many traditional pedagogies have advocated an approach based on one or more of these factors. For teachers, this
means attention to the coordination between vocal fold adduction, breath
management, and vocal tract conformation.

Registration and voice classification

Much of the preceding discussion on breath management, phonation, and
resonance makes clear that vowel formant frequency, vocal tract morphol-
ogy, and subglottal pressure may all relate to voice type (Cleveland, 1977;
Ågren & Sundberg, 1978; Dmitriev & Kiselev, 1979; Cleveland & Sundberg,
1985). Cleveland (1993a, 1993b) cited range, timbre, and tessitura as factors
to be considered in classifying voices. The comfortable tessitura of the voice is
related to register events, and teachers have often included the pitch at which
register transitions occur as another factor to be considered.

Sundberg (1987) nominated the range of overlap between male 'modal'
and 'falsetto' registers as in the vicinity of G_3 (200 Hz) to F_4 (350 Hz) but went
on to state that 'these ranges of register overlap, and the register boundaries
vary substantially among individuals' (p. 51). Titze (1994), however, demonstrated that all investigators show a register transition between D_4 (294 Hz)
and G_4 (392 Hz), spanning six voice categories. Neither Sundberg (1987) nor
Titze (1994) nominated particular pitches as register boundaries for the different voice types. Miller (1986), while not ruling out individual variation,

did suggest D_4 (294 Hz) as the *passaggio* for bass, $E\flat_4$ for sopranos and dramatic baritones, E_4 for mezzo-sopranos and dramatic tenors, and G_4 for lyric tenor, spinto tenor, and contralto. While it may not be possible to state with certainty the pitch at which a register shift will occur in a given voice, the general pattern across voice types is clear: the major shift occurs lowest in the bass and highest in tenor and contralto. This may serve as a guide for teachers in the classification of voices.

The centre frequency of the singer's formant could also serve as an objective guide to voice classification (Dmitriev & Kiselev, 1979; Sundberg, 2001). The centre frequency of the singer's formant varies with voice classification, being lowest for basses and highest for tenors. As mentioned in Chapter 5, the centre frequency for tenors is around 2.8 kHz, for baritones around 2.7 kHz, and for altos around 3.2 kHz.

A recent study using long-term average spectrum (Johnson & Kempster, 2010) found a strong correlation between the centre note of the singing range and voice classification, suggesting that long-term average spectrum might also prove an objective way of classifying voices.

For singing teachers, voice classification is a subtle, complex matter, involving multiple vocal factors: vocal range, timbre, tessitura, and register transition locations.

> Higher voices have shorter vocal folds and vocal tracts; lower voices have longer vocal folds and vocal tracts. Hybrid classifications occur when long-necked singers have short vocal folds, producing dark, high voice; or when short-necked singers have long vocal folds, producing bright, low voice. (Callaghan et al., 2012, p. 566)

Opera *Fach* casting also involves weight and flexibility of the voice, and body type and general physical appearance. While voice classification is more flexible in music theatre, appearance is even more important.

References
Ågren, K., and Sundberg, J. (1978). An acoustic comparison of alto and tenor voices. *Journal of Research in Singing, 2*(1), 26–33.

Bunch Dayme, M. (1995). *Dynamics of the Singing Voice* (5th edn.). Vienna: Springer-Verlag.

Caccini, G. (1970). *Le nuove musiche* (H. Wiley Hitchcock, ed.). Madison: A-R Editions. (Original work published 1602.)

Callaghan, J. (1996). The implications of voice science for the teaching of singing: vocal registers. *Australian Voice, 2*, 27–31.

Callaghan, J., Emmons, S. & Popeil, L. (2012). Solo voice pedagogy. In G. E. McPherson & G. F. Welch (eds.), *The Oxford Handbook of Music Education*, Vol. I (pp. 559–80). New York, NY: Oxford University Press.

Cleveland, T.F. (1977). Acoustic properties of voice timbre types and their influence on voice classification. *Journal of the Acoustical Society of America*, *61*(6), 1622–29. doi:10.1121/1.381438

Cleveland, T.F. (1993a). Voice pedagogy for the twenty–first century: toward a theory of voice classification (Part 1). *The NATS Journal*, *49*(3), 30–31.

Cleveland, T.F. (1993b). Voice pedagogy for the twenty-first century: the importance of range and timbre in the determination of voice classification. *The NATS Journal*, *49*(5), 30–31.

Cleveland, T.F. & Sundberg, J. (1985). Acoustic analysis of three male voices of different quality. In A. Askenfelt, S. Felicetti, E. Jansson & J. Sundberg (eds.), *Proceedings of Stockholm Music Acoustics Conference, 1983* (pp. 143–56). Stockholm: Royal Swedish Academy of Music.

David, M. (1995). *The New Voice Pedagogy*. Lanham, MD: Scarecrow Press.

Dmitriev, L. & Kiselev, A. (1979). Relationship between the formant structure of different types of singing voices and the dimensions of supraglottic cavities. *Folia Phoniatrica et Logopaedica*, *31*, 238–41. doi:10.1159/000264170

Doscher, B. (1994). *The Functional Unity of the Singing Voice* (2nd edn.). Metuchen, NJ: Scarecrow Press.

Echternach, M. & Richter, B. (2012). Passaggio in the professional tenor voice: evaluation of perturbation measures. *Journal of Voice*, 26(4), 440–46. doi:10.1016/j.jvoice.2011.03.004

Echternach, M., Sundberg, J., Arndt, S., Breyer, T., Markl, M., Schumacher, M. & Richter, B. (2008). Vocal tract and register changes analysed by real-time MRI in male professional singers: a pilot study. *Logopedics Phoniatrics Vocology*, *33*(2), 67–73. doi:10.1080/14015430701875653

Echternach, M., Sundberg, J., Arndt, S., Markl, M., Schumacher, M. & Richter, B. (2010). Vocal tract in females registers: a dynamic real-time MRI study. *Journal of Voice*, *24*(2), 133–39. doi:10.1016/j.jvoice.2008.06.004

Echternach, M., Traser, L., Markl, M. & Richter, B. (2011). Vocal tract configurations in male alto register functions. *Journal of Voice*, *25*(6), 670–77. doi:10.1016/j.jvoice.2010.09.008

Estill, J. (1991). Compulsory figures for the master voice technician in speaking, acting, or singing. Unpublished course notes. Adelaide, Australia: Voice Craft.

Estill, J. (1995). *Voice Craft: A User's Guide to Voice Quality*. Vol. 2: *Some Basic Voice Qualities*. Santa Rosa, CA: Estill Voice Training Systems.

Estill, J. (1996a). *Voice Craft: A User's Guide to Voice Quality*. Level One: *Primer of Compulsory Figures*. Santa Rosa, CA: Estill Voice Training Systems.

Estill, J. (1996b). *Workshop: Compulsory Figures for Voice*, 28 January to 2 February. Sydney, Australia: National Voice Centre.

Garcia, M. (1982). *Hints on Singing* (B. Garcia, trans.) (rev. edn.). New York, NY: Joseph Patelson Music House. (Original work published 1894.)

Hertegård, S., Gauffin, J. & Sundberg, J. (1990). Open and covered singing as studied by means of fiberoptics, inverse filtering & spectral analysis. *Journal of Voice*, *4*(3), 220–30.

Hill, S. (1986). Characteristics of air-flow during changes in registration. *The NATS Journal*, *43*(1), 16–17.

Hirano, M. (1988). Vocal mechanisms in singing: laryngological and phoniatric aspects. *Journal of Voice*, *2*(1), 51–69. doi:10.1016/S0892-1997(88)80058-4

Hollien, H. (1974). On vocal registers. *Journal of Phonetics*, *2*, 125–43.

Hollien, H. (1984). A review of vocal registers. In V.L. Lawrence (ed.), *Transcripts of the Twelfth Symposium, Care of the Professional Voice, 1983*, Pt. I (pp. 1–6). New York, NY: The Voice Foundation.

Johnson, A.M. & Kempster, G.B. (2011). Classification of the classical male singing voice using long-term average spectrum. *Journal of Voice*, *25*(5), 538–43. doi:10.1016/j.jvoice.2010.05.009

Johnson, B. (1982). To have or have not: that is the question. In H. Hollien (ed.), *Report on Vocal Registers*. New York, NY: Collegium Medicorum Theatri.

Keidar, A. (1986). An acoustic-perceptual study of vocal fry using synthetic stimuli. *Journal of the Acoustical Society of America*, *73*(Suppl 1), S3. doi:10.1121/1.2020366

Keidar, A., Hurtig, R. & Titze, I.R. (1987). The perceptual nature of vocal register change. *Journal of Voice*, *1*(3), 223–33.

Lehmann, L. (1952). *How to Sing (Meine Gesangskunst)* (R. Aldrich, trans.). New York, NY: Macmillan. (Original work published 1902.)

Lindestad, P.-Å. & Södersten, M. (1988). Laryngeal and pharyngeal behavior in countertenor and baritone singing: A videofiberscopic study. *Journal of Voice*, *2*(2), 132–39.

MacCurtain, F. & Welch, G. (1985). Vocal tract gestures in soprano and bass: a xero-radiographic-electro-laryngographic study. In A. Askenfelt, S. Felicetti, E. Jansson & J. Sundberg (eds.), *Proceedings of the Stockholm Music Acoustics Conference, 1983*, Vol. 1 (pp. 219–38). Stockholm: Royal Swedish Academy of Music.

McKinney, J.C. (1982). *The Diagnosis and Correction of Vocal Faults*. Nashville, TN: Broadman Press.

Miller, R. (1986). *The Structure of Singing: System and Art in Vocal Technique*. New York, NY: Schirmer Books.

Miller, R. (1989). Sotto voce: 'covering' in the singing voice. *The NATS Journal*, *46*(2), 14–17.

Mörner, M., Fransesson, N. & Fant, G. (1964). Voice register terminology and standard pitch. *Speech Transmission Laboratory Quarterly Status Progress Report* (KTH, Stockholm), 4, 12–15.

Nix, J. (2012). Commentary: vocal and choral music. In G.E. McPherson & G.E. Welch (eds.), *The Oxford Handbook of Music Education*, Vol. I (pp. 551–58). New York, NY: Oxford University Press.

Roubeau, B., Chevrie-Muller, C. & Arabia, C. (1991). Control of laryngeal vibration in register change. In J. Gauffin & B. Hammarberg (eds.), *Vocal Fold Physiology* (pp. 279–86). San Diego, CA: Singular Publishing Group.

Roubeau, B., Chevrie-Muller, C. & Arabia-Guidet, C. (1987). Electroglottographic study of the changes of voice registers. *Folia Phoniatrica et Logopaedica, 39*(6), 280–89. doi:10.1159/000265871

Schoenhard, C., Hollien, H. & Hicks, J.W., Jr. (1984). Spectral characteristics of voice registers in female singers. In V.L. Lawrence (ed.), *Transcripts of the Twelfth Symposium, Care of the Professional Voice, 1983*, Pt. I (pp. 7–10). New York, NY: The Voice Foundation.

Sundberg, J. (1987). *The Science of Singing*. Dekalb, IL: Northern Illinois University Press.

Sundberg, J. (2001). Level and center frequency of the singer's formant. *Journal of Voice, 15*(2), 176–86. doi:10.1016/S0892-1997(01)00019-4

Sundberg, J. & Skoog, J. (1996). Dependence of jaw opening on pitch and vowel in singers. *Journal of Voice, 11*(3), 301–6.

Thurman, L., Welch, G., Theimer, A., Grefsheim, E. & Feit, P. (2000). The voice qualities that are referred to as 'vocal registers.' In L. Thurman and G. Welch (eds.), *Bodymind and Voice: Foundations of Voice Education* (rev. edn.), Vol. 3 (pp. 421–48). Collegeville, MN: The VoiceCare Network.

Timberlake, C. (1990). Practica musicae: terminological turmoil: the naming of registers. *The NATS Journal, 47*(1), 14–26.

Titze, I.R. (1983). Vocal registers. *The NATS Bulletin, 39*(4), 21–22.

Titze, I.R. (1985). The importance of vocal tract loading in maintaining vocal fold oscillation. In A. Askenfelt, S. Felicetti, E. Jansson & J. Sundberg (eds.), *Proceedings of the Stockholm Music Acoustics Conference, 1983*, Vol. 1 (pp. 61–72). Stockholm: Royal Swedish Academy of Music.

Titze, I.R. (1988). A framework for the study of vocal registers. *Journal of Voice, 2*(3), 183–94.

Titze, I.R. (1994). *Principles of Voice Production*. Englewood Cliffs, NJ: Prentice Hall.

Traser, L., Burdumy, M., Richter, B., Vicari, M. & Echternach, M. (2013). The effect of supine and upright position on vocal tract configurations during singing: a comparative study in professional tenors. *Journal of Voice, 27*(2), 141–48. doi:10.1016/j.jvoice.2012.11.002

Vennard, W. (1967). *Singing: The Mechanism and the Technic* (rev. edn.). New York, NY: Carl Fischer.

Walker, J. S. (1988). An investigation of the whistle register in the female voice. *Journal of Voice*, 2(2), 140–50.

Chapter 7: Vocal Health

Recent publications on singing pedagogy make explicit what was in earlier works implicit in the whole approach to vocal technique: a concern for the maintenance of vocal health. Doscher (1994), David (1995), and Bunch Dayme (2009) have sections on this subject. Thurman and Welch (2000) devote a complete volume to it, as does Sataloff (2005). For all singers, a knowledge of how to care for the voice is necessary for the instrument to be available and in good condition whenever it is needed.

For professional singers, keeping the voice in peak condition is necessary for earning a living, and yet the pressures of busy schedules, demanding repertoire, and constant travel make that a difficult task. Many singers working at an elite level may not earn a living from singing and need to supplement their income in occupations such as teaching, hospitality, and sales. That heavy voice use then puts them at particular risk of vocal damage.

Studies on vocal health for singers have produced prescriptions relating to maintaining hydration, managing general health, fitness, and lifestyle, avoiding vocal strain and fatigue, and using good technique to achieve efficient voice use.

Hydration

Water is of extreme importance to the normal functioning of the respiratory tract and of the vocal tract in particular. Hydration is essential to the vocal folds because of the effects of friction. As the tissue vibrates, mechanical energy is dissipated into heat. The higher the frequency and the higher the intensity, the greater the friction. Loud high notes therefore pose particular problems. Well-irrigated vocal folds cope better with these problems, because they dissipate less energy (Titze, 1983b).

The greater part of the watery thin mucous manufactured by the nose is evaporated into the air that is breathed in through the nose. In this way, dry room air is moistened and filtered, and warmed by the time it arrives at pharyngeal level. This fluid must be replaced, as must the fluid lost through exhalation and in the waste products of the body (Lawrence, 1986). Hydration requires particular attention in air-conditioned buildings or in the artificial atmosphere in aeroplane cabins, where usually the only humidity is produced by passengers exhaling moisture. Body hydration can be maintained by drinking copious amounts of water and by inhaling steam. Room atmosphere made dry by air conditioning can be made humid by use of a humidifier. When the body is well hydrated, urine will be dilute, non-odorous, and clear.

Occupational disorders

It only takes a small imbalance of the factors involved in respiration, phonation, and resonance for singers to experience vocal problems. Occupational disorders in singers include muscle tension dysphonia, vocal nodules, vocal haemorrhage, polyps, or general deterioration. Unlike instrumental playing,

> mastering singing involves making reflexive activity voluntary and voluntary activity reflexive. Specifically, the singer must learn to contract groups of muscles in isolation while simultaneously relaxing muscles which are either antagonistic or not involved in phonation. . . . The overall aim is to produce the greatest spectrum of vocal pitch and intensity with the least effort. (Jahn, 2009, p. 4)

If excess muscle tension is employed, muscle tension dysphonia may result, with a loss of resonance and dynamic range, and then hoarseness and

116

sometimes nodules. Nodules are more common in women and children, whose vocal folds are not as resilient as those of males.

Vocal haemorrhage may result from a particular incident (such as coughing, vomiting, weight lifting, or childbirth), and may be exacerbated by the use of blood thinners or by menstruation. Healing requires complete vocal rest. If the singer continues to sing, a polyp may develop. Polyps may resolve with voice rest and steroids, or may require laser removal. Young professional singers who have pushed themselves, or been pushed by management, may experience a weak and tremulous voice, as may older singers whose voices are declining. Therapy and good teaching may assist.

General fitness, health, and lifestyle

For singers, the instrument is the whole body. Thus, the integrity and quality of the instrument are tied to the physiological and emotional well-being of the whole person (Holt & Holt, 1989). Singers require respiratory fitness, endurance, and general good health. Excess weight, lack of general condition, or failure to maintain good abdominal and thoracic muscle strength all undermine the power source of the voice and predispose the singer to vocal difficulties (Sataloff, 1985). Dehydration, fatigue, and other general medical conditions may affect the mucosa covering the vocal folds, alter lubrication, and decrease vocal efficiency (Sataloff, 1986).

Good diet and sufficient sleep are an important part of maintaining general health and promoting vocal health and efficiency. Some singers find that the voice is adversely affected by certain foods, such as dairy products, chocolate, and nuts (Sataloff, 1987a).

Dental problems or problems to do with the jaws may have harmful effects on the voice. Temporomandibular joint dysfunction, for example, introduces muscle tension in the head and neck, which is transmitted to the larynx directly through the muscular attachments between the mandible and the hyoid bone, and indirectly as generalized increased muscle tension (Sataloff, 1987a). These problems may affect tongue movement and may also result in decreased range, vocal fatigue, and change in the quality or placement of the voice.

Any medical condition that interferes with efficient respiration and breath management may alter performance and cause voice abuse. When a singer complains to the laryngologist about changes in the voice, the problem is often not in the vocal folds, but rather in the production of adequate airflow. Minor alterations in respiratory function that would barely be noticed in the general population can have significant effects on a singer, causing vocal fatigue, loss of range, and hyperfunctional voice use (Spiegel et al., 1988). Alterations in respiratory function may be the result of asthma (most commonly), obstruction of the nasal airway, the pharynx or the larynx, and chest diseases (Spiegel et al., 1990).

Allergies are becoming increasingly common, with many people reacting adversely to substances they inhale, ingest, or come into contact with. Allergic reactions may include upper respiratory problems (allergic rhinitis) and lower respiratory problems (asthma). Individuals may suffer seasonal allergic reactions or may be ill perennnially, depending on what causes their hypersensitivity (Sataloff, 1997). Unfortunately, singers may be sensitive to both the effects of their allergy and to the medications prescribed for it. They need to be referred to a medical specialist with a knowledge of voice.

In asthma, inflammation causes a narrowing of the airways and bronchospasm. This airway narrowing may be induced by the increased ventilation of exercise, including singing. Bronchospasm and airway narrowing plainly present problems to an artist relying on both stamina and subtlety in respiratory control. Physicians primarily direct treatment at reducing airway inflammation; therapy may also involve secondary treatment of bronchospasm. Because asthma can be life-threatening, asthmatic singers need treatment. From a vocal point of view, however, the cure may be worse than the complaint. The most common forms of asthma treatment involve long-term use of inhaled medication, which may affect the vocal folds and larynx. Inhaled corticosteroids seem to be particularly problematic for singers. Orally administered anti-inflammatory drugs and bronchodilator drugs are now available (Cohn, 1998). Allergy-directed therapy may also be appropriate. Plainly, asthmatic singers need to receive expert advice on the best management of their condition.

Conditions altering abdominal function, such as muscle spasm, constipation, or diarrhoea, might be overlooked as a cause of vocal problems, but any condition interfering with efficient use of abdominal support may have deleterious effects on the voice (Sataloff, 1987a). Decrease in respiratory efficiency with ageing may also affect the voice (Boone, 1993).

Singers need good medical advice on the prescription drugs that can be used to treat general medical problems without having an adverse effect on vocal function. In their chapter on pharmacological effects on voice, Titze and Verdolini Abbott (2012) have included a comprehensive series of tables on commonly prescribed medications and the effects these may have on the voice (2012, pp. 106–22). Singing teachers need to be alert to the fact that singers may be using prescribed drugs to control health problems that they see as having no relation to the voice.

Drugs may affect the voice by influencing proprioception and coordination, airflow, fluid balance, the secretions of the upper respiratory tract, and the structure of the vocal folds (Martin, 1984). Many commonly used prescription drugs may have a harmful effect on the voice. Those with a dehydrating effect include antihistamines, diuretics, indigestion medications, sleeping pills, and some antibiotics (Holt & Holt, 1989; Lawrence, 1983; Sataloff, 1987a; Boone, 1993; Caputo Rosen & Sataloff, 1995). Large doses of vitamin C may also have a dehydrating effect (Lawrence, 1981). Recreational drugs, too, may adversely affect the voice. Alcohol, tobacco, and marijuana, for example, all have local irritant effects as well as blunting body sensation (Lawrence, 1983; Boone, 1993). Caffeine and alcohol, in addition, are dehydrating. While there are many medical conditions where treatment is obviously vital, the Titze and Verdolini Abbott motto is: 'when in doubt, don't medicate' (2012, p. 105).

The voice is extremely sensitive to even slight hormone changes. Many of these are reflected as alterations of fluid content in the lamina propria of the vocal folds. This causes alteration in the mass and shape of the vocal folds and results in voice change, particularly muffling, sluggishness, decreased range, and loss of vocal efficiency (Sataloff, 1993). Hormonal changes in menopause, in menstruation, and in diseases such as hypothyroidism may cause such problems (Sataloff), as may changes induced by the use of drugs such as steroids, oestrogen, and testosterone (Titze, 1994).

Voice problems related to sex hormones are seen most commonly in female singers. Vocal changes associated with the normal menstrual cycle have been the subject of a number of studies over the last 40 years (Brown & Hollien, 1984; Isenberger et al., 1984; Abitbol et al., 1989). While these changes have proven difficult to quantify, they are perceptually evident. Most ill effects are seen in the immediate premenstrual period in response to endocrine changes. These may include decreased vocal efficiency, loss of notes high in the range, vocal instability and fatigue, uncertainty of pitch, slight hoarseness, reduced vocal power and flexibility, and some muffling of the voice (Sataloff, 1993, 1996). While the effects of menopause have not been as widely studied, it is likely that the endocrine changes following menopause would have similar effects to those of the premenstrual phase (Sataloff, 1996). Pregnancy commonly results in voice changes similar to premenstrual symptoms (Sataloff, 1993). Birth control pills composed predominantly of oestrogen seem not to affect the larynx, but those that are progestin-dominant may have a masculinizing or virilizing effect on the female larynx (Lawrence, 1983; Martin, 1988). Androgenic hormonal treatments are also used in the treatment of endometriosis, hormonal imbalances, and fibrocystic breast disease. Singers and their teachers need to be aware that when synthetic derivatives of testosterone are used, there is a risk of vocal fold changes, and in the case of long-term use, investigators have reported irreversible deepening of the voice (Martin, 1988).

Sataloff (1987b) suggested that steroids may be helpful for short-term use in treating cases of acute inflammatory laryngitis associated with oversinging, exposure to smoke, or the dehydrating effects of air travel.

Anything that affects sensory feedback may cause a loss of vocal control. Hearing loss interferes with auditory feedback and may result in altered vocal production, particularly if the singer is unaware of the hearing loss (Sataloff, 1987a). Even the common cold, when it affects internal hearing, may cause difficulties in vocal control (Lawrence, 1983). Medications that blunt sensation, such as throat sprays and lozenges containing topical anaesthetics, tranquillizers, antidepressants, and some types of blood pressure medication, should be avoided if possible (Lawrence). Psychoactive medications need to be carefully monitored, since nearly all such medications have effects that can interfere with vocal tract physiology (Caputo Rosen & Sataloff, 1995).

Most voice disorders are related to tissue changes in the vocal fold cover (Titze, 1994). Changes may result from viral or bacterial infection (as in laryngitis associated with colds or influenza, or in bronchitis or croup), from irritation by pollutants in the atmosphere, or from smoking.

Aspirin is a drug that may affect vocal fold tissue. Commonly used alone for pain relief and also in combination with other drugs in many over-the-counter medications, aspirin (and other anti-inflammatories) may have a direct effect on blood coagulation by binding the calcium ion with which it comes in contact so that the calcium is not as immediately available for blood clotting. It also increases the fragility of capillaries, which may cause haemorrhage into the vocal folds in loud or high singing (Lawrence, 1983; Martin, 1984; Boone, 1993). Recovery from vocal fold haemorrhage usually requires at least two weeks voice rest (Lawrence).

Gastroesophageal reflux may also have an adverse effect on the vocal folds. Ross et al. (1998) found that 49 patients with suspected laryngopharyngeal reflux disease all showed significantly increased abnormal perceptual voice characteristics, which they termed musculoskeletal tension, hard glottal attack, glottal fry, restricted tone placement, and hoarseness. While gastroesophageal reflux may be caused by a hernia, it may also arise from the lifestyle of a performer (Lawrence, 1983; Sataloff, 1987a; Boone, 1993). Many singers avoid eating before a performance, eating the major meal of the day at night to relax after the performance, and then going straight to bed. Digestion then occurs with the body in a prone position, and gastric reflux may result. This may cause reddening and swelling of the vocal folds, with consequent hoarseness the next morning. Cleveland (1990) found a history of reflux and allergy in singers with intermittent pitch problems.

The eating disorder bulimia nervosa can cause a range of problems, from edema through granulomas, nodules, polyps, and contact ulcers. Reflux may be a contributing factor to vocal disorders in singers with bulimia (Rothstein, 1998). Alterations in the mucosa of the larynx and pharynx similar to those found in reflux laryngopharyngitis have also been found in fungal infections such as candidiasis (Forrest & Weed, 1998).

Vocal strain and fatigue

It is not known why vocal endurance is widely variable, with some singers able to endure prolonged voice use without risk while others succumb early to fatigue. Titze (1983a) postulated that vocal fatigue is linked to inefficient use of the mechanism, to muscular fatigue, and to dehydration. Fatigue may result when the mechanism is asked to perform a task requiring unaccustomed muscle use. Some muscle fatigue can be expected to occur after prolonged periods of phonation, regardless of how well the muscles are developed.

It is probable that vocal fatigue is physiologically similar to muscle fatigue in any other part of the body (Titze, 1983b). Vocal fatigue may result both from the fatiguing of respiratory and laryngeal muscles and from biomechanical changes in nonmuscular tissues that cause the vocal folds to vibrate less efficiently (Titze, 1983c). It is likely that many of the principles associated with muscle growth, maintenance, and deterioration in athletics may also apply to vocal performance.

The risk of vocal strain is minimized by warming up the voice before use and avoiding noisy environments that encourage overuse, such as singing over loud electric instruments, talking or singing in noisy nightclubs, and shouting at sporting events. Cooling down has long been advocated after extended athletic effort. While it is rarely mentioned in the vocal literature, it would seem a sensible procedure after extended vocal effort.

The effects of ageing on the voice

Because the body is the vocal instrument, anything that affects the body may affect the voice. Ageing affects heart, brain, and all other body organs, so plainly it has an effect on the voice. However, often ageing brings a range of illnesses and the medications that deal with them, and it can be difficult to establish exactly what cause to assign to particular vocal effects. Ageing is associated with deteriorating bodily functions,

> including accuracy, speed, endurance, stability, strength co-ordination, breathing capacity, nerve conduction velocity, heart output, and kidney function. Muscle and neural tissues atrophy, and the chemicals responsible for nerve transmission change. Ligaments atrophy, and cartilages turn to bone (including those in the larynx). Joints develop irregularities that interfere with smooth motion (Sataloff & Linville, 2005 p. 503).

Plainly these deteriorations have a negative effect on the fine motor coordination that is singing.

There are also changes specific to the vocal mechanism: the vocal folds thin and deteriorate. They lose their elastic and collagenous fibres, becoming stiffer and thinner, and the vocal fold edge becomes less smooth. These changes account for the voice changes often noted with ageing. Sundberg et al. (1998) studied the effects of ageing on singers' voices. They used commercial recordings of internationally famous singers who had been recorded over a period ranging from their 20s to their 60s. There were four basses, four baritones, four tenors, four altos/mezzo-sopranos, and four sopranos. Excerpts from the recordings were analysed acoustically for vibrato rate and extent, and the centre frequency of a spectrum envelope peak near 3 kHz (the singer's formant) and also rated for age by a panel of experts. Since these professional singers had continued to get recording contracts over a 30-year span, presumably they failed to show typical vocal signs of ageing. The age was overestimated for young singers and underestimated for the older singers. The rated age correlated with vibrato rate and extent and with the centre frequency of the singer's formant. The results corroborated the general observation that with increasing age vibrato rate decreases and vibrato extent increases. The centre frequency of the singer's formant showed a rather weak correlation with rated age. This relation may reflect a descent of the larynx with increasing age, as such a descent should lower all formant frequencies.

However, it cannot be assumed that these declines are linear. With a growing ageing population, more research is being done, and this research suggests that if general fitness and health can be maintained, vocal changes can be minimized. In singing, as with many other activities, those who acquired the skill early in life and maintained it exhibit a lesser decline than novices beginning late in life.

Vocal efficiency

Vocal efficiency in singing relies on both good health and good technique to supply energy and stamina and to regulate the fine changes in balance between respiratory and laryngeal function necessary to meet musical demands. Continuing vocal efficiency can be promoted by maintaining a regular practice schedule, by warming up before performance, by cultivating good speech habits, and by employing strategies to deal with the demands of performance. Optimum vocal conditioning requires following a specific regimen of daily vocalization to promote stamina in the respiratory system, coordination of voice onset and release, unification of the registers, resonance balancing, pitch, and dynamic control (Miller, 1986).

122

Sabol et al. (1995) investigated the effects of isometric-isotonic vocal function exercises, practised regularly for four weeks, on parameters of voice production in the healthy singer. Their 20 subjects were graduate-level voice majors of similar age and vocal training. They were divided into experimental and control groups, each containing three men and seven women. Each group continued their regular singing practice regimen, and the experimental group added the vocal function exercise program. Beginning from an assumption that exercise of the isometric type is not always an essential ingredient in singers' practice regimens, the researchers introduced the following exercises to be performed in the very soft part of the dynamic range:

5. Sustain /i/ as long as possible on a comfortable note (F_4).
6. Glide from the lowest to the highest note in the frequency range using /o/.
7. Glide from the highest to the lowest note in the frequency range, using /o/.
8. Sustain the musical notes middle C and D, E, F, G above middle C for as long as possible, using /o/ (one octave lower for males). Repeat these notes two times. (p. 29)

At the end of the programme, the experimental subjects showed significant positive changes in vocal function. They displayed significantly increased phonation volumes at all pitch levels, with a decreased flow rate. Maximum phonation times also improved. In other words, voice use became much more efficient.

This 1995 study displayed an interest in vocal efficiency and how to achieve it. Both the interest in vocal efficiency and the means used to achieve it are those advocated by traditional pedagogies over hundreds of years. Tosi, for example, writing in the 18th century, gave these directions to the student:

> Let him learn the Manner to glide with the Vowels and to drag the Voice gently from the high to the lower Notes, which, tho' Qualifications necessary for singing well, cannot possibly be learned from Sol-fa-ing only, and are overlooked by the Unskilful. (1743/1987, pp. 29–30)

It is likely that the success of the vocal function exercises used in the study was attributable not only to the type of exercises used, but also to the fact that a short sequence was repeated twice, done twice a day, every day of the week, with progress monitored three times a week. These conditions are ideal for the acquisition of a physical skill and closely model those adopted by the old Italian School. While participants were asked to list the vocal exercises they usually practised, they were not asked to describe the duration or frequency of practice, nor how often it was monitored. These factors may be just as decisive, or even more decisive, in the positive result than the actual exercises performed.

In maintaining optimum vocal functioning, warming up before rehearsal and performance is necessary, as is avoiding fatigue by 'marking' in lengthy production rehearsals. Titze (1993) suggested that vocal athletes need to adopt the warm-up principles of gymnasts, figure-skaters, and dancers, stretching joints, tendons, ligaments, and muscles. Glides over a large range of pitches and intensities constitute laryngeal and respiratory stretching exercises. Arpeggios, scales, and glissandos serve this purpose. As in developing any motor skill, exercises to increase accuracy of targeting, stability of posturing, speed of transitions, and dynamic range are advisable (Titze, 1993). Singers can practise the accuracy of pitch targeting by attacking notes at various pitches; the stability of posturing by singing long, sustained notes; and the speed of transition by executing rapid scales or arpeggios. Singers can extend range by executing quick leaps between high and low notes. Finally, singers can practise independence of phonation and articulation through consonant–vowel alterations, rapidly executed on scales or arpeggios. Having accessed the entire range of pitch and vocal quality, the singer should complete the warm-up with some loud singing.

Miller's (1990) prescription for a 20-minute warm-up procedure had much in common with that outlined above. He recommended that the singer begin with gentle, brief onsets and offsets in a comfortable range of the voice, progressing to humming in medium range and syllables with nasals and vowel sequences. Next, the singer performs exercises for flexible tongue and jaw action, followed by agility patterns, both ascending and descending. Miller suggested a few minutes rest before turning to passages that deal with vowel definition and modification or with sostenuto. Registration and *passaggio* vocalizes follow. Undertaking an established warm-up routine before performance offers psychological as well as physical security to the singer. Singing teachers and choral conductors should also use a warm-up routine before beginning work with the voice (Miller, 1990). Titze (1993) summarized the purpose of the warm-up as obtaining, as quickly as possible, a uniform vocal quality over a wide pitch range. Estill (1996b) recommended sirening up and down the range on /ŋ/, using 'thin folds, a tilted thyroid and maximum effort, i.e., as hard a feeling of effort in the head with as soft a sound as possible in the larynx, without any break or roughness or change of quality either ascending or descending the scale' (1996a, p. 91) as the only warm-up necessary to achieve this.

Singers and singing teachers sometimes underestimate the effect of the speaking voice on the singing voice. Misuse of the speaking voice, or use of a tired speaking voice, has both direct and indirect effects on the singing voice.

Teachers need to be alert to the risks posed by some occupations, such as teaching or aerobics instruction (Smith et al., 1997; Smith et al., 1998; Kostyk & Rochet, 1998; Long et al., 1998). Direct effects are hoarseness and vocal fatigue. An indirect effect may be uncertainty about the reliability of the voice in singing, or even fear of singing (Cooper, 1982). Using the speaking voice at its optimal pitch is important to vocal health (Gregg, 1990; Titze, 1994). Boone (1977) suggested about 100 Hz (A$\flat_2$) as appropriate for basses, about 135 Hz (C$\sharp_3$) for tenors, about 200 Hz (G$\sharp_3$) for altos, and about 256 Hz (C$_4$) for sopranos. Researchers have identified speaking at too low a pitch as a significant factor in voice problems (Drew & Sapir, 1995).

While teachers of singing cannot be expected to have detailed knowledge of pathologies and medications, they do need to be sufficiently informed and aurally aware to distinguish between poor vocal technique and possible vocal damage. They need a knowledge of fitness and lifestyle management both to maintain their own vocal fitness in what has been identified as a high-risk profession and to advise their students on such issues. They also need to be in contact with a wider network of professionals in related fields – teachers of spoken voice; body use professionals such as Alexander, Feldenkrais, and yoga teachers; dentists and orthodontists; otolaryngologists, speech therapists, and voice care teams – with whom they can work and to whom students with vocal problems can be referred.

References

Abitbol, J., de Brux, J., Millot, G., Masson, M.-F., Mimoun, O., Pau, H. & Abitbol, B. (1989). Does a hormonal vocal cord cycle exist in women? Study of vocal pre-menstrual syndrome in voice performers by videostroboscopy-glottography and cytology on 38 women. *Journal of Voice, 3*(2), 157–62.

Boone, D.R. (1977). *The Voice and Voice Therapy.* Englewood Cliffs, NJ: Prentice-Hall.

Boone, D.R. (1993). Biologic enemies of the professional voice. *Journal of Research in Singing and Applied Vocal Pedagogy, 16*(2), 15–24.

Brown, W.S. and Hollien, H. (1984). Effects of menstruation on the singing voice. In V.L. Lawrence (ed.), *Transcripts of the Twelfth Symposium, Care of the Professional Voice, 1983*, Pt. I (pp. 112–16). New York, NY: The Voice Foundation.

Bunch Dayme, M. (2009). *Dynamics of the Singing Voice* (5th edn.). Vienna: Springer-Verlag.

Caputo Rosen, D. & Sataloff, R.T. (1995). Laryngoscope: psychoactive medications and their effects on the voice. *The NATS Journal, 52*(2), 49–53.

Cleveland, T.F. (1990). Vocal pedagogy in the twenty-first century: some new observations on pitch problems. *The NATS Journal, 46*(3), 34–35, 52.

Cohn, J. (1998). Laryngoscope: asthma and the serious singer. *Journal of Singing, 54*(3), 51–53.

Cooper, M. (1982). The tired speaking voice and the negative effect on the singing voice. *The NATS Bulletin, 39*(2), 11–14.

David, M. (1995). *The New Voice Pedagogy*. Lanham, MD: Scarecrow Press.

Doscher, B. (1994). *The Functional Unity of the Singing Voice* (2nd edn.). Metuchen, NJ: Scarecrow Press.

Drew, R. & Sapir, S. (1995). Average speaking fundamental frequency in soprano singers with and without symptoms of vocal attrition. *Journal of Voice, 9*(2), 134–41.

Estill, J. (1996a). *Voice Craft. A User's Guide to Voice Quality*. Level One: *Primer of Compulsory Figures*. Santa Rosa, CA: Estill Voice Training Systems.

Estill, J. (1996b). *Workshop: Compulsory Figures for Voice*, 28 January to 2 February. Sydney, Australia: National Voice Centre.

Forrest, L. & Weed, H. (1998). Candida laryngitis appearing as leukoplakia and GERD. *Journal of Voice, 12*(2), 91–95.

Gregg, J.W. (1990). From song to speech: on pitch. *The NATS Journal, 46*(3), 37, 50, 52.

Holt, G.A. & Holt, K.E. (1989). Laryngoscope: Medications: Aids to singing health? *The NATS Journal, 45*(4), 21–24.

Isenberger, H., Brown, W.S. & Rothman, H. (1984). Effects of menstruation on the singing voice. Part II: Further developments in research. In V.L. Lawrence (ed.), *Transcripts of the Twelfth Symposium, Care of the Professional Voice, 1983*, Pt. I (pp. 117–23). New York, NY: The Voice Foundation.

Jahn, A. (2009). Medical management of the professional singer. *Medical Problems of Performing Artists, 24*(1), 3–9.

Kostyk, B.E. & Putnam Rochet, A. (1998). Laryngeal airway resistance in teachers with vocal fatigue: a preliminary study. *Journal of Voice, 12*(3), 287–99.

Lawrence, V.L. (1981). Laryngoscope: vitamin C. *The NATS Journal, 37*(5), 24–25.

Lawrence, V.L. (1983). Laryngoscope: when all else fails, read the instructions. *The NATS Journal, 39*(3), 16–19.

Lawrence, V.L. (1986). Laryngoscope: marijuana and cocaine. *The NATS Journal, 43*(2), 26–27.

Long, J., Williford, H.N., Scharff Olson, M. & Wolfe, V. (1998). Voice problems and risk factors among aerobics instructors. *Journal of Voice, 12*(2), 197–207.

Martin, F.G. (1988). Drugs and vocal function. *Journal of Voice, 2*(4), 338–44.

Martin, F.G. (1984). Drugs and the voice. In V.L. Lawrence (ed.), *Transcripts of the Twelfth Symposium, Care of the Professional Voice, 1983*, Pt. I (pp. 124–32). New York, NY: The Voice Foundation.

Miller, R. (1986). *The Structure of Singing: System and Art in Vocal Technique*. New York, NY: Schirmer Books.

Miller, R. (1990). Sotto voce: warming up the voice. *The NATS Journal, 46*(5), 22–23.

Ross, J.-A., Noordzji, J. & Woo, P. (1998). Voice disorders in patients with suspected laryngo-pharyngeal reflux disease. *Journal of Voice, 12*(1), 84–88.

Rothstein, S. (1998). Reflux and vocal disorders in singers with bulimia. *Journal of Voice*, *12*(1), 89–90.

Sabol, J.W., Lee, L. & Stemple, J.C. (1995). The value of vocal function exercises in the practice regimen of singers. *Journal of Voice*, *9*(1), 27–36.

Sataloff, R.T. (1985). Laryngoscope: ten good ways to abuse your voice: a singer's guide to a short career (Part 1). *The NATS Journal*, *42*(1), 23–25.

Sataloff, R.T. (1986). Laryngoscope: voice rest. *The NATS Bulletin*, *43*(5), 23–25.

Sataloff, R.T. (1987a). The professional voice, Part I: anatomy, function, and general health. *Journal of Voice*, *1*(1), 92–104.

Sataloff, R.T. (1987b). Laryngoscope: a 'first aid kit' for singers. *The NATS Journal*, *43*(4), 26–29.

Sataloff, R.T. (1993). Laryngoscope: hormones and the voice. *The NATS Journal*, *50*(1), 43–45.

Sataloff, R.T. (1996). The effects of menopause on the singing voice. *Journal of Singing*, *52*(4), 39–42.

Sataloff, R.T. (1997). Laryngoscope: allergy. *Journal of Singing*, *53*(4), 39–43.

Sataloff, R.T. (ed.) (2005). *Professional Voice: The Science and Art of Clinical Care* (3rd edn.), Vol. 3. San Diego, CA: Plural Publishing.

Sataloff, R.T. & Linville, S.E. (2005). The effects of age on the voice. In R.T. Sataloff (ed.), *Professional Voice: The Science and Art of Clinical Care* (3rd ed.), Vol. 3 (pp. 497–511). San Diego, CA: Plural Publishing.

Smith, E., Gray, S.D., Dove, H., Kirchner, L. & Heras, H. (1997). Frequency and effects of teachers' voice problems. *Journal of Voice*, *11*(1), 81–87.

Smith, E., Kirchner, H.L., Taylor, M., Hoffman, H. & Lemke, J.H. (1998). Voice problems among teachers: differences by gender and teaching characteristics. *Journal of Voice*, *12*(3), 328–34.

Spiegel, J.R., Sataloff, R.T., Cohn, J.R. & Hawkshaw, M. (1988). Respiratory function in singers: medical assessment, diagnoses and treatments. *Journal of Voice*, *2*(1), 40–50.

Spiegel, J.R., Sataloff, R.T. & Hawkshaw, M.J. (1990). Laryngoscope: respiratory function and dysfunction in singers. *The NATS Journal*, *46*(4), 23–25.

Sundberg, J., Thörnvik, M.N. & Söderström, A.M. (1998). Age and voice quality in professional singers. *Logopedics Phoniatrics Vocology*, *23*(4), 169–76. doi: 10.1080/140154398434077

Thurman, L. & Welch, G. (eds.) (2000). *Bodymind and Voice: Foundations of Voice Education* (rev. edn.), Vol. 3. Collegeville, MN: The VoiceCare Network.

Titze, I.R. (1983a). Vocal fatigue. *The NATS Bulletin*, *39*(3), 22–23.

Titze, I.R. (1983b). A further look at vocal fatigue: Part I. *The NATS Bulletin*, *40*(1), 33–34.

Titze, I.R. (1983c). A further look at vocal fatigue: Part II. *The NATS Bulletin*, *40*(2), 29–30.

Titze, I.R. (1993). Voice research: warm-up exercises. *The NATS Journal*, *49*(5).

Titze, I.R. (1994). *Principles of Voice Production*. Englewood Cliffs, NJ: Prentice Hall.

Titze, I.R. & Verdolini Abbott, K. (2012). *Vocology: The Science and Practice of Voice Habilitation*. Salt Lake City, UT: National Center for Voice and Speech.

Tosi, P.F. (1987). *Observations on the Florid Song* (Galliard, trans., M. Pilkington, ed.). London: Stainer and Bell. (Original work published 1743.)

Chapter 8: The Voice of the Mind

> I marvel at the ancient wisdom of referring to what we now call mind by the word *psyche* which was also used to denote breath and blood.
>
> (Damasio, 2000, p. 30)

> The voice is not a mechanical instrument separated from the innermost nature of an individual communicator. . . . Technical skills are eventually integrated into an artistic and kinaesthetic whole dictated by the holistic imagination.
>
> (Miller, 2004, pp. 247, 248)

> All of us possess — or if you are a thoroughly modern mentalist, all of us are — our ideas, concepts, stories, theories, and skills.
>
> (Gardner, 2004, p. 22)

The title of this chapter borrows the title of a book first published in 1951 by Herbert-Cesari. This was a ground-breaking work not only in its attention to vocal mechanics:

> *Correct sensations of vocal tone*, interpreted in their proper light, will be found to *reflect with extraordinary fidelity the mechanical adjustments obtaining within the vibrator and resonator systems*. An accurate knowledge of the working of both systems is indispensable (Herbert-Cesari, 1963, p. 30, emphasis in original)

but also in addressing the role of the mind in singing:

> It is the intangible that is inclined to be overlooked or ignored; consequently, a disproportionate amount of attention is devoted to purely physical effort, forgetting that singing is mainly mental (p. 286).

And then:

> And what is a correct sensation but a right thought or idea translated into concrete actuality. Physically speaking it is the grosser manifestation of vocal cord undulation transformed, aye, transfigured, into the finer substance of focused resonance. It is thought resolved into thing: The Voice of the Mind, a correct thing rising from a correct thought (p. 360).

Singing differs from other types of musical performance in that the performer *is* the instrument. Yet, while vocal production and vocal acoustics continue to be investigated, such matters as mental control of the vocal instrument, and coordination of this with interpretation and communication of musical and verbal texts, have been somewhat neglected. This chapter explores aspects of brain and body, body and mind, and musical perception and cognition that are relevant to these neglected subjects and hence deserve more attention from singers and teachers of singing.

All musical performers need to hone technical skills, sharpen aural perception, analyse musical structure, and understand a range of styles and musical literature. Singers also need to understand and articulate a verbal text, often in a foreign language. Those technical and musical skills are in rehearsal translated into intentional movements, brought together as a somatic experience, and then communicated as meaning grounded in the body in the social context of performance (Davidson & Correia, 2001).

In singing, the performer uses the whole body as an instrument. While it may be possible to play (badly) a musical instrument without musical thought, relying purely on mechanical movement, it is not possible to sing without it (Callaghan, 2002). Nevertheless, there has been little investigation into the most efficient way of teaching the full range of skills required by singers and how these skills may best be incorporated into musical performance.

Experimental studies in neuroscience, music perception, and cognition are casting light on the mind and how it works in the body. The results of experimental studies can clarify how aural perception may be enhanced, how musical memory may be improved and used, how practice regimes may be structured, when and how feedback may best be given, and how the learning of vocal performance can be made more efficient.

The meaning of meaning

For singers the issue of meaning and how it is conveyed is crucial to their art. And it crucially affects how teachers work with singers in bringing together vocal, musical, and linguistic skills. What kind of meaning is it? How is it understood, felt, created, conveyed?

Understanding the mind, human consciousness, and the feeling of self has occupied scientists, psychologists, and philosophers for centuries. A large part of the problem has been that, historically, Western scholarship and research have pursued objective theories of meaning, rationality, and behaviour, based on the traditional separation of mind and body. This raises the difficulty of the perspective of the investigator: how to conduct an objective investigation. Damasio characterizes the problem thus: 'The body and its brain are public, exposed, external, and unequivocally objective entities. The mind is a private, hidden, internal, unequivocally subjective entity' (2002, p. 4).

What have enabled a different perspective on the intertwined operations of the human mind and body are the advances in neuroscience over the last 25 years or so. These advances are beginning to impact on work in philosophy, cognition, psychomotor learning, musical performance, and linguistics that can be brought together to form a working theory of embodied meaning for singers.

Meaning and imagination

Writing in 1987, Johnson challenged traditional objectivist thinking and its rigid separation of mind from body, cognition from emotion, and reason from imagination. He referred to a crisis in the theory of meaning and rationality and put forward imagination as occupying a central role in all meaning, understanding, and reasoning (Johnson, 1987, p. ix).

If meaning is regarded strictly as a relation between abstract symbols (words) and things, then how 'human beings grasp things as meaningful – the way they understand their experience – is held to be incidental to the nature of meaningful thought and reason' (Johnson, 1987, p. x). And yet many of the ways in which we categorize things are 'formed on the basis of imaginatively structured cognitive models, and their nature is such that they could not correspond directly to anything in reality external to human experience' (p. xi). Many of these models depend on the nature of the human body, particularly perception and motor skills. Concepts are defined and understood within frameworks and structures dependent on the nature of human experience in different cultures at different times.

It is time to bring the body back into our understanding of how the mind works.

Consciousness and the brain

Consciousness is that first-person phenomenon that allows owners to be aware of their thoughts and feelings. It is the basis of mind. The link between the first-person mind and the third-person behaviour is the brain. Damasio identifies two kinds of consciousness: core consciousness and extended consciousness (2000, p. 16). Both are biological phenomena, but while core consciousness is simple, extended consciousness is complex, having several levels of organization and evolving across the lifetime of the organism, utilizing both conventional memory and working memory. This extended consciousness is what is required for human creativity, and its 'peak' is also enhanced by language. This is a bodily thing: 'The organism in the relationship play of consciousness is the entire unit of our living being, our body as it were; and yet, as it turns out, the part of the organism called the brain holds within it a sort of model of the whole' (Damasio, 2000, p. 22).

The shared essence of the processes of emotion, feeling, and consciousness is the body, and the body is the singer's instrument. Relevant to musical performance is the fact that remembered objects and situations evoke particular emotions. 'The classes of stimuli that cause happiness or fear or sadness tend to do so fairly consistently in the same individual and in individuals who share the same social and cultural background . . . there is a rough correspondence between classes of emotion inducers and the resulting emotional state' (Damasio, 2000, pp. 56–57). It is this that allows the communication of meaning (verbal, musical, and emotional) through singing.

The theory of multiple intelligences

For much of the 20th century, 'intelligence' was viewed as a single property of the human mind. Hodges and Gruhn suggest intelligence can be defined in terms of cognitive brain functions, creative strategies, and processing speed. A person shows evidence of intelligence through broad knowledge, the ability to evaluate situations based on rational thought, to create practical solutions for new problems, to develop innovative ideas in special domains, and to recognize causal links between facts and ideas quickly and precisely (2012, pp. 208–9).

Howard Gardner's work on 'multiple intelligences' situated these abilities within a cultural setting. In response to a growing body of biological and anthropological evidence, he first put forward a theory of multiple intelligences in 1983, defining 'an intelligence' as 'the ability to solve problems, or to create products, that are valued within one or more cultural settings' (1993, p. xiv). He saw individuals as having a profile of intelligences, or intellectual proclivities, expressed in the context of specific tasks, domains, and disciplines (p. xx).

Gardner and his collaborators (Kolb, 1984; Lazear, 1991) have investigated individual differences in profiles of intelligences and how these are linked to ways of learning. While people are attracted to domains related to their particular intelligences, success in a specific domain requires proficiency in a set of intelligences. For example, people with musical intelligence may be attracted to the domain of music, but for success in this domain they require proficiency in a set of seven intelligences. For a singer, these would include:

- **verbal/linguistic:** understanding order and meaning of words, memory and recall, story-telling;
- **logical/mathematical:** abstract pattern recognition, discerning relationships and connections;
- **musical/rhythmic:** appreciating the structure of music, schemes or frames in the mind for hearing music, sensitivity to sounds, recognition, creation, and reproduction of melody and rhythm, sensing characteristic qualities of tone;
- **visual/spatial:** active imagination, forming mental images;

- **bodily/kinaesthetic:** control of 'voluntary' movements, control of 'pre-programmed' movements, the mind–body connection, expanding awareness through the body, communication through gesture;
- **social/interpersonal:** effective verbal/nonverbal communication, sensitivity to others' moods, temperaments, motivations, and feelings; and
- **solidarity/intrapersonal:** concentration of the mind, mindfulness, metacognition (thinking and learning about knowing what you know), awareness and expression of different feelings.

Music and language

Music and language exhibit significant, and certainly not accidental, commonalities in their material substance (the organization of sound), physiological bases, cultural significance, and cognitive processing. Music and language are both expression systems produced by the body and used for human communication.

Links between musical and linguistic intelligence

In Gardner's schema, musical intelligence is the ability to discern meaning and importance in sets of pitches rhythmically arranged and also to produce such metrically arranged pitch sequences as a means of communicating with others. Both audition (hearing) and audiation (mental hearing, or auditory imagery) are essential to singing. The ear is the organ essential to this process, not only in providing auditory input, but in its control of symmetry and balance. Tomatis' (1991) finding that the right ear is dominant in singing (refer to Chapter 2) is relevant to teaching.

Crowder proposed that the difference between audition and auditory imagery lies in the sensory qualities underlying the two processes. In audition, both spectral and dynamic cues are salient; in auditory imagery it is spectral cues that are salient (Crowder, 1989). Musical imagery for relative pitch is related to musical perception for the same stimuli – an issue of vital importance for singers. Loudness information, too, is vital in that it has been identified as being relevant in onset times.

Crowder found that differences in timbre impair the detection of identical pitches, with some of his subjects unable to separate timbre from pitch. This finding has important implications for the teaching of singing. Many beginner singers have difficulty matching pitch, particularly when the note is played on a piano; children with treble voices may have difficulty matching the pitch of an adult voice; men may have difficulty matching the pitch of a female voice.

Musical intelligence and linguistic intelligence are both closely tied to the auditory–oral tract. Singing competency is the example par excellence of auditory–oral musical intelligence. The process of hearing, perceiving, and remembering sound forms a loop with the production of sound. In speaking and singing, the sounds being produced by the vocal mechanism are constantly being fed through this loop – the phonological loop – dictating what is produced by the vocal apparatus.

Cognition of music and language

An understanding of cognition in both music and language lies in the nature of these modes of communication and how they are learnt. Both music and language rely on the oral–aural channel and early learning can proceed without relation to physical objects. Neurobiological research suggests that children's learning of both modes is achieved by the establishment of mental representations that are reflected by cortical activation patterns (Deacon, 1997; Gruhn, 1997). Hodges and Gruhn point out that 'the brain does not simply store information, rather it generates rules and higher order structures from the incoming input. That is, the brain productively develops the structures that are needed for cognitive processing' (2012, p. 212).

An adequate model of language cognition is one that would account for linguistic universals and culturally diverse languages, spoken and written language, and linguistic production and linguistic reception. Given the similarities identified between music and language, one would expect models of music cognition to meet these same criteria. This, however, is rarely the case. Many focus more on perception than cognition, many are grounded in understandings of music based on the written tradition of Western art music that are then not generalizable to other musical traditions, and many address musical reception while neglecting musical production. Fiske (1992) has identified three types of theories of music cognition: psychoacoustic theories that explain musical behaviour in respect of the mechanisms involved in auditory perceptual activity, pattern structure theories concerned with musical thinking in relation to the perceptual identification of features or components related to the recognition and recall of musical patterns, and those that assume the presence of language-like grammatical protocols underlying mental construction of musical patterns.

This last type seems better to answer the case, subsuming the theories of the other two types. I assume that music cognition refers to the mental processes that take place following psychoacoustic processing, that is to musical thinking. The theories of Heller and Campbell, of Lehrdahl and Jackendoff, of Serafine and of Fiske are worth consideration. In a series of publications (Heller & Campbell, 1976; Campbell & Heller, 1980; Campbell & Heller,

135

1981; Heller & Campbell, 1982), Heller and Campbell put forward the view that music cognition is pattern construction and pattern management, having both universal and style-specific components, with musical understanding being the product of music acculturation. They see music processing as similar to language processing. They (and many other writers on music cognition) assume that the musical process is a tripartite one involving composer, performer, and listener. This raises problems in relation to the many musical traditions in which composer and performer are one; few theories of music cognition account for improvised music-making and oral traditions.

Psychologist Aniruddh Patel theorizes that the link between music and language is their processing in the brain: 'what is shared by linguistic and musical syntactic processing is derived from comparison of cognitive theories of syntactic processing in the two domains' (2003, p. 677). He postulates that 'structured integration is a key part of syntactic processing: that is mentally connecting each incoming element X to another element Y in the evolving structure' (p. 678). Presumably structured integration is essential to any kind of thinking in any kind of system, so, while this is no doubt true of music and language, it doesn't explain particular connections. Patel's assumptions about the particular connections do not stand up to scrutiny. For example, he states that 'every human infant is born into a world with two distinct systems. The first is linguistic and includes the vowels, consonants, and pitch contrasts of the native language. The second is musical and includes the timbres and pitches of the culture's music' (Patel, 2008, p. 9). That infants are born with a sensitivity to sound and have the ability to organize it mentally seems likely; that they come equipped with two culturally-specific sound systems seems unlikely. Similarly, the link between linguistic and musical syntax is too neat and implies a very Western-harmonic view of musical structuring (Patel, 2003). Syntax is defined as 'a set of principles governing the combination of discrete structural elements (such as words or musical tones) into sequences' (2003, p. 674). That is no doubt true, but applies to many other types of syntactic thinking, that is, the ordering or structuring of symbols. For example, Richard Miller talks of voice pedagogy as syntax:

> Voice pedagogy can be thought of as a form of syntax, the ability to devise and follow complex programs of action, using tools, signs, words, and physical coordination. Some dictionary definitions of syntax: to put together, to put in order, a connected system or order, an orderly arrangement; or a harmonious adjustment of parts or ambient factors. Although generally associated with grammatical construction, syntax occurs in all learning, including learning to sing. (Miller, 2004, p. 189)

Lerdahl and Jackendoff (Lerdahl & Jackendoff, 1983; Jackendoff, 1987) agree with Heller and Campbell and with Serafine (1988) that music is heard as organized patterns and that processing these patterns depends on knowledge of a particular music system. The Lerdahl and Jackendoff theory derives from Noam Chomsky's school of generative linguistics (Chomsky 1965, 1975). Jackendoff (1993) postulates a universal mental grammar comprising an innate and a learned component. However, while in relation to language the theory accounts for generation and reception, in relation to music it is difficult to see how the theory accounts for generation outside the written tradition of Western tonal music.

Serafine proposes a bipartite model. She is unusual in insisting that 'the critical interaction is not that between composer and listener, or performer and listener, or composer and performer, but rather that between one of those actors and a piece of music' (1988, p. 6). Her central claim is that 'music is a form of thought and that it develops over the life span much as other forms of thought develop, principally those such as language, mathematical reasoning, and ideas about the physical world' (Serafine, 1988, p. 5). Serafine's theory better accounts for cultural diversity and for musical performance (i.e. musical creation, including composition, improvised performance, and interpretation of another's composition).

Fiske identifies in the theories of Heller and Campbell, Lerdahl and Jackendoff, and Serafine two components (the first, the innate – processing – component; and the second the learned component, comprising a description of the perceived tonal-rhythmic patterns resulting from exercising the rules of the first component). He proposes a third component which he identifies as a generic decision-making mechanism, 'a description of the activity that leads to realizing those musical structures and interstructural relationships' (1992, p. 371).

Music and language as semiotic systems

While it is useful to compare music and language in terms of their organization of sound, their physiological bases, their cultural significance, and their cognitive processing, these are incomplete models, ignoring the fact that both language and music are essentially semiotic systems, that is systems which link perceptible expressions to meaningful interpretations, in both cases the paradigmatic means of expression being the human voice.

Saussure's seminal work (1916/1959), although based on the study of language, called for the creation of a new science of signs which he called 'semiology,' of which language would only be one instance. As he explained:

> What is natural to mankind is not oral speech but the faculty of constructing a language, i.e. a system of distinct signs corresponding to

distinct ideas. . . . The faculty of articulating words . . . is exercised only with the help of the instrument created by a collectivity and designed for its use . . . (1916/1959, pp. 10–11)

Although Saussure's challenge has been taken up by a number of scholars and applied to music (Ruwet, 1967, 1972; Nattiez, 1973, 1990), they have found it difficult to get away from simplistic notions of the 'language of music' (McDonald, 2005, 2012). The main stumbling block here has been the notion of 'musical meaning' (McDonald, 2011), and the difficulties of defining something that corresponds only peripherally to common denotational, referential understandings of linguistic meaning (Zuckerandl, 1956). The most promising avenue here is Burrows' 'three field' model of language and music (1990) which grounds both systems in the semiotic affordances of the human body, and in particular of vocal sound. Burrows speaks of the voice as (literally) expression, 'a pressing outward past the partially yielding obstacle of the vocal folds' (1990, p. 30).

Meaning in music and language

In recent years linguistic models have been applied to music, producing either a verbal model of musical meaning (e.g. Swain, 1997) or a model of musical organization divorced from meaning (e.g. Lerdahl & Jackenoff, 1983). An adequate model would account for universals and cultural diversity, oral and written forms, and production and reception. For all musical performers, but particularly for singers, who use the human voice to express a dual music/language 'text,' the issue of meaning cannot be ignored. Singers are concerned with simultaneously conveying both musical and verbal meanings.

From a semiotic point of view, the question in relation to the two semiotic systems of language and music is whether the similar expression substance of language and music embodies comparable types of meaning. In order to deal with this question, a conception of meaning broader than the traditional one is needed. In traditional semantics, meaning is largely equated with 'reference,' that is the relationship of expression to the external world. A useful approach for this purpose has been developed in the school of linguistics known as systemic functional linguistics (e.g. Halliday, 1978, 1994), whose major contribution to the understanding of meaning in language can be summarized in the concept of metafunction (Callaghan & McDonald, 2003). Metafunction refers to the different general functional types of meaning according to which linguistic patterns may be interpreted: ideational, construing a model of the world; interpersonal, enacting social relationships; and textual, creating relevance to context (Halliday, 1994). Such a notion has obvious relevance outside language, and more recently has been applied to other semiotic systems such as visual imagery and displayed art (Kress & van

Leeuwen, 1996; O'Toole, 1994) and music (van Leeuwen 1999; McDonald, 2011, 2012).

Skill acquisition and memory

'Skill is goal-directed, well-organized behaviour that is acquired through practice and performed with economy of effort' (Proctor & Dutta, 1995, p. 18). Skill acquisition and skilled performance involve perceptual, cognitive, and motor mechanisms. Once the sensorimotor skills of singing have been acquired, the cognitive demands required for that task are reduced, freeing mental resources for the tasks of musical and textual interpretation.

Fitts (1964; Fitts & Posner, 1967) identifies three phases of complex skill acquisition: cognitive, associative, and autonomous. In the cognitive phase, the learner employs cognitive processes in understanding the nature of the task and how it should be performed, and attending to outside cues, such as the pitch to be matched and the teacher's instructions and feedback. This is the phase typical of learning basic vocal skills. In the associative phase, inputs are linked more directly to appropriate actions, with less direction and feedback required. This is the phase typical of learning to bring vocal, musical, and linguistic skills together in singing connected phrases. When the task can be performed automatically, without conscious control, the autonomous phase has been reached and skilled music-making is possible.

Practice

There is now an accumulation of studies on how practice affects motor learning. Generally, the amount learnt increases with the amount of time devoted to practice, and distributed practice is more effective than massed practice (Baddeley, 1997). Practice needs to be deliberate: structured and goal-oriented. Results support the generalization that skills are best learnt when practised a little and often. In many studies blocked practice improved performance during acquisition but retarded long-term learning.

Pitts et al. (2000) found young instrumentalists used a complex range of practice strategies. They concluded that practice strategies need to be taught systematically by example and explanation. Practice needs to employ both routine procedures and musical experimentation, a combination of formal and informal practice.

An understanding of vocal and musical patterns allows smaller or simpler patterns to be learned first, followed by increasingly larger patterns. Given the patterned structure of musical performance tasks, this principle is important in learning vocal skills and in practising songs.

Important in the acquisition of vocal skills is how perception and movement are related and integrated. While it is clear that perception guides movement, there is also evidence that perception is influenced by the nature of the movements that the human motor system is capable of producing.

With practice, performance is improved as perceptual judgments are made faster and more accurately. Proctor & Dutta (1995) ascribe this to the learning of distinctive features and the possible 'unitisation' of features. This is an important finding for learning singing, where the learning of motor skills that bring together a cluster of musical features using functionally related muscle groups is essential for skilled performance (Callaghan, 1995).

Research shows that memory actually shapes experience and that the outcomes reflect changes in understanding (Davidson & Scripp, 1992). Long-term musical memory is influenced by a range of musical and technical concepts that allow the performer to retain an image of the shape of a piece and its kinaesthetic realization. Short-term memory, on the other hand, relies on chunking into small units. It is effective to partition the music in meaningful parts, based on its formal structure and the complexity of the technical or musical execution, with the more complex parts subject to more division than less complex parts (Lehmann & Jørgensen, 2012). It would be helpful to singers if music publishers were to change their practice to take into account that beaming musical notes into distinct metric patterns, as opposed to single flagged notation, assists comprehension and memory of whole structures.

A combination of physical and mental practice is most effective in improving skill acquisition. Ross (1985) points out that mental practice focuses the performer's attention on the cognitive aspects of music performance, with physical practice being required to improve motor skills. Given what is known about sub-vocalisation, mental practice may be even more effective for singers than for instrumentalists.

Rosenthal et al. (1988) compared listening, singing, and silent analysis as practice techniques for advanced instrumentalists. They found listening to a model alone (even without the opportunity for practice) about as effective as practising with the instrument. Coffman (1990) also found mental practice effective with less advanced piano students, although, for superior psychomotor skill improvement, physical practice was also necessary.

In a comparative study of guided model, model only, guide only, and practice only treatments on the accuracy of advanced instrumentalists' musical performance, Rosenthal (1984) found that subjects in the model only group performed better than those in all other groups, and those in the guided model group did better than those in the guide only and practice groups.

For these more advanced performers, direct modelling, without any added verbiage, was the most successful practice aid. It is likely that for less advanced students, providing a model within the lesson, with verbal explanation, would prepare the student for using the model in practice sessions.

Feedback

Feedback has been identified as an important element in learning a motor skill. For singers, feedback may come from either external or internal sources. External sources include the human response of auditors, and the feedback supplied by technology. Internal feedback – tactile, kinaesthetic, and proprioceptive – is supplied through sensory receptors located throughout the entire body. Auditory feedback, transmitted from the ear through the brain stem to the cerebral cortex, is also used as a control, allowing the singer to match the sound produced with the sound intended.

Feedback and technology

Technology now offers a wide range of external feedback to professional singers, teachers, and students of singing. Many students make digital sound or video recordings of their lessons. Such recordings can provide a valuable learning tool, so long as the information is interpreted in an informed way. Linklater (1997) found videotape models more useful than audiotape models as a practice tool, but suggests that students need musical discrimination skills to benefit from either type of model. Henley's results suggested that recorded audio models may well prove an effective way of guiding practice in the absence of an instructor (2001).

For less experienced students it is useful for singer and teacher to listen and dissect together, and then compare notes on what is working well and what not so well in order to devise better practice strategies. It can also be a good way for the teacher to link directions given during a lesson and the expected outcome.

For decades now computers have been widely employed as an adjunct for neuromuscular skills training in such areas as sports, speech pathology, and non-native language teaching, and more recently as an additional tool in the teaching of singing. Vocal sound can be displayed in a near real-time display which, if displayed in a meaningful way, can be an effective learning tool for singers (Wilson et al., 2008). We live in a very visually-oriented world, dominated by film, television, and computer displays, so it makes sense to use this form of communication in the teaching of singing.

While experienced musicians become very aurally and kinaesthetically oriented, beginner singers are predominantly visual learners. In using these tools it is important for the singer to be able to make aural and kinaesthetic sense of visual displays, to be able to relate what is seen to the vocal aesthetic appropriate for the genre and style being sung, and to be able to contextualize the information in the holistic act that is singing. Just how the visual displays are interpreted needs to be meaningful for the individual learning style of the singer (see Himonides, 2012). For that reason it is good for singer and teacher

to work together using the technology, and to use software that comes with an explanatory manual, such as *Voice Tradition and Technology* (Nair, 1999), *Your Voice: An Inside View* (McCoy, 2004), *Resonance in Singing* (Miller, 2008), or *How to Sing and See* (Callaghan & Wilson, 2010).

Learning a song

Learning a song requires the memory and physicalization of musical and verbal text. Studies in cognition suggest that this is assisted by pattern recognition, auditory memory, sub-vocal rehearsal, knowledge of results and knowledge of performance, and use of metaphor and modelling.

An understanding of vocal and musical patterns allows smaller or simpler patterns to be learned first, followed by increasingly larger patterns. Given the patterned structure of musical performance tasks, this principle is important in learning vocal skills and in practising songs.

In the development of singing skills, children begin with the words, then add the rhythm, and finally add the pitch. In vocal music, rhythm – and particularly the rhythm of word-setting – often proves easier to learn when separated from the pitch contours of a song. The overall topology comes before the detail, with pitch information being stored in contour schemes (Hargreaves & Zimmerman, 1992). Once known, melody and text seem to be remembered together (Serafine et al., 1986).

Shepard (1982) proposed pitch space as an important component of auditory imagery, accounting for the representation of melody and harmony in auditory images. In the Western tradition, memory for harmony is important in song-learning, as the harmonic context affects vocal timbre, and harmonic voice-leading may affect pitch. Memory for harmonic movement assists the learning of the sequence of phrases and assists in shaping the song.

The process of hearing, perceiving, and remembering sound forms a loop with the production of sound. In speaking and singing, the sounds being produced by the vocal mechanism are constantly being fed through this loop – the phonological loop – dictating what is produced by the vocal apparatus. The phonological loop is assumed to comprise two components: a phonological store that is capable of holding speech-based information; and an articulatory control process based on inner speech. While the phonological store is an aspect of short-term memory, the memory trace can be refreshed by a process of reading off the trace into the articulatory control process, which then feeds it back into the store, the process underlying sub-vocal rehearsal. As sub-vocal rehearsal assists the retention of sounds in a particular order, it is obviously important in learning a song.

Also important, at different stages, are knowledge of results and knowledge of performance. In providing knowledge of results, time needs to be allowed for intrinsic feedback to be processed before the teacher supplies feedback on the performance. Knowledge of results merely provides information on whether the performance was successful or not. Knowledge of performance, however, gives detailed information on what aspects of the movement contributed to successful performance, and directs the singer's attention to those aspects that are critical to performance.

In identifying modelling and metaphor as two approaches to performance teaching which develop cognitive skills and the links between them (Davidson & Scripp, 1992), research supports traditional practice. In both cases reflective thinking during and beyond the performance is used to enhance perceptual and performance skills.

Embodiment

> By profound meditation, the knower, the knowl-
> edge and the known become one. The seer, the sight
> and the seen have no separate existence from each
> other. It is like a great musician becoming one with
> his instrument and the music that comes from it.
>
> (Iyengar, 2001, p. 3)

Individually appropriate body alignment and integrated body use are essential for vocal mastery in any style. Body alignment influences breath management, and the two together affect lung volume, larynx height and tilt, and tracheal pull. All these influence the integrated function of phonation and resonance. Alignment of the head is particularly important, as it affects all postural reflexes (Callaghan et al., 2012, p. 561).

There are many systems of integrated body use that may optimize vocal function. Currently, Alexander Technique (Alexander, 1910, 1923), Feldenkrais Method (Feldenkrais, 1949), yoga (Iyengar, 2001) and Pilates (Pilates, 1934; Pilates & Miller, 1945) are commonly used. While their emphases and methodology may differ, what these body-use approaches have in common is changing habitual use through conscious mental control and retraining of the kinaesthetic sense. Through vertical alignment of the spine, alignment of the head, activation of the abdominal and pelvic floor muscles, release and widening of the ribcage, a holistic connection of mind and body is achieved. This facilitates the integrated working of brain, breath, and emotion basic to vocal communication.

Many pedagogies refer to Alexander Technique as the template for conscious creation of upright body use. In addition to fostering optimal vertical alignment, the release and widening of the ribcage afforded by Alexander principles is beneficial for projected voice. The Alexander Technique aims to retrain movement and postural habits to decrease compression stress and increase ease of movement (Hudson, 2002a, p. 9). Alexander Technique emphasizes 'forward and up' head movement, which implies lengthening the spine and widening the back. Alexander used a method of projecting mental directions as a way to change habitual responses to stimuli. He aimed to create a method of consciously inhibiting undesirable responses and replacing them with more appropriate and productive ones (Hudson, 2002a, p. 10). Alexander was always concerned about breathing and emphasized coordinated use of the whole body.

Using mental directions to let the neck muscles release, the head move forward and up and the torso lengthen and widen improves the coordinated use of the body's postural and respiratory mechanisms. It helps the singer develop a more efficient relationship with gravity. Alexander reinforced these mental directions with manual guidance. The combination of these two strategies helps performers replace inefficient actions with new more efficient ones and develop mental representations that facilitate efficient movement (Hudson, 2002a, pp. 12-14).

Alexander's concept of Primary Control emphasized the use of the head and neck in relation to the rest of the body, providing an integrating force allowing freedom of movement throughout the system. For singers this primary control allows free control of the laryngeal muscles and breathing mechanism (Hudson, 2002a, p. 12). With Primary Control breathing becomes 'a wavelike movement from top to bottom, both on inhalation and exhalation' (Hudson, 2002a, p. 15). The spine gathers on inhalation and lengthens on exhalation. Spinal movement adds a dynamic to the respiratory act that allows the natural movement and function of the structure of respiration to occur without added effort. Hudson points out that many singers have a false brain map of this movement and 'any mismapped use of the spine and torso can produce a compromise in the efficiency and coordination of the body's holistic response to the respiratory impulse' (2002a, p. 15).

Hudson criticizes the concept of posture taught by some vocal pedagogues as implying putting the body in a position and maintaining that position (2002b, p. 107). She sees the body use created by Primary Control and the upright reflexes 'differing from that of the singer's noble posture in that when the head finds its balance on top of the spine and the spine is allowed to lengthen, the pelvis and legs release in the opposite direction from the head' (2002b, p. 106). This seems to me a misunderstanding of that historic term 'noble posture' oft advocated by Richard Miller (1986, pp. 30, 32, 153), who also states that 'The two poles of bel canto are the ability to move and the ability to sustain the voice. A successful breath-management system cannot be constructed on rigidity' (Miller, 2004, p. 12).

The Feldenkrais Method emphasizes the development of kinaesthetic awareness. While most teachers aim to guide students to associate certain sensations with a free, expressive sound, often the approach to achieving this is to use particular physical manoeuvres. Unfortunately, the singer's brain may not respond to conscious, analytical commands to change. 'The Feldenkrais Method uses the body's neurological language to break down those subtle barriers, resulting in almost magical adjustment that truly frees the singer and the voice' (Blades-Zeller & Nelson, 2002, p. 33).

The Feldenkrais Method aims to produce an individual 'organized to perform with minimum effort and maximum efficiency' (Blades-Zeller & Nelson, 2002, p. 34). Like Alexander Technique, Feldenkrais Method comprises two components: guided group movement lessons called Awareness Through Movement and individual hands-on sessions with a practitioner called Functional Integration. There are sequences addressing such movements as sitting, breathing, and so on, with students focused on discovering a more efficient way to perform everyday movements. As in Alexander Technique, the idea is that students learn through doing, the discovery involving 'the part of the nervous system that controls movement, as opposed to conceptual consciousness, "thinking."' Thus, 'changes tend to be retained and often amplified' (Blades-Zeller & Nelson, p. 34).

The Feldenkrais Method focuses on: (1) life as a process; (2) effective movement involving the whole self; (3) learning as a key activity; (4) the necessity of choice; and (5) the logic of human development (Blades-Zeller, & Nelson, p. 35). Feldenkrais wrote of ingrained faulty functioning that is learnt early in life and then becomes an inherent characteristic of the person. For this to change 'the nervous paths producing the undesirable pattern of motility' need to be 'undone and reshuffled into a better configuration' (Feldenkrais, 1949, p. 40). He emphasized the necessity to imagine another way of being and doing – developing kinaesthetic awareness and accurate kinaesthetic imagery. This is an essential aspect of singing: the relationship between the kinaesthetic sense, effort, and good sound (Nelson & Blades, 2005, p. 145).

Feldenkrais addresses the importance of the alignment and support of the pelvis in achieving full vocal potential, since the spine has its base in the pelvic girdle, and the ribs hang off the spine (Nelson & Blades, 2005, p. 153).

The Pilates Method of body conditioning was developed by Joseph Pilates beginning during the First World War and continuing until his death in 1967. His system contains stretching and strengthening exercises performed either on a mat or using various types of apparatus. Pilates work aims to improve posture and improve balance. Pilates-inspired work emphasizes strengthening of the 'box,' 'core,' or 'powerhouse.' The box is the pelvis and trunk: the abdominal muscles in the front, the paraspinals and gluteals in the back, the diaphragm as the roof, and the pelvic floor and hip girdle musculature as the bottom (Johnson et al., 2007, p. 129). The core, or powerhouse, extends from the pelvic floor inferiorly to the ribcage superiorly – the centre of the body (Muscolino & Cipriani, 2004, p. 17). Strengthening postural muscles such as the transverse abdominis and internal and external oblique muscles provide core stability and core control (Johnson et al., 2007; Critchley, et al., 2011), which are essential to singing. The aim is to work the muscles and joints of the pelvis and lumbar spine, not only in static posture, but also in dynamic strength and flexibility (Muscolino & Cipriani, 2004, p. 24).

As with Alexander Technique and Feldenkrais Method, Pilates' Contrology is concerned not just with strengthening the body, but is also a 'balanced regimen for strengthening and conditioning the mind as well' (Muscolino & Cipriani, 2004). The six key principles of Contrology are: centring, concentration, control, precision, breath, and flow – all essential to singing. Pilates called Contrology a 'complete coordination of body, mind, and spirit' (Lange et al., 2000).

Pilates was influenced by many movement systems including hatha yoga, gymnastics, physical therapy, and somatics. Throughout his career he worked with athletes and with modern dance professionals such as George Balanchine and Martha Graham. 'Pilates training opens the back portion of the ribs and develops awareness and strength in that part of the body' (Melton, 2001, p. 14). It was perhaps Pilates' work with dancers that caused him to emphasize closing the ribs and centring the breath in the chest, with no abdominal release and anterior expansion of the lower ribs discouraged. Contemporary practitioners do not necessarily follow these directions.

While in the last few decades various versions of yoga have in the West been adopted as exercise regimes, 'yoga is one of the six orthodox systems of Indian philosophy,' that teaches the means by which the individual spirit can be united with the Supreme Universal Spirit, and so secure liberation (Iyengar, 1991, p. 1). Borg-Olivier and Machliss (2011, p. 20) point out that there are many types of yoga and each type of yoga has many styles. However, whatever the type, yoga addresses both the physical and the mental and unity of the two. Physical yoga concerns body exercises (asana) and breath control (pranayama). The mental aspects concern ethical disciplines and meditative practices.

The practices of yoga address every facet of the whole person in a way that can facilitate the holistic music-making that is singing. Iyengar describes yoga as 'a timeless pragmatic science evolved over thousands of years dealing with the physical, moral, mental and spiritual well-being of man as a whole' (2001, Preface). In its translation into Western cultures and English language, yoga has been defined in many different ways. Carman lists three:

- yoga as the movement from one level to a higher level;
- yoga as the bringing together, the unifying of two or more things; and
- yoga as action with undivided, uninterrupted attention (2012, p. 3).

The integrated practice that is yoga is similar to the integrated practice that is singing: 'both yoga and singing are grounded in the breath, in its extension and control, and in its flexible use' (Carman, 2004, p. 435). The asanas (physical postures) of yoga help with body alignment, strength and flexibility, and overall co-ordination. Pranayama (breathing exercises) build command of the breath, the ability to use the breath as a focus of concentration, and the control of energy. Humming and chanting assist with the connection of breath to phonation and resonance. The concentration practices of pratyahara and dharana focus the mind and the meditation practices of dhyana and samadhi develop the ability to let go of old thought patterns and form new habits (Carman, 2004, 2012).

The role of the teacher

The ultimate role of the teacher is as facilitator. Singing is a means of expression and communication: it requires psychomotor skills that embody musical and linguistic meanings and the mind to direct these skills. The teacher needs to be able to enable the student to acquire the particular physical skills involved in breath management, phonation, resonance, and registration. The teacher needs to know how vocal health and stamina are developed and maintained and be able to communicate that knowledge to the student. But of paramount importance is the ability to enable students of different backgrounds, experience, education, age, and physicality to build the mental skills that will allow them to make singing a holistic means of communication, the voice of the mind. These issues of teaching and learning are examined in Chapter 9.

References

Alexander, F.M. (1910). *Man's Supreme Inheritance*. New York, NY: E.P. Dutton.

Alexander, F.M. (1923). *Constructive Conscious Control of the Individual*. London: Methuen.

Baddeley, A. (1997). *Human Memory: Theory and Practice* (rev. edn.). Hove, UK: Psychology Press.

Barthes, R. (1977). *Image, Music, Text* (S. Heath, trans.). New York, NY: Hill and Wang.

Blades-Zeller, E. & Nelson, S. (2002). Relating the Feldenkrais Method to teaching of singing: an introduction. *Australian Voice*, *8*, 33–40.

Borg-Olivier, S. & Machliss, B. (2011). *Applied Anatomy and Physiology of Yoga*. Sydney: Yoga Synergy.

Burrows, D. (1990). *Sound, Speech and Music*. Amherst, MA: University of Massachusetts Press.

Callaghan, J. (1995). Fundamental teaching units: building blocks of vocal pedagogy. *Australian Voice*, *1*, 1–5.

Callaghan, J. (2002). Learning to sing. In C. Stevens et al. (eds.), *Proceedings of the 7th International Conference on Music Perception and Cognition*, Sydney, 2002, pp. 744–47.

Callaghan, J., Emmons, S. & Popeil, L. (2012). Solo voice pedagogy. In G. E. McPherson and G. F. Welch (eds.), *The Oxford Handbook of Music Education*, Vol. I (pp. 559–80). New York, NY: Oxford University Press.

Callaghan, J. & McDonald, E. (2003). The singer's text: music, language and the expression of meaning. *Australian Voice*, *9*, 42–48.

Callaghan, J. & Wilson, P. (2010). *How to Sing and See: Singing Pedagogy in the Digital Era*. Sydney: Cantare Systems.

Campbell, W. & Heller, J. (1980). An orientation for considering models of musical behavior. In D. Hodges (ed.), *Handbook of Music Psychology* (pp. 29–36). Lawrence, KS: National Association for Music Therapy.

Campbell, W. & Heller, J. (1981). Psychomusicology and psycholinguistics: parallel paths or separate ways? *Psychomusicology*, *1*(2), 3–14.

Carman, J. E. (2004). Yoga and singing: natural partners. *Journal of Singing*, *60*(5), 433–41.

Carman, J. E. (2012). *Yoga for Singing. A Developmental Tool for Technique & Performance*. New York, NY: Oxford University Press.

Chomsky, N. (1965). *Aspects of the Theory of Syntax*. Cambridge, MA: MIT Press.

Chomsky, N. (1975). *Reflections on Language*. New York, NY: Pantheon.

Coffman, D. D. (1990). Effects of mental practice, physical practice and knowledge of results on piano performance. *Journal of Research in Music Education*, *38*(3), 187–96. doi:10.2307/3345182

Critchley, D. J., Pierson, Z. & Batterxby, G. (2011). Effect of pilates mat exercises and conventional exercise programmes on transversus abdominis and obliquus abdominis activity: pilot randomised trial. *Manual Therapy*, *16*(2) 183–89. doi: 10.1016/j.math.2010.10.007

Crowder, R. G. (1989). Imagery for musical timbre. *Journal of Experimental Psychology*, *15*(3), 472–78. 10.1037/0096-1523.15.3.472

Damasio, A. (2000). *The Feeling of What Happens: Body, Emotion and the Making of Consciousness*. London: Vintage.

Damasio, A. (2002). How the brain creates the mind. *Scientific American: The Hidden Mind*, *12*(1), 4–9.

Davidson, J. W. & Correia, J. S. (2001). Meaningful musical performance: a bodily experience. *Research Studies in Music Education*, *17*(1), 70–83. doi:10.1177/1321103X010170011301

Davidson, L. & Scripp, L. (1992). Surveying the co-ordinates of cognitive skills in music. In R. Colwell (ed.), *Handbook of Research on Music Teaching and Learning*, pp. 392–413. New York, NY: Schirmer Books.

Deacon, T. W. (1997). *The Symbolic Species: The Co-evolution of Language and the Brain*. Harmondsworth: Penguin.

Eco, U. (1976). *A Theory of Semiotics*. Bloomington, IN: Indiana University Press.

Feldenkrais, M. (1949). *Body and Mature Behavior: A Study of Anxiety, Sex, Gravitation and Learning*. New York, NY: International Universities Press.

Fiske, H. (1992). Structure of cognition and music decision-making. In R. Colwell (ed.), *Handbook of Research on Music Teaching and Learning* (pp. 360–76). New York, NY: Schirmer Books.

Fitts, P.M. (1964). Perceptual-motor skill learning. In A.W. Melton (ed.), *Categories of Human Learning* (pp. 243–85). New York, NY: Academic Press.

Fitts, P.M. & Posner, M.I. (1967). *Human Performance*. Belmont, CA: Brooks/Cole.

Gardner, H. (1993). *Multiple Intelligences: The Theory into Practice*. New York, NY: Basic Books.

Gardner, H. (2004). *Changing Minds: The Art and Science of Changing Our Own and Other People's Minds*. Boston, MA: Harvard Business School Press.

Gruhn, W. (1997). Music learning: neurobiological foundations and educational implications. *Research Studies in Music Education*, *9*(1), 36–47. doi:10.1177/1321103X9700900105

Halliday, M.A.K. (1978). *Language as Social Semiotic*. London: Edward Arnold.

Halliday, M.A.K. (1994). *An Introduction to Functional Grammar* (2nd edn.). London: Edward Arnold.

Hargreaves. D.J. & Zimmerman, M.P. (1992). Developmental theories of music learning. In R. Colwell (ed.), *Handbook of Research on Music Teaching and Learning* (pp. 377–91). New York, NY: Schirmer Books.

Heller, J. & Campbell, W. (1976). Models of language and intellect in music research. In A. Motycka (ed.), *Music Education for Tomorrow's Society* (pp. 149–80). Jamestown, VA: GAMT Music Press.

Heller, J. & Campbell, W. (1982). Music communication and cognition. *Bulletin of the Council for Research in Music Education*, *7*, 1–15.

Henley, P.T. (2001). Effects of modeling and tempo patterns as practice techniques on the performance of high school instrumentalists. *Journal of Research in Music Education*, *49*(2), 169–80. doi:10.2307/3345868

Herbert-Cesari, E. (1963). *The Voice of the Mind* (2nd edn.). London: Lowe and Brydone.

Himonides, E. (2012). The misunderstanding of music-technology-education: A meta perspective. In G.E. McPherson & G.F. Welch (eds.), *The Oxford Handbook of Music Education*, Vol. 2 (pp. 433–56). New York, NY: Oxford University Press.

Hodges, D. & Gruhn, W. (2012). Implications of neurosciences and brain research for music teaching and learning. In G.E. McPherson and G.F. Welch (eds.), *The Oxford Handbook of Music Education*, Vol. 1 (pp. 205–23). New York, NY: Oxford University Press.

Hudson, B. (2002a). The effects of the Alexander Technique on the respiratory system of the singer/actor, Part I: F.M. Alexander and concepts of his technique that affect respiration in singer/actors. *Journal of Singing*, *59*(1), 9–17.

Hudson, B. (2002b). The effects of the Alexander Technique on the respiratory system of the singer/actor, Part II: Implications for training respiration in singer/actors based on concepts of the Alexander Technique. *Journal of Singing*, *59*(2), 105–10.

Iyengar, B.K. S. (2001). *Light on Yoga*. London: Thorsons.

Jackendoff, R. (1987). *Consciousness and the Computational Mind*. Cambridge, MA: MIT Press/Bradford.

Jackendoff, R. (1993). *Patterns in the Mind: Language and Human Nature*. New York, NY: Harvester/Wheatsheaf.

Johnson, M. (1987). *The Body in the Mind: The Bodily Basis of Meaning, Imagination, and Reason*. Chicago, IL: The University of Chicago Press.

Johnson, E.G., Larsen, A., Ozawa, H., Wilson, C.A., Kennedy, K.L. (2007). The effects of Pilates-based exercise on dynamic balance in healthy adults. *Journal of Bodywork and Movement Therapies*, *11*(3), 238–42. doi:10.1016/j.jbmt.2006.08.008

Kolb, D.A. (1984). *Experiential Learning: Experience as the Source of Learning and Development*. Englewood Cliffs, NJ: Prentice-Hall.

Kress, G. & van Leeuwen, T. (1996). *Reading Images: The Grammar of Visual Design*. Geelong, Australia: Deakin University Press.

Lange, C., Unnithan, V., Larkam, E. & Latta, P.M. (2000). Maximizing the benefits of Pilates-inspired exercise for learning functional motor skills. *Journal of Bodywork and Movement Therapies*, *4*(2), 99–108. doi:10.1054/jbmt.1999.0161

Lazear, D. (1991). *Seven Ways of Knowing: Teaching for Multiple Intelligences*. Palatine, IL: IRI/Skylight Publishing, Inc.

Lehmann, A.C. & Jørgensen, H. (2012). Practice. In G.E. McPherson & G.F. Welch (eds.), *The Oxford Handbook of Music Education*, Vol. 1 (pp. 677–93). New York, NY: Oxford University Press.

Lerdahl, F. & Jackendoff, R. (1983). *A Generative Theory of Tonal Music*. Cambridge, MA: MIT Press.

Linklater, F. (1997). Effects of audio- and videotape models on the performance achievement of beginning clarinetists. *Journal of Research in Music Education*, *45*(3), 402–14. doi:10.2307/3345535

McCoy, S. (2004). *Your Voice: An Inside View*. Princeton, NJ: Inside View Press.

McDonald, E. (2005). Through a glass darkly: a critique of the influence of linguistics on theories of music. *Linguistics and the Human Sciences*, *1*(3), 463–88.

McDonald, E. (2011). Dealing with musical meaning: towards an embodied model of music. In D. Shoshana, S. Hood & M. Stenglin (eds.), *Semiotic Margins: Reclaiming Meaning*, 101–23. London: Continuum.

McDonald, E. (2012). Embodiment and meaning: moving beyond linguistic imperialism in social semiotics. *Social Semiotics*, *23*(3), 318–34. doi:10.1080/10350330.2012.719730

Melton, J. (2001). Pilates training and the actor/singer. *Australian Voice*, *7*, 13–15.

Miller, D.G. (2008). *Resonance in Singing*. Princeton, NJ: Inside View Press.

Miller, R. (1986). *The Structure of Singing: System and Art in Vocal Technique.* New York, NY: Schirmer Books.

Miller, R. (2004). *Solutions for Singers: Tools for Performers and Teachers.* New York, NY: Oxford University Press.

Muscolino, J. E. & Cipriani, S. (2004). Pilates and the 'powerhouse' – I. *Journal of Bodywork and Movement Therapies, 8*(1), 15–24. doi:10.1016/S1360-8592(03)00057-3

Nair, G. (1999). *Voice Tradition and Technology: A State-of-the-Art Studio.* San Diego, CA: Singular Publishing Group.

Nattiez, J.-J. (1973). Linguistics: a new approach for musical analysis? *International Review of the Aesthetics and Sociology of Music, 4*(1): 51–68.

Nattiez, J.-J. (1990). *Music and Discourse: Towards a Semiology of Music.* Princeton, NJ: Princeton University Press.

Nelson, S. & Blades, E. (2005). Singing with your whole self: the Feldenkrais Method and voice. *Journal of Singing, 62*(2), 145–57.

O'Toole, M. (1994). *The Language of Displayed Art.* London: Leicester University Press.

Patel, A.D. (2003). Language, music, syntax and the brain. *Nature Neuroscience, 6*(7), 674–81. doi:10.1038/nn1082

Patel, A.D. (2008). *Music, Language, and the Brain.* New York, NY: Oxford University Press.

Pilates, J.H. (1934). *Your Health.* Incline Village, NV: Presentation Dynamics.

Pilates, J.H. & Miller, W. (1945). *Pilates' Return to Life Through Contrology.* Incline Village, NV: Presentation Dynamics.

Pitts, S., Davidson, J. & McPherson, G. (2000). Developing effective practise strategies: case studies of three young instrumentalists. *Music Education Research, 2*(1), 45–56. doi:0.1080/14613800050004422

Proctor, R.W. & Dutta, A. (1995). *Skill Acquisition and Human Performance.* Thousand Oaks, CA: Sage Publications.

Rosenthal, R.K. (1984). The relative effects of guided model, model only, guide only and practice only treatments on the accuracy of advanced instrumentalists' musical performance. *Journal of Research in Music Education, 32*(4), 265–74. doi:10.2307/3344924

Rosenthal, R.K., Wilson, M., Evans, M. & Greenwalt, L. (1988). Effects of different practice conditions on advanced instrumentalists' performance accuracy. *Journal of Research in Music Education, 36*(4), 250–57. doi:10.2307/3344877

Ross, S.L. (1985). The effectiveness of mental practice in improving the performance of college trombonists. *Journal of Research in Music Education, 33*(4), 221–31. doi:10.2307/3345249

Ruwet, N. (1967). Musicology and linguistics. *International Social Science Journal, 19*(1), 79–87.

Ruwet, N. (1972). *Langage, musique, poésie.* Paris: Le Seuil.

Saussure, E. de (1959). *Course in General Linguistics* (W. Baskin, trans.). London: Peter Owen. (Original work published in 1916.)

Serafine, M.L. (1988). *Music as Cognition: The Development of Thought in Sound*. New York, NY: Columbia University Press.

Serafine, M.L., Davidson, J., Crowder, R.G. & Repp, B.H. (1986). On the nature of melody-text integration in memory for songs. *Journal of Memory and Language*, *25*(2), 123–35. doi:10.1016/0749-596X(86)90025-2

Shepard, R.N. (1982). Geometric approximations to the structure of musical pitch. *Psychological Review*, 89(4), 305–33. doi:10.1037/0033-295X.89.4.305

Swain, J.P. (1997). *Musical Languages*. New York, NY: Norton.

Tomatis, A.A. (1991). *The Conscious Ear: My Life of Transformation through Listening* (S. Lushington, trans., B.M. Thompson, ed.). New York, NY: Station Hill Press.

van Leeuwen, T. (1999). *Speech, Music, Sound*. London: Macmillan.

Wilson, P., Lee, K., Callaghan, J. & Thorpe, W. (2008). Learning to sing in tune: does real-time visual feedback help? *Journal of Interdisciplinary Music Studies*, *2*(1–2), 157–72.

Zuckerkandl, V. (1956). *Sound and Symbol: Music and the External World*. Princeton, NJ: Princeton University Press.

Chapter 9: Teaching and Learning

Your body is not just a vehicle for your brain to cruise around in.

(Blakeslee & Blakeslee, 2007, p. 12)

Feeling is an inseparable part of everything that happens in the conscious life of the psychophysical organism. One of the most important aspects of this is the relation of feeling to cognition.

(Reid, 1986, p. 18)

Research neither destroys the magic of music nor trivialises educational transactions.

(Swanwick, 1994, p. 71)

Singing as brain maps

Blakeslee and Blakeslee's 2007 book, *The Body Has a Mind of Its Own*, examines the science emerging on how mind and body are connected in producing the embodied, feeling self. Blakeslee and Blakeslee define a map as 'any scheme that spells out one-to-one correspondences between two different things' (2007, p. 7) and point out that 'aspects of the outside world and the body's anatomy are systematically mapped onto brain tissue' (pp. 7–8).

This mapping is a reciprocal activity, with meaning 'rooted in agency (the ability to act and choose) and agency depending on embodiment . . . In real life there is no such thing as a disembodied consciousness' (p. 12). The brain maps the body's surface, its musculature, its intentions, and its actions, building a body schema through the interaction of touch, vision, proprioception, balance and hearing. The capacity of the brain to change, adapt, and reorganize these maps means that physical practice increases the size of the brain map involved in the new physical skill and the body schema can be changed. The action of singing, in terms of vocalizing, is thus a realization of a body schema in the brain.

The singer possesses mental representations consisting of both content and form or format, with different people finding some forms easier to decode than others, and being better persuaded by different factors (Gardner, 2004). This is an essential link to multiple intelligences and a vital aspect of teaching and learning. Changing mind means changing mental representations. And because mental representations can be combined in many ways, there is the potential for an almost limitless range of changes. Changing mental representations results in changed behaviour, i.e. learning.

Teaching, learning, and mind change

Howard Gardner, in *Changing Minds* (2004), built on his knowledge of neurology and cognitive psychology, and his previous publications on multiple intelligences (first edition 1983; second edition 1993), to address the issue of how minds are changed: one's own and those of other people. Learning to sing is changing one's own mind; teaching singing is changing the minds of others and, perhaps in the process, changing one's own mind. This, of course, implies changing behaviour, which in turn involves changing mental representations, related to what other authors call brain maps.

Gardner brings together a wide range of factors in a comprehensive model of mind changing, socially contextualised, that serves well as a model of teaching and learning. He identifies '(1) the various agents and agencies of mind change, (2) the tools that they have at their disposal, and (3) the seven factors that help to determine whether they succeed in changing minds' (Gardner, 2004, p. 5).

A teacher wanting to convey information to a student needs to try different formats to address the intelligences of the student. This could mean trying words, numbers, bulleted lists, graphs, drawings, etc. Then there are the different factors (levers) that may be involved in mind changing – reason, research, resonance, representational redescriptions, resources and rewards, real world events, and resistance (Gardner, 2004, pp. 14-18). These are the factors involved in motivating a student to effect a change.

While reason and research may be important, my teaching experience suggests that for the majority of singers resonance and representational redescriptions are even more important, as is overcoming resistance. Reason and research appeal to the logical mind; resonance has to do with emotion. The idea or perspective needs to appeal to the singer's point of view and feel right to the singer. Employing rhetoric that draws on other factors, such as reason and research, and representing the idea in a number of different forms is likely to make the idea feel right and help overcome resistance. The older the singer, the more entrenched the habits of mind that resist change. Change is easier when an individual is in a new environment (a new job, a new life partner), and surrounded by peers of a different persuasion. Gardner identifies different agents and institutions that may change minds, from large-scale changes involving the diverse population of a region or an entire nation, to changing one's own mind (Gardner, 2004, p. 63). For singing, most likely are 'changes brought about through works of art or science,' 'changes within formal instructional settings,' 'intimate forms of mind changing,' and 'changing one's own mind.' Early in the process, hearing an amazing singer, attending a brilliant opera production, or reading a book on singing may open a whole new brain space for a learner singer. Singers studying within the formal setting of a university or conservatoire may well be influenced by their studies in other subjects, by their fellow students, by their teachers, and by the overall culture of the institution. But within those formal settings, resistances may be very strong if new theories are introduced.

In singing, the teacher in the one-to-one setting of the studio is the agent of an intimate form of mind changing (teaching), and students, both within that setting, but also in their practice, performance, and observation of others, are the agents in changing their own mind (learning). Singers need to be lifelong learners able to change the content of their own minds in response to changes in the different domains relevant to what they do. In order to learn, one must be able to change one's own mind, which requires sufficient self-knowledge to understand how one's own mind works: 'It is important to know as much as one can about one's own mind, one's own learning proclivities and quirks, and to seize on these in finding the optimal "pedagogy" and "curriculum" for one's own idiosyncratic array of intelligences and stupidities' (Gardner, 2004, p. 148).

Since teachers need to be learning all they can about individual students, in order to address their particular intelligences, their particular modes of learning, and their favoured mental representations, this is a complementary endeavour. Gardner identifies several crucial dimensions that are relevant to the mind-changing that is teaching singing. These include:

- identifying the current content (idea, concept, story, theory, skill) and the desired content, in order to deal with competing counter-contents; and
- employing levers of change and tipping points appropriate to the particular student (2004, pp. 209-211).

Transferring technical and musical skills into performance

In skill-based behaviour, integrated patterns of behaviour produce smooth, automated performance (Smith et al., 1992). This is the level of skill required for expert singing performance. In learning vocal skills that can be employed in performance, it is important to distinguish between factors that produce temporary changes in performance and those that produce the relatively permanent changes that comprise learning. For the clusters of vocal skills and chunks of musical patterns to become elements of a learned skill, sequence learning is necessary. In singing, this sequence is usually triggered by implicit memory and auditory imagery as the breath for each phrase is taken. Each phrase is cued in that way and linked to other phrases by the mental image of the overall shape of the musical structure.

While schedules of practice and extrinsic feedback have been shown to aid the acquisition of motor skills, for long-term learning the performer needs to rely on intrinsic feedback. That is, singers need to be skilled enough to rely on their own auditory image of, and sensory feedback on, the vocal sound they are producing, as the performance situation may well not provide any extrinsic feedback.

For a singer to be able to perform well in a multiple-task context (such as singing in a foreign language while moving on stage, managing costume and props, watching a conductor, and interrelating with other singers) depends on the level of skill attained in each component task and the relative amount of attention each requires. The ability to multitask is a skill that develops with practice in multiple-task contexts and that is assisted by automaticity in one or more of the tasks. Eventually, correlations among multiple cues are learned in many situations, with performance enhanced as a consequence.

The singer's text and the expression of meaning

The link between meaning in language and meaning in music is the body. And the embodiment of these meanings comes through voice, the singer's instrument.

Voice is always about the body, in that vocal sound is produced by body movement. The sound of a human body producing music is a sensual, perhaps even sexual, experience for the listener. Auditors respond to what Barthes called the 'grain of the voice': 'The "grain" is the body in the voice as it sings . . . I am determined to listen to my relation with the body of the man or woman singing or playing and that relation is erotic' (Barthes, 1977, p. 188).

Two researchers who have recently evolved sophisticated theories of meaning related to language and music are David Burrows in *Sound, Speech, and Music* (1990) and Horst Ruthrof in *The Body in Language* (2000). Burrows states as his aim 'to consider what influence the specific character of the means, in the case of sound, may have had on the form taken by its ends of communication in man; and what the consequences for man's nature may have been of adapting to sound's unique potential for communication' (1990, pp. 3-4). His approach is based on the phenomenology of sound, speech, thought, and music and characterizes the individual, living human body as a centre with a strong tendency to treat everything else as peripheral to it. This centre/periphery scheme is projected in three basic fields. Field 1 is physical space; Field 2 is the invisible and intangible space where thought takes place; Field 3 is the field of the spirit – the sense of self as diffused through the full range of awareness.

His argument is that 'the chief vehicle of thought is speech, and of speech, sound' and therefore 'sound is far more to speech than a passive conveyance' (p. 9). It is, rather, the means through which human thought has evolved, exploiting 'the unique capacity of vocal sound for rapidity of articulation in detachment from the world of enduring spatial objects' (p. 9). Through an examination of sound, voice, and words Burrows develops a complex and convincing theory of thought, expression, and meaning. As he says, sound is like the self and 'by means of the articulated sound of speech we can hear each other think' (p. 54). Burrows suggests that the Cartesian duality of mind and matter is more a duality of degrees of manipulability running from ideas to things, with the greater manipulability of ideas a function of the ease with which sound can be articulated.

Like Burrows, in *The Body in Language* (2000) Ruthrof is concerned with what it is about language that allows it to process non-linguistic material so successfully. He proposes two possibilities: either language is a highly abstract or even formal system capable of subsuming anything and everything in a certain generalized way; or, since the body and other forms of materiality are graspable via language, linguistic meaning must already have some kind of corporeality. It is the latter proposition which is argued in *The Body in Language*, an investigation of the role played by the body in meaning events. Thus, like Burrows, he takes a phenomenological approach.

The body is always already 'part of language as discourse' (p. vi). It is present in discourse in the form of non-linguistic signs – olfactory, tactile, gustatory, aural, visual, and other non-verbal readings of the world. Ruthrof maintains that when we learn a language as part of a community, we are guided to systemically link the sounds of language expressions with non-verbal signs. While criticizing most traditional theories of language for their failure to accommodate mental projections of the world, Ruthrof acknowledges that cognitive science is beginning to address issues of the body, but in visual ways: 'cognitive science appears to be offering a new corporeal turn . . . [it is] not yet able to address the body in its entirety but favours its visual mechanisms' (p. 17). He argues that language as a mere sequence of signifiers cannot mean. 'We have to add something to make language mean. This additional ingredient [the body] moves language from the level of signifiers to that of signifieds, from the plane of syntax to that of semantics' (p. 30): 'nonverbal signs are the deep structure of language' (p. 34), with the verbal being dependent at least in certain respects on the perceptual and its imaginative variations. Signs are modified by perception, which in turn enriches language with non-verbal modifications.

Mark Johnson is another author who, in *The Body in the Mind* (1987), takes issue with the propositional nature of language and proposes analogue reasoning grounded in imagination. He sees meaning as arising from understanding, imagination, and embodiment.

This is the singer's text: meaning grounded in the body, expressed through the body.

Dealing with performance anxiety

Performers and sports people speak of 'performing in the zone,' 'flow,' or 'peak performance' (Davidson & Correia, 2001; Gorrie, 2009; Kenny, 2011; Wrigley, 1999). This is the experience where mind, body, emotion, and soul merge as one in the activity. A flow experience comes out of tackling a challenging activity requiring a degree of skill that has been learned, that is perceived as joyful and important, that has a definite goal or purpose, that is totally self-absorbing, that requires such control that self-consciousness disappears, and that is in itself rewarding. For singers this means having made the detailed cognitive, physical, and emotional preparation so that in performance they can totally immerse themselves in the activity.

When these preparations have not been done, performance anxiety may result. Dealing with that requires mind change, since it is the singer's thoughts and predictions that cause the physical symptoms of anxiety (Desberg & Marsh, 1988), that are the physiological realizations of the fight-or-flight response. These may include: muscle tension, shaking, increased heart rate, high, rapid breathing, sweating, hot or cold flushes, nausea, or dry mouth. For any performer these symptoms militate against a good performance; for singers, such problems as high, rapid breathing and dry mouth are disastrous.

The mental symptoms of performance anxiety may include negative thoughts, distraction, a feeling of impending doom, memory blanks, or a feeling of panic (Roland, 1997, p. 4). Singers feeling anxious about a performance may mentally create 'threats' such as overestimating the consequences of potential failure or underestimating their ability to cope with the demands of the performance (Roland, 1997, p. 9). The mental symptoms then trigger behavioural and physiological responses. Managing both physical and mental symptoms involves mind change, requiring self-knowledge, self-monitoring, and the ability to change mental representations.

Gorrie identifies four variables involved in this: cognitive attributes, physical attributes, external interference, and performance arousal (2009, p. 25). He identifies cognitive attributes as 'performance intelligence' or the knowledge the performer has about the material and the field of performance, and physical attributes as the physical capacity to carry out that performance intelligence, and performance arousal as the state of mind before and/or during performance. It could be argued that those three variables are all cognitive in nature. Traditional studio teaching most often gives great emphasis to the 'performance intelligence' aspects (knowing the music, performance style, etc.) and the physical attributes (technique). And these are well within the control of the singer.

External interference is rarely mentioned, but knowing that such interference is a possibility can in itself help control anxiety. For example, an opera audition may involve singing on a stage occupied by the set of the current production, with people moving around the auditorium. These factors are outside the singer's control, but merely knowing that they are quite normal in the situation is reassuring.

Performance arousal is the cognitive attribute most involved in performance anxiety. While some arousal may be beneficial to performance, the negative arousal of fear is not. The most complex part of the equation is the appropriateness of performance arousal, which Gorrie labels 'the variable which governs whether you perform in The Zone or not' (2009, p. 26). Some anxiety may increase the singer's ability to perform simple tasks better and more quickly, up to a tipping point. If anxiety goes beyond this point, the performance becomes worse (Roland, 1997, p. 6). The essential difference between a positive performance experience and a negative performance experience is the singer's focus: in a positive experience the singer is self-focused, in a negative experience the singer is externally focused. In the positive experience the singer is focussed on physicalizing the music in her head, in the negative experience the singer is focused on the supposed negative attributes of the audience (Kenny, 2011, p. 2).

The state of arousal that may become stage fright can be interpreted as a challenge rather than a threat. That arousal immediately before a performance can help the singer become alert and focused. If the focus is on bringing to life a piece of music for an appreciative audience, then the anxiety level falls immediately and the experience is a positive one. Singers can use their expertise in breath management to control the anxiety response of fast, rapid breathing (Callaghan, in press). Less experienced singers reach the peak of anxiety during the performance, which then leads to their negative predictions being fulfilled, thus fuelling their performance anxiety. This is the real problem with performance anxiety: it 'feeds off itself' and becomes stronger even though the 'threat' hasn't changed (Roland, 1997, p. 11).

The main cause of performance anxiety is the fear of negative evaluation, and if the consequences of that negative evaluation are serious the anxiety may be more severe (Callaghan, in press). Different situations may provoke performance anxiety, depending on the singer's experience and performance level. For a first-year conservatoire student, performance anxiety may strike at the assessment recital at the end of first year, for a seasoned professional it may strike with a change of genre, style, or voice classification. Knowing the performance will be evaluated, or performing in a new guise may invoke feelings of insecurity. Singers performing in small groups or in front of fellow-students, if they feel musically or vocally inadequate, may fear negative evaluation by their peers. All singers, no matter how experienced, are particularly vulnerable when auditioning.

Performance anxiety is a vicious cycle where the prediction that something will go wrong and lead to failure produces anxiety, which then leads to behaviours and physiological responses that lead to failure. Mind change involves rethinking that mindset and possibly changing aspects of the situation. For example, for the first year student facing an assessment recital, the teacher can help examine whether the singer's estimate that she may fail in performance is realistic. If it is, a change in repertoire and more work on technique may militate against this. If failure is still a possibility, what are the consequences? It may be possible to redo the performance at a later date. If the student's estimate of her ability is unrealistic, then the teacher can point out in what ways the student has the ability to cope with the demands of the performance. But it rests with the student to work on the mindset.

Voice knowledge

What scientists know about singing

It is difficult to draw firm conclusions about the implications for singing pedagogy of many scientific studies. The utility of experimental findings for the teaching of singing depends on their incorporation into a theory of the singing voice and on their relation to current practice. Apart from this, other difficulties arise from researchers neglecting experimental detail that is important from the singing teacher's point of view.

One difficulty is that much of the experimental work exists as studies of discrete aspects of voice using a small number of subjects. In some cases, it is difficult to identify what pedagogical tradition the singers represent and to link the vocal strategies used with a perceptual result. Generalizing from such studies is difficult.

A second difficulty is that in many studies, singers produce only isolated syllables or sustained vowels, or they may sing in only a limited pitch range. It is then unclear what conclusions may be made about singing connected phrases over a wider pitch range.

A third difficulty relates to sample populations. While in the last 20 years or so it has become more common to give details of subjects' voice type, years of training, and singing experience, many studies still compare amateur singers with postgraduate students and retired professionals. It is then difficult to generalize from the findings. A similar consideration is that studies often do not distinguish between different categories of voice belonging to the same general voice type (e.g. between a lyric tenor and a Heldentenor, or between a coloratura soprano and a spinto soprano). Nor, in most cases, do they distinguish between different voice types (e.g., a baritone and a bass-baritone). In some studies, a singer is a singer is a singer and a baritone is a baritone is a baritone. This is unfortunate, because such more subtle categorizations may well be relevant to register, range, voice quality, or flexibility and have a significant impact on results.

A fourth difficulty is that most studies say nothing about how much preparation or warm-up was done by the subjects. Nor, when invasive experimental techniques are used, is it clear how these techniques may have affected participants' performances.

A fifth difficulty is that it is not clear from most studies what consequences different vocal strategies might have for vocal sound or for vocal control. For example, do 'belly-in' and 'belly-out' strategies of breath management produce any difference in sound quality? What is their comparative effectiveness in relation to sustained singing in different pitch ranges, to executing leaps, or to singing coloratura passages?

Perhaps the most important difficulty in interpreting results of experimental investigations is the fact that male and female voices differ in many respects. Historically, most investigators have been men, as have most subjects (often the experimenters or their colleagues). This has led to construction of a model of the singing voice that is essentially a model of the male voice. So many instances have accumulated in which the female voice represents a deviation from this model that it is time to rethink the model. Titze (1994) advocated use of the adult female voice as a standard because for women, vocal physiology represents a strong connection with units of the metric system. For example, the vibrating vocal fold length is of the order of 1 cm; the vibration amplitude is of the order of 1 mm; the mass of a vocal fold is of the order of 1 g; the maximum aerodynamic power in phonation is of the order of 1 W, and so on. Another solution would be to devise a much more complex and sophisticated model, based on extensive work with all types of voices, to replace the inadequate gender-based model in use at present. This is beginning to happen.

Nevertheless, with respect to some aspects of vocal functioning, results from an accumulation of studies do allow generalization. Some important findings can be identified.

In relation to respiration, basic research has provided insight into optimal methods of inspiration, relative posturing of the chest and abdomen, and muscular control of expiration. Because the respiratory mechanism provides the airflow and subglottal pressure for singing, phonatory problems often have their origin in either airflow or subglottal pressure, or in the fine balance between the two necessary for laryngeal efficiency. An important finding is that flow phonation, resulting from less adductory force of the vocal folds and more airflow, allows production of vocal intensity with economic use of the breath and places less mechanical stress on the vocal folds.

Research has not yet, however, determined what is involved in 'support' of the voice. Since control of subglottal pressure relies on a complex system of passive recoil forces and active muscular forces to achieve an ideal operation of the thoracic, diaphragmatic, and abdominal aspects of respiration, there is no simple formula for support. It is more likely that control of respiration for singing needs to be a dynamic coordination related to body type and specific musical demands.

While the area of vocal registration still presents problems of definition and terminology, the pitch range within which the major register change occurs has been identified. Control of involuntary timbre transitions can be achieved through coordination of subglottal air pressure, laryngeal operation, and formant tuning. With the benefit of instrumental acoustic analysis, it is now possible to be quite specific about the effect of particular articulatory manoeuvres on vocal resonance for this purpose, for the production of the singer's formant, and for control of vocal timbre. Voice classification may be assisted by data on the frequencies at which register changes and the singer's formant occur in the different voice types.

Experimental research on the relationship between airflow, laryngeal operation, and vocal tract resonances confirms the traditional wisdom that singers should adopt strategies that decouple the articulatory and phonatory systems. Such strategies contribute to control of fundamental frequency while maintaining the vibrancy of the voice.

In the area of physical efficiency and vocal health, there is a body of voice science knowledge readily available to practitioners. Findings on the utility of visual feedback from instrumentation are also of immediate applicability in the teaching of vocal skills in the studio setting.

What singing teachers know about voice

The vocal instrument is unlike any other musical instrument in that much of it cannot normally be seen, and its workings cannot normally be observed. For hundreds of years, therefore, teachers of singing, unlike teachers of any other musical instrument, have practised their profession without any detailed knowledge of how the vocal instrument works. In the absence of such knowledge, teachers have relied on their informed auditory discrimination, their musical judgment, the extensive body of practical knowledge developed by the profession, and their own experience of singing. Teaching has been a matter of demonstrating and describing what has to be achieved and what sensations are felt in achieving it, and thus conveying experiential knowledge – the soma of singing – to students.

What most singing teachers know about voice, then, is based on use of the whole body as a musical instrument. They are concerned about body alignment and use, the mental skills of audiation, and fine control of vocal tone. They strive to develop these qualities in their students through general music education, informed listening, and observation of master singers.

Beginning singing teachers are usually much older than beginning voice scientists. While many singers teach a little to supplement their income, those who devote themselves to teaching usually do so after some kind of career as a singer. There are probably three reasons for this: first, performing is valued above teaching; second, teachers feel an obligation to have experienced the demands of performance and to have a wide knowledge of music, of vocal repertoire, and of the languages used in the standard repertoire before embarking on a teaching career; and, third, many retired singers are still eager to work and naturally turn to teaching as a way of using their professional skills and continuing to contribute to the world of singing.

Practitioners are aware that singing is an intensely personal experience, involving the whole person – mind, body, emotions. They also are mindful of the need to understand and communicate with a range of personalities, to facilitate development of a range of intellects, and to provide a supportive environment in what can be a testing professional environment. They know that anything that threatens physical, mental, or emotional well-being is a threat to the voice.

While historical writings make plain that teachers have always been interested in how the vocal mechanism works, it has only been since late in the 20th century that technology has allowed scientists to examine the workings of the singing voice in detail. Dissemination to a wider community of the body of knowledge developed by voice scientists in recent decades has only recently begun. Some of today's teachers of singing were trained as singers before that process became established; the majority have never had formal training in singing pedagogy. In many cases, they see the physical skills of voice production as important, but because they see those skills in the context of musical imagination and whole-body use, they assume that these can be acquired through listening, observation, practice, and coaching from an expert trained in the tradition.

In a study of singing teaching in Australian tertiary education institutions (Callaghan, 1998) I investigated teachers' knowledge of voice production, analysed in relation to breath management, phonation, resonance and articulation, registration, vocal health, and control of the voice. The highly experienced teachers interviewed saw a knowledge of voice production as important in allowing singers to perform freely and easily, in maintaining vocal health, and in facilitating control of the voice. While many teachers felt that a knowledge of vocal physiology and acoustics was important for teaching singing, most of them assumed this knowledge could be acquired by studying singing and by performing as a singer. Most of them acquired knowledge of vocal function through doing, listening, observing, and consulting with colleagues. While they thought scientific information about the voice would be of use to singing teachers, they were concerned that such information might interfere with the hearing and feeling aspects of the art and with helping their students to experience singing as an holistic sensory activity.

Vocal control depends on a complex of fine motor coordinations directed by neurological signals and monitored by a range of external and internal feedback. Feedback may come from external sources such as the response of listeners, or from internal feedback such as hearing, vision, touch, kinesthesia, or proprioception. A major source of control is the singer's sensations of vibration.

It is in this way – through audiation, sensory feedback, and mental image – that most singers and teachers of singing understand vocal functioning and control. This is pivotal in understanding the relationship between the voice knowledge of scientists and that of musicians.

Professional education of singing teachers

Role perceptions and values

The practice of any occupation is mediated by the values and judgments inherent in practitioners' perceptions of themselves, of their relation to the body of knowledge and skills used in the practice of that occupation, of their roles in the institutions that employ them, of their relation to professional training or accrediting bodies, of the day-to-day practice of that occupation, of the occupation's function in society and (in service occupations) of their role with respect to clients. These perceptions are in turn influenced by practitioners' personal circumstances and interests, their training, their experience, and their current employment. Comparison at a general – and necessarily simplistic – level indicates a marked difference between the values of voice teacher and voice scientist, highlighting the lack of fit between the two roles.

The role perception of singing teachers carries with it particular values through which voice knowledge and approaches to teaching are moderated. It implies particular attitudes to the nature of vocal knowledge and how it is best transmitted. Evidence from interviews (Callaghan, 1998) suggests that voice teachers value artistry and individual expression. They value 'knowing how' over 'knowing that' and assume the oral transmission of knowledge. They emphasize experiential, holistic, sense-based learning. Voice teaching is caring and communicative. It deals with the soma.

Voice scientists, on the other hand, value the technical and technological. They value 'knowing that' over 'knowing how' and assume the written transmission of knowledge. They emphasize experimental, reason-based learning, which may often be fragmented. Voice science is experimental and rigorous. It deals with the body.

Craft knowledge
Bensman and Lilienfeld contended that

> major 'habits of mind,' approaches to the world, or in phenomenologi-
> cal terms, attitudes towards everyday life, and specialized attitudes, are
> extensions of habits of thought that emerge and are developed in the
> practice of an occupation, profession, or craft. We emphasize craft since
> we focus upon the methods of work, techniques, methodologies, and
> the social arrangements which emerge in the practice of a profession as
> being decisive in the formation of world views. (1991, p. xv)

They identified as indigenous to an occupation 'an autonomy in the development of craft technique, attitudes towards materials and media, and the development of skill and virtuosity' which give it 'distinct and peculiar characteristics of its own' (p. xvi). Bensman and Lilienfeld defined the artistic attitude as
one that attempts to create an image of the world in such a way that it can be
experienced directly, intuitively, emotionally, and 'naively' (p. 5). Important in
this world view is a consciousness of and pride in highly developed technique,
but a concealing of this technique in an apparent spontaneity, one of the elements by which a great performer is judged (p. 6). There is nothing in such a
world view that predisposes practitioners in the arts to take an interest in the
sciences, even where scientific knowledge is relevant to their work.

It is this artistic 'habit of mind' that I saw in the respondents to my survey of singing teachers in Australian tertiary institutions (Callaghan, 1998).
It was clear that respondents identified themselves as singers. That is, they saw
themselves primarily as performing artists and identifed with the techniques,
attitudes, and skills of musical performers, rather than with those of teachers.
Hence their priorities were in developing in their students a whole-body
sensation of singing that works at the behest of the imagination and inner
ear to meet the demands of musical performance. They felt that to achieve
that, a teacher needed experiential knowledge of singing technique, together
with a knowledge of vocal repertoire and style, and, for teachers working in
classical styles, a knowledge of the main languages of the international reper-
tory of classical vocal music – English, French, German, and Italian. Many
of them also saw knowledge of related areas such as body use, acting, and
performance-skills enhancement as important. The acquisition and maintenance of knowledge in all these fields represents a major commitment and has
a daily relevance; such relevance is not always obvious to teachers in relation
to voice science.

Professional knowledge

As Donald Schön (1983, 1987) pointed out, the view of professional know-ledge implemented by the majority of institutions of higher learning is based on a model of 'technical rationality' derived from the long tradition of positivist thought:

> According to the model of Technical Rationality – the view of profes-sional knowledge which has most powerfully shaped both our thinking about the professions and the institutional relations of research, educa-tion, and practice – professional activity consists in instrumental prob-lem solving made rigorous by the application of scientific theory and technique. (1983, p. 21)

The systematic knowledge base of a profession, he says, 'is thought to have four essential properties. It is specialized, firmly bounded, scientific, and standardized' (1983, p. 23). Schön sees this last feature as particularly impor-tant in relating the profession's knowledge base to its practice (i.e. profession-als apply standardized knowledge to particular problems).

This scientific model of professional knowledge is alien to the artistic models held by most singing practitioners. Because they derive their know-ledge of voice from their own experience as singers and then apply that know-ledge to the particular problems of individual students, many practitioners do not have a concept of a scientific, standardized knowledge of voice. For most of us, our model of voice is performance-related: our training and experience are in the world of musical performance and our teaching is directed toward that world.

In that world of musical performance, practitioners regard voice as a sub-ject of study in the same way that trumpet or violin are subjects of study. Musicians apply technical facility on their instrument to playing music (or in this case singing music). The ability to play or sing is then combined with a range of musical knowledge and performance skills in the world of musical performance. It is not surprising, then, that some teachers of singing view scientific knowledge of voice as irrelevant, or uncongenial, or too difficult to understand.

Voice knowledge

In order to teach vocal technique effectively, it is necessary to understand how the voice works. The puzzle is what 'to understand' means in this context. Are practitioners' understandings of vocal technique, learned through their own singing study and performance experience, sufficient for teaching? If a teacher understands through sensation and is able to convey this to the student, is this adequate? While in some cases such an approach may work, given the wide-ranging demands of professional music-making today and the context of contemporary education, with its emphasis on economic and educational accountability, this approach is inadequate. It is dependent on the level of understanding – in one mode only – of the teacher and on the teacher's ability to convey this understanding – again, in one mode only – to the student. Even if such an approach does work, it is doubtful whether it is the most efficient approach for all students and for all musical styles. It is usually slow; depending on the student's innate abilities and learning style and the teacher's level of technical competence, it may also be ineffective.

In the preface to *The Relevance of Education*, Jerome Bruner wrote: 'I confess I am puzzled . . . about the relationship between knowledge as detached (competence?) and knowledge as a guide to purposeful action (performance?)' (1972, p. 16). An understanding of this relationship is essential in approaching the professional education of singing teachers. I propose that competence and performance exist only in relation to each other: competence is the sum of skills needed for performance, and performance is not possible without competence. This is supported by Reid's assertion that 'there is an essential interplay between reflective thinking (which is discursive) and direct intuitive experiences: they need each other.' (1986, p. xi). Although vocal technique needs to be felt, there is no reason why it cannot be verbally explained, and no reason why the content of that knowledge cannot be related to the content of voice science knowledge. As Bruner went on to say, 'It can also be said of knowledge that, though it is constrained by the very mode of its expression, it can be expressed in various modes' (p. 16).

Many teachers are concerned that if they become too analytical about vocal technique, it will destroy students' ability to learn 'by feel.' There seem to be two confusions here, a confusion of the teacher's state of mind with the student's, and an assumption that intuitive and analytic ways of knowing are antithetical.

> What then of analysis? Does it really force intuitive knowledge out, is holistic response inevitably left behind? . . . Not necessarily. We must remember that analysis has two complementary definitions. On the one hand analysis is sometimes pulling things apart to find the separate elements, the component parts. . . . On the other hand analysis identifies general principles that may link and underlie individual phenomena. (Swanwick, 1994, p. 31).

Identification of general principles is surely important for both teacher and student. Swanwick (1994) suggested picturing 'sensation, intuitive knowledge and what Croce calls logical knowledge as a cumulative continuum, with intuitive knowledge as the bridge between the others, a link made of dynamic forms, images, representations of many types' (1994, pp. 30-31). To efficiently perform a whole-body task, one needs an objective, an overview of the task, a knowledge of the component parts, a knowledge of how they fit together, and a system of cueing, such that one activity automatically cues the next. It is the teacher's overview of the task, combining intuitive knowledge and logical knowledge – the 'knowing how' and 'knowing that' of singing – and how these modes of knowing are linked in representations of many types that allows construction of an 'explanatory model' of voice (Bruner, 1972, p. 16) to assist the student's learning. The difficulty is that teachers who identify them-selves primarily as singers, although they are well aware that teaching singing is not just a matter of imparting discrete items of knowledge or technique, do not see it as their responsibility to construct explanatory models.

> Even at the level of 'knowing how' – the psycho-motor technical man-agement of an instrument – there are insights to be won into how we actually learn complex skills and sensitivities, gaining control over sound materials. The simple view of what happens would be to assume that a skilled action . . . is the result of tying together into one bundle a number of smaller technical bits into a larger whole, rather like mak-ing a broom or a peg rug. But do we really build up a technique from individual bristles, from atoms of muscular behaviour? The element of truth in this is rather small and needs a massive correction. Above all the performance of a skill requires a plan, a blueprint, a schema, an action pattern. (Swanwick, p. 144)

However, in order to be able to construct an explanatory model for the stu-dent, the teacher needs both intuitive and analytic knowledge. Teachers' con-cern about being 'too analytical' involves confusion of what a teacher needs to do with what a student needs to do. Forming a plan is helped by the use of metaphors, mental images, and mind pictures of the action, but teachers are not always aware that the images need to belong to the student and to be linked to the physical realities of the task: 'In developing images of action a student is learning how to manage music, becoming autonomous, learning how to learn' (Swanwick, 1994, p. 146).

Likewise, the technical vocabulary of singing teaching needs to be clear and consistent. Concern over the terminology of singing pedagogy has been expressed at many voice meetings in recent years. While a concern with the individual learning needs of students is important, and the development of individual artistic expression is essential, differences in terminology create confusion. Moreover, even where singing teachers may share an understand-ing of a particular term, a more objective terminology that relates physical function to logic in pedagogical use is needed to facilitate cross-disciplinary communication.

A flexible model of professional education for singing teachers needs to take account of both the craft knowledge currently employed by practitioners in skill teaching and the voice knowledge accumulated through experimental and qualitative research. It needs to take into account the clients of the singing teaching profession and the setting in which their work will be done. Schön advocated that:

> university based professional schools should learn from such deviant traditions of education for practice as studios of art and design, conservatories of music and dance, athletics coaching, and apprenticeship in the crafts, all of which emphasize coaching and learning by doing. Professional education should be redesigned to combine the teaching of applied science with coaching in the artistry of reflection-in-action. (1987, p. xii)

The 'deviant tradition' of singing teaching already incorporates the best of coaching and learning by doing. I propose that a solid basis of content could be incorporated by adopting some aspects of the traditional applied science model in which practitioners learn the body of knowledge of the discipline and how to apply it to particular professional problems. Implementation of such a model relies on respect for the professional orientation of singing teachers as artists preparing students for musical performance. That is, skills teaching needs to be based on cognitive knowledge, and voice knowledge needs to be acquired in a way that serves the learning-by-doing orientation of the profession.

It is no longer adequate for practitioners to base their teaching solely on the directives that were used in their own training, or that they have heard used by famous singers in masterclasses, or on the personal imagery that has worked for them in their own singing. The directives may not be well-based in physical function or vocal acoustics, and the images may not suggest the appropriate coordination to the student. This approach may well be ineffective; at the very least, it is likely to be inefficient. Moreover, it may well be deficient in imparting some essential skills such as those needed to prevent vocal damage.

Adoption of an approach that takes into account the findings of voice science will have various benefits. First, it will eliminate much trial-and-error teaching and will lead to more consistent and predictable results in less time than more traditional methods do. Second, it will enable practitioners to deal with a wider range of singing styles and student requirements than can be accomplished with the traditional methods, whose roots are in the bel canto tradition. Third, it will provide a secure basis for the diagnosis and correction of technical problems. Fourth, it will better equip teachers to teach singing practices based on optimum function and safe voicing, thus reducing the risk that students will develop habits that could cause undue fatigue, produce less than optimum results, or perhaps cause vocal damage. Fifth, it will promote development of standard terminology for the physical skills of singing, thus greatly assisting communication of teachers with students, with other teachers and with other voice professionals. Finally, it will provide a basis for assessing the competing claims and counter-claims of different approaches to singing, both current and historical.

There are signs that these advantages are becoming more widely appreciated by singing teachers, and the findings of voice science will come to have a much greater influence on the profession than they have done in the past. Conversely, voice scientists are displaying greater awareness of the relevance to their discipline of the craft knowledge of singing teachers. Such developments will benefit not only both professions, but ultimately everyone – teachers, scientists, executants, and listeners alike – with a serious interest in the art of singing.

References

Barthes, R. (1977). *Image, Music, Text* (S. Heath, trans.). New York, NY: Hill and Wang.

Bensman, J. & Lillienfeld, R. (1991). *Craft and Consciousness: Occupational Technique and the Development of World Images* (2nd edn.). New York, NY: Aldine de Gruyter.

Blakeslee, S. & Blakeslee, M. (2007). *The Body Has a Mind of Its Own. How Body Maps in Your Brain Help You Do (Almost) Everything Better*. New York, NY: Random House Trade Paperbacks.

Bruner, J. (1972). *The Relevance of Education*. London: Allen and Unwin.

Burrows, D. (1990). *Sound, Speech and Music*. Amherst, MA: University of Massachusetts Press.

Callaghan, J. (1998). Singing teachers and voice science: an evaluation of voice teaching in Australian tertiary institutions. *Research Studies in Music Education, 10*(1), 25–41. doi:10.1177/1321103X9801000103

Callaghan, J. (in press). Teaching the professional singer. In G. Welch, D. Howard & J. Nix (eds.), *The Oxford Handbook of Singing*. New York, NY: Oxford University Press.

Davidson, J.W. & Correia, J.S. (2001). Meaningful musical performance: a bodily experience. *Research Studies in Music Education, 17*(1), 70–83. doi:10.1177/1321103X010170011301

Desberg, P. & Marsh, G. (1988). *Controlling Stagefright*. Oakland, CA: New Harbinger Publications.

Gardner, H. (2004). *Changing Minds: The Art and Science of Changing Our Own and Other People's Minds*. Boston, MA: Harvard Business School Press.

Gorrie, J. (2009). *Performing in the Zone*. CreateSpace Independent Publishing Platform.

Johnson, M. (1987). *The Body in the Mind: The Bodily Basis of Meaning, Imagination, and Reason*. Chicago, IL: The University of Chicago Press.

Kenny, D. (2011). *The Psychology of Music Performance Anxiety*. Oxford: Oxford University Press.

Reid, L.A. (1986). *Ways of Understanding and Education*. London: Heinemann Educational.

Roland, D. (1997). *The Confident Performer*. Sydney: Currency Press.

Ruthrof, H. (2000). *The Body in Language*. London: Cassell.

Schön, D.A. (1983). *The Reflective Practitioner: How Professionals Think in Action*. New York, NY: Basic Books.

Schön, D.A. (1987). *Educating the Reflective Practitioner: Toward a New Design for Teaching and Learning in the Professions*. San Francisco: Jossey-Bass.

Smith, J.D., Reisberg, D. & Wilson, M. (1992). Subvocalization and auditory imagery: interactions between the inner ear and inner voice. In Daniel Reisberg (ed.), *Auditory Imagery* (pp. 95–119). Hillsdale, NJ: Lawrence Erlbaum Associates.

Swanwick, K. (1994). *Musical Knowledge: Intuition, Analysis and Music Education*. London: Routledge.

Titze, I.R. (1994). *Principles of Voice Production*. Englewood Cliffs, NJ: Prentice Hall.

Wrigley, B. (1999). *Peak Music Practice Handbook*. Brisbane, Australia: R Fortescue.

Index

About the author

Dr Jean Callaghan is an Australian singing voice specialist with advanced degrees in singing, a PhD in vocal pedagogy, and a second postgraduate research degree in music and language theory. She has sung and taught around Australia and in New Zealand, Singapore, Sweden, England, and Germany, working in universities, privately with individual singers and teachers, and giving recitals, masterclasses, lectures, workshops, and short courses for voice professionals. For the University of Western Sydney she designed and delivered Australia's first full postgraduate qualification in singing pedagogy.

Jean Callaghan has served as president of the Australian National Association of Teachers of Singing, the Australian Voice Association, and the Australian Association for Research in Music Education.

Her research interests are interdisciplinary and concern vocal pedagogy and the relationship between music and language. She was part of the research team that developed *Sing&See™*, specialised computer software providing acoustic feedback on the singing voice, and author (with Pat Wilson) of the accompanying manual, *How to Sing and See* (2004). In *Perspectives on Teaching Singing* (S. Harrison, ed., 2010) she has chapters on 'Singing Teaching as a Profession' and, with Diane Hughes, a chapter advocating interdisciplinary voice studies in Australian school education. With Shirlee Emmons and Lisa Popeil she wrote the chapter on 'Solo Vocal Pedagogy' in the *Oxford Handbook of Music Education* (G. Welch & G. McPherson, eds., 2012) and as solo author the chapter on 'Teaching the Professional Singer' in the forthcoming *Oxford Handbook of Singing* (G. Welch, D. Howard & J. Nix, eds.).

Lightning Source UK Ltd.
Milton Keynes UK
UKOW06f1302080816

280200UK00002B/535/P